WEAPONISATION OF SPACE

An Inevitable Reality and Plausible Fallout

WEAPONISATION OF SPACE

An Inevitable Reality and Plausible Fallout

Group Captain PA Patil

Introduction by

Air Marshal Vinod Patney SYSM PVSM AVSM VrC (Retd)

KNOWLEDGE WORLD
KW Publishers Pvt Ltd
New Delhi

in association with

Centre for Air Power Studies
New Delhi

The Centre for Air Power Studies is an independent, non-profit, academic research institution established in 2002 under a registered Trust to undertake and promote policy-related research, study and discussion on the trends and developments in defence and military issues, especially air power and the aerospace arena, for civil and military purposes. Its publications seek to expand and deepen the understanding of defence, military power, air power and aerospace issues without necessarily reflecting the views of any institution or individuals except those of the authors.

Centre for Air Power Studies
P-284, Arjan Path
Subroto Park
New Delhi 110010

Tele: (91-11) 25699131

E-mail: capsnetdroff@gmail.com
website: www.capsindia.org

ISBN 978-93-86288-42-4 Hardback
ISBN 978-93-86288-43-1 ebook

Published in India by Kalpana Shukla

KNOWLEDGE WORLD

KW Publishers Pvt Ltd
4676/21, First Floor, Ansari Road
Daryaganj, New Delhi 110002
Phone: +91 11 23263498/43528107
Marketing: kw@kwpub.com
Editorial: jose@kwpub.com
Website: www.kwpub.com

2011 FPBA BEST PUBLISHERS AWARD (ENGLISH)

Printed in India by Gopsons Papers Ltd

CENTRE FOR AIR POWER STUDIES

VISION

To be an independent **centre of excellence on national security** contributing informed and considered research and analyses on relevant issues.

MISSION

To encourage independent and informed research and analyses on issues of relevance to national security and to create a pool of domain experts to provide considered inputs to decision-makers. Also, to foster informed public debate and opinion on relevant issues and to engage with other think-tanks and stakeholders within India and abroad to provide an Indian perspective.

Contents

Acknowledgements

It is with immense gratitude that I acknowledge the opportunity provided to me by Air Mshl Vinod Patney, SYSM PVSM AVSM VrC (Retd.), Director General, Centre for Air Power Studies (CAPS) to take on this challenging research work and stimulating my thought process from time to time. I feel greatly indebted to Air Mshl KK Nohwar PVSM VM (Retd), Additional Director General, CAPS, for the valuable inputs and overall review of the project.

My special and exclusive thanks to my supervisor and mentor Air Vice Mshl Manmohan Bahadur (Retd.) who not only offered his valuable guidance, assistance and advice from time to time, but offered his comments and suggestions at every stage in the course of my work. Without his painstaking efforts and constructive criticism, it would have been extremely difficult for me to shape my project to its conclusion.

I am grateful to the Indian Air Force (IAF) for providing me with the opportunity to undertake this research programme at CAPS. I would also like to acknowledge and thank all my colleagues for the lengthy discussions and deliberations on subjects of varied choices during the lunch hour, which opened up, and provided me with, new directions to the research. Special thanks to my colleague Gp Capt AK Gupta who made this book richer by offering comprehensive and superior arguments and comments while critically reviewing it.

I would like to thank all the staff at CAPS for providing me with unstinted support that went a long way in offering me a comfort zone in terms of Information Technology (IT) support, administrative procedures and canteen facilities that made the environment conducive and helped me focus on research every day. I would also like to thank Mrs. Sushma Zutshi, Ms. Surbhi Sareen and the library staff for helping me in getting hold of varied research material.

Finally, my sincere thanks to Ms Kalpana Shukla and Mr Jose Mathew at KW Publishers Pvt Ltd for publication of this book. I owe my deepest gratitude to Ms Rehana Mishra who undertook painstaking efforts in editing the script over sleepless nights.

Introduction

The importance of 'high ground' was understood and appreciated by military strategists and practitioners from times immemorial. With the advent of air power, aircraft could now get well over the hilltops and see far and wide. The disposition of enemy forces could be seen and monitored. Reconnaissance, in its varied dimensions, became, and remains, an important role of air power. Thus, little wonder that there was consternation in the US and the West when on October 4, 1957, the Sputnik took to the skies and beyond. Space represented the ultimate high ground. Within a few short weeks, the US created the then highly classified National Reconnaissance Office. The race for space supremacy was well and truly joined, and continues to this day. The number of satellites in orbit increased and the capabilities improved at a rapid pace. Soon, the US boasted that with their 'keyhole satellites' they could read the licence plate numbers on cars on the ground. Such boasts notwithstanding, it became patently evident that space assets would play a significant part in the planning and prosecution of future conflicts. With the capability to place satellites in geostationary orbit and rapid advances in miniaturisation, communication systems and data processing, the utility of space assets increased manifold. The 1991 "Operation Desert Storm" has been dubbed the "first space war" and emphatically brought to light the advantages that accrue with the use of space assets. The potential of space assets was recognised and the 2001 Report of the Rumsfeld 'Space Commission' unequivocally stated that the US must stay a generation ahead of others in space capabilities and the US armed forces a further generation ahead. The report and the environment of the times heralded that competition in, and of, space was now a fact of life. Space assets comprises a real force multiplier. At the same time, space commerce took root and increased at a fast rate till, in the year 2015, the civilian space business was worth as much as $ 312 billion, and growing. It is often mooted that in space, the 3Cs apply—space is getting competitive, congested, and contested. History teaches us that competition follows commerce and competition could degenerate into conflict. At the same time, as the dependence of the militaries on space increases, one side or the other would like to interfere in the space capabilities of the adversary in order to preserve own use of space and significantly deny its use to the other side. Thus, it is often argued that both commercial and military requirements make a 'space war' inevitable. Space-faring nations still comprise a small club but there are many other nations dependent on space assets for military purposes and, indeed, for their very way of life. All will be significantly affected by a space war.

At the beginning of the space age, the attempts at conquest of space had a purely military dimension. It was somewhat later that the potential for commercial exploitation became manifest. Military use of space or militarisation of space occurred very early in the space age. Use of space for reconnaissance, communications and navigation altered the planning and conduct of war. Better communications implied better and deeper command and control. Radar and electro-optical satellites could aid in early warning. The space-based constellation of satellites that gives us the Global Positioning System (GPS), aids in better accuracy of weapon delivery and is the basis of precision strikes. With enough satellites in orbit, a global coverage for military requirements is feasible. Militarisation of space is now an incontrovertible fact of life and the impact of space assets on military planning will increase with time. What does weaponisation imply? Strictly speaking, weaponisation of space, by definition, must mean the placement of weapons in space or on satellites. However, if weaponisation of space also implies the ability to interfere with, or cause damage to/destruction of, the space assets of an adversary, then the ground-based systems or airborne systems that could target space assets must also be included. Similarly, ballistic missiles or hypersonic missiles that travel through space to attack targets on the ground that control or monitor space assets should also be included.

It is generally accepted that space is a global commons. The UN Committee on the Peaceful Uses of Outer Space (UNCOPUOS) was established in 1959 and that led to the "Outer Space Treaty" that defined the basic framework of international space law and came into force in January 1967. Those were the early days of the space age and the treaty dictates were readily accepted. Four other conventions/ agreements followed, with the last being the Moon Agreement of 1979. There have been major transformations in capabilities since that date and there are infirmities in the space treaty but no further agreement has had formal acceptance. Countries are hesitant to limit their freedom of action and sign on to a treaty that they could regret at a future date. The quest for space supremacy remains as live as ever. For instance, the space treaty prohibits the placement of weapons of mass destruction in space or on celestial bodies but there is no embargo on conventional weapons. Banning of all types of weapons in space will be for the good of humanity but no progress has been made towards implementation of such initiatives. A treaty for the Prevention of Arms Race in Outer Space (POROS) was mooted but remains in the doldrums. All this indicates that a space war is not beyond imagination, immaterial of the grave consequences that will inevitably result.

Weaponisation of space or attempts at weaponisation do not comprise a recent phenomenon. The erstwhile USSR experimented with co-orbital satellites as early as 1973. On board the space station Salyut 3, a 23 mm machine gun was placed, ostensibly for offensive and defensive purposes. Experiments were also carried out on the efficacy of jamming, the use of lasers, and Electro-Magnetic Pulse (EMP) as well. In 1985, the US launched a two-stage rocket from an F-15 aircraft to destroy an obsolete satellite and the USSR followed with the use of a three-stage missile on board a MiG-31 aircraft. Ground launched kinetic kill vehicles are of more recent origin and the Chinese Anti-Satellite (ASAT) test of January 2007 was notable as some 20,000 pieces of debris were left in space that could impact movement of satellites through space to their intended altitude or during recovery of space vehicles. The debris will affect the Chinese as well as the other space-farers and it is generally accepted that jamming, temporary or permanent disabling, use of misinformation techniques and the like should be the preferred means of waging space wars in case such wars become inevitable. In the times to come, use of lasers and Direct Energy Weapons (DEWs) could also reach maturity and become operationally viable. Cyber attacks also show promise. It may be possible to hack, jam, eavesdrop, seize control of satellites, effect disinformation, etc, and all under the cloak of deniability. With cyber attacks, it may be possible to inflict only temporary impairment of capabilities but it cannot be said with a measure of assurance that in the flush of war, the attacker will restrict himself to causing only temporary damage.

What is the possible course of a space war? It is difficult to answer the poser as much will depend on relative capabilities and how dependent a state is on space assets. The side that wrests control in space will have a decided edge in future operations. However, there is no doubt that the impact of a space war will be severe and, hence, is avoidable. As the more powerful space nation will be at an advantage in waging the war but, paradoxically, more vulnerable to the impact of space attacks on its space assets, both sides would hopefully resort to a strategy of deterrence and dissuasion. However, if one side has an overpowering capability and attacks on the other's space capabilities are likely to be largely unchallenged, the temptation to gain the advantage in a space war will be difficult to resist except for the possible apprehension that international condemnation may result. As a rule, the strong are not troubled by such opinions. The weaker space powers have little option other than to have a strong deterrent capability in space or otherwise.

The impact of continued weaponisation of space demands attention. It is essential that all those interested in national security have a fair idea of the physics involved in weaponisation, the state

-of-the-art at present, and what the future holds. The author has done a signal service to bring home to us, within the covers of a single book the history and state of play at present. The status and capabilities of space-faring nations, particularly the US and China, are discussed.

The chapter on legal issues gives a graphic picture of how, quite often, the self-interests of nations trump the principles of common good. In February 2008, Russia and China put up a proposal for a "Treaty on Prevention of the Placement of Weapons in outer Space" (PPWT) but little progress has been made. The problem of enforceability also remains intractable.

The Indian space scenario is covered in the last chapter of the book. Our space industry is on an upward slope but the author argues that we cannot be blind to the need for at least a deterrent capability against an inimical space war. This requirement will only increase as we begin to make increasing military use of space. The opinions offered are those of the author and not necessarily the views of any organisation and that makes the reading of the book that much more compelling.

Air Mshl **Vinod Patney** SYSM PVSM AVSM VrC (Retd)
Director General

Centre for Air Power Studies, New Delhi

Acronyms

UAV	Unmanned Aerial Vehicle
RAF	Royal Air Force
RPV	Remotely Piloted Vehicle
ICBM	Inter-Continental Ballistic Missile
SCORE	Signal Communication by Orbiting Relay Equipment
GSNS	Global Satellite Navigation Systems
NCW	Network-Centric Warfare
GPS	Global Positioning System
PNT	Positioning, Navigation, and Timing
ESA	European Space Agency
ESRO	European Space Research Organisation
EDA	European Defence Agency
SST	Space Surveillance and Tracking
BMD	Ballistic Missile Defence
GSLV	Geosynchronous Satellite Launch Vehicle
AMOS	Afro-Mediterranean Orbital System
ASAT	Anti-Satellite
SAINT	Satellite Interceptor
IRBM	Intermediate-Range Ballistic Missile
FOBS	Fractional Orbit Bombardment System
BMEW	Ballistic Missile Early Warning
EMP	Electromagnetic Pulse
LEO	Low Earth Orbit
ALMV	Air-Launched Mini Vehicle
EW	Electronic Warfare
OST	Outer Space Treaty
MIRACL	Mid-Infrared Advanced Chemical Laser
ALL	Airborne Laser Lab

PTBT	Partial Test Ban Treaty
PAROS	Prevention of Arms Race in Outer Space
CD	Conference on Disarmament
PLA	People's Liberation Army
ABL	Airborne Laser
DEW	Directed Energy Weapon
IW	Information Warfare
SBI	Space-Based Interceptor
DACS	Divert and Attitude Control System
MRBM	Medium Range Ballistic Missile
IIR	Imaging Infra-Red
MEO	Medium Earth Orbit
HEO	Highly Elliptical Orbit, High Earth Orbit
GEO	Geostationary Earth Orbit
MIRV	Multiple Independently Reentry Vehicle
MSLV	Micro Satellite Launch Vehicle
SDI	Strategic Defence Initiative
OTV	Orbital Test Vehicle
ALTV	Approach and Landing Test Vehicle
SMV	Space Manoeuvre Vehicle
RASCAL	Responsive Access, Small Cargo, Affordable Launch
DARPA	Defence Advanced Research Projects Agency
MIPCC	Mass Injection Pre-Compressor Cooling
ERV	Expendable Rocket Vehicle
EM	Electromagnetic
DE	Directed Energy
HPL	High Power Laser
RAM	Rockets, Artillery, Mortar
DFL	Deuterium Fluoride Laser
COIL	Chemical Oxygen Iodine Laser
HFL	Hydrogen Fluoride Laser
ATL	Advanced Tactical Laser
AEW&C	Airborne Early Warning and Control
ISR	Intelligence, Surveillance and Reconnaissance

AFRL	Air Force Research Laboratory
CHAMP	Counter-electronics High-powered Advanced Microwave Missile Project
UHF	Ultra High Frequency
VHF	Very High Frequency
HF	High Frequency
ARM	Anti-Radiation Missile
TT&C	Telemetry, Tracking and Command
SSN	Space Surveillance Network
THEL	Tactical High Energy Laser
MLD	Maritime Laser Demonstrator
MATRIX	Mobile Active Targeting Resource for Integrated eXperiments
JHPSSL	Joint High Power Solid State Laser
LADS	Laser Area Defence System
HELLADS	High Energy Liquid Laser Area Defence System
CD	Conference on Disarmament
C4ISR	Command, Control, Communications, Computers, Intelligence, Surveillance and Reconnaissance
PLAAF	People's Liberation Army Air Force
DESBW	Directed Energy Space-Based Weapon
KKSBW	Kinetic Kill Space-Based Weapon
UNSC	United Nations Security Council
UNGA	United Nations General Assembly
UNCOPUOS	United Nations Committee on the Peaceful Uses of Outer Space
CBRN	Chemical, Biological, Radiological or Nuclear
WMD	Weapons of Mass Destruction
PPWT	Prevention of the Placement of Weapons in outer space and Threat of use of force against outer space objects
ICoC	International Code of Conduct
TCBM	Transparency and Confidence-Building Measures

1
Pursuit for Space Supremacy

Mankind will not forever remain on Earth, but in the pursuit of light and space, will first timidly emerge from the bounds of the atmosphere, and then advance until he has conquered the whole of circumsolar space.[1]

– Konstantin Tsiolkovsky, 1911,
Father of Russian rocketry

The expansion and development of great civilisations is attributable to a multitude of facets involving utilisation of available and potential resources, spirit of exploration and venturing off the beaten track into the unforeseen for the benefit of mankind. The basic nature of man is to explore undefined territories, often driven by ideas seemingly unconceivable. Civilisations, during the process of evolution, made inroads across the globe with an impetus to gain control of unchartered areas for sustenance, subsistence and sustainability. *Intellectually and technologically* sophisticated societies advanced from one level of growth to the next. This pattern of growth in the middle of the 20th century coerced humans to explore, and step into, the new dimension of space. During the last six decades, human presence and interest in space has been exponentially growing in frequency and duration, driven with a purpose and a focussed approach. Today, space tourism, asteroid mining and inhabiting remote planets no longer comprise a fantasy but are *realisable* ideas. Space technology in these years has advanced considerably; however, when compared to the aspirations, dreams and proposals for further space adventures, technology seems to be continually evolving. Expansion of the frontiers of knowledge from our immediate surroundings to the edge of the universe unfolds vast potential benefits to enhance the quality of life on Earth. In today's modern society, use of outer space expands a country's scientific, security and economic objectives while contributing to national power and as a corollary, to national security. Enormous investments have been made by a number of countries in space-based assets and programmes. All growing economies are driven by the use of these space-based assets.

Supremacy: The Incessant Propeller

The race for developing and possessing superior capability over that of competitors or improvising the ones existing, has been one of the driving forces that has led to the growth and prosperity of mankind. To prosper amongst peer circles, it becomes obligatory on the part of individuals, groups or communities to showcase achievements in a mutual field of interest or innovate something that is desired. These achievements, while expanding economic objectives and improving the social structure, bring about a sense of domination over rival partners. This domination paves the way to command and control while instigating a sense of anxiety to preserve and protect this upper edge. Safeguarding of status introduces the need for security. Achieving a secure environment is complementary to growth and gives rise to a parallel race in the design and development of arsenals and war-waging capabilities. Attainment of superior capability, exploiting it to own advantage, and protecting this for potential benefit over an opponent beget supremacy.

> ***Supremacy can be defined as having a discernible advantage over an adversary in a sphere of influence or area of interest while denying this edge to the adversary on purpose or by design.***

The race for supremacy in varied spheres of influence has propelled nations to explore the unforeseen and fuelled the thought process of human curiosity and ingenuity. It is this quest of supremacy that has ignited the human imagination to explore the unseen and accomplish feats for the greater benefit of mankind over generations. Space is one such area having vast potential yet to be exploited.

Graduating on the Aerial Route: The Early Rocketry

The idea of using incendiary aerial weapons can be traced back to the use of bows for the launch of arrowheads carrying flames. However, these arrows used passive means of propulsion. The idea of the use of rockets as a weapon seems to have evolved from fire crackers, wherein, the fire cracker took an aerial route owing to the thrust generated from the burning of combustible material. The early use of rocketry in war can be traced back to the year 1232 CE when a barrage of "arrows of flying fire"[2], a crude form of solid propelled rockets were used by the Chinese forces of the Sung Dynasty against the Mongols in the battle of Kai-Feng-Fu[3]. The curious and mystified Mongols improvised on these rockets and as they fought across Asia and Europe, introduced this new and effective weaponry to others. With this, the use of rockets as standoff weapons to destroy and degrade enemy fortifications had set in. Rockets were developed in various forms in the period of the 13th to 15th centuries. However, due to lack of progress and effect, interest in rockets technology slowly dwindled. It was in the 16th century that Johann Schmidlap[4], a German fireworks maker developed a twin-stage rocket, where a smaller rocket was used to piggyback on a larger rocket. This basic concept formed the pedestal of multi-stage rocket technology in the years to come.

Interest in rocket technology got rekindled in the last three decades of the 18th century, this time in India. Rockets were used against enemy fortifications, what we call centres of gravity, targeting palaces, cavalries, ammunition dumps and advancing combatants. Though the use of rockets did not change the outcome of wars, the advantage of creating panic and psychological effect was not lost. In the battle of Pollilur on September 10, 1780, the second Anglo-Mysore War, Col William Braille's ammunition store was detonated and destroyed by one of the Mysore forces' rockets, contributing to the British defeat.[5] Haidar Ali, the king of Mysore, gauging their importance, raised a dedicated rocket contingent in 1788 and used rockets effectively against the invading British troops. As per an eyewitness account, one of the rockets killed three people and injured four others.[6] These rockets, 10 ft long and weighing in excess of 5 kg, used metal tubes with bamboo sticks for stability and could be launched over half a mile. Tipu Sultan, son of Haidar Ali, used rockets in the battle of Srirangapatnam in 1792 and then again in 1799, creating panic and disarray amongst the British forces. Though the battle was ultimately lost by Tipu Sultan, the innovative use of rockets aroused the interest of British artillery expert Col William Congreve who improvised on the design and increased the size of the rockets for launching from ships. On October 8, 1806, British forces fired more than 2,000 rockets against the French to burn a considerable portion of the city of Boulogne.[7] Congreve rockets were used effectively by the British forces in the battle of Copenhagen (1807), the naval battle of Basque Roads (1808), the Walcheren Island Expedition (1809) and the battle of Fort Mc Henry in 1812. The use of rockets in conflicts continued over the next two decades, however, it was in 1844 that the technique of "spin stabilisation"[8] was introduced by William Hale of England. This principle technique continues to be used even today in various weapon delivery systems. Hale rockets were employed in the Mexican-American War (1846-48)[9], when the important Mexican port of Veracruz fell to American forces post firing of a barrage of rocket bombs. Thus, from elementary fire crackers, a lot of headway was made to evolve the rocket into a credible weapon system.

Conception of Advanced Rocketry

As considerable advancement in artillery technology was achieved, development and innovation in rocket technology took a backseat. Work on rocket technology progressed, albeit at a slow pace, during this period as artillery systems were able to cater to the military requirements of the time. In 1898, a Russian school teacher, Konstantin

Tsiolkovsky floated the idea of space exploration. In a report published by him in 1903, he suggested the use of liquid propellants for improving the rockets' range.[10] World War I (1914-18) saw the emergence of new weapons with technological developments in the fields of engineering, chemistry and metallurgy. It was during this time that the efficacy of machine guns, artillery, tanks and mortars came to the fore. This was also the first time that aircraft were used in dogfights and Germany used large bomber planes as well as dirigibles or zeppelins to bomb British and French cities. This period also witnessed large scale use of chemical weapons for the very first time. Modern war technology, which evolved during this time gave rise to a very different kind of warfare and necessitated the changes in tactics and strategy. Spurred by these advances, work in the field of modern rocketry was initiated in the early 20th century by an American, Robert H Goddard. He conducted a series of experiments, and in year 1919, published his research "A Method of Reaching Extreme Altitudes". In his study, he concentrated on achieving ejection of gases from rockets at high velocity with a majority of the mass constituted of propellant material. Through a series of experiments using steel chambers with tapered nozzles, he was able to demonstrate that trapped gases could attain an exhaust velocity to the tune of 8,000 ft per second. Introducing the concept of successive charges, he mathematically proved that rockets capable of reaching extreme altitudes could be developed.[11] Continuing his work in improving the efficiency and range of rockets, Goddard was able to design rockets with larger sizes capable of achieving farther ranges.

At the same time, Hermann Oberth, called the "German Father of Rocketry", proposed the theory of recoil rockets and in 1917, proposed the use of liquid fuelled rockets as long range missiles for the German Army. In 1922, he submitted a thesis titled "By Rockets into the Planetary Space", wherein he proved mathematically the capability of rockets to escape the Earth's atmosphere and once outside the Earth's atmospheric influence, the rockets could travel faster than their exhaust.[12] He also proposed that man-made objects could be placed in an orbit using rockets.[13] Thus, the notion of placing artificial objects in an orbit was floated and was followed up in the years to come.

Early Developments in Unmanned Aerial Vehicles (UAVs)

Design and developments in early pilotless aircraft seem to have played a significant role in rocket technology. Unlike airplanes, which could be manoeuvred to their destinations, the rockets developed till then did not possess the capability of active control and could not be steered in flight for correcting their trajectory. The use of airplanes, loaded with explosives and steering them with improved accuracy for a devastating effect on the target must have played in the minds of many. The challenge was the recovery of the pilot. In the year 1916, British Professor Archibald Mongomery Low,[14] working for the Royal Flying Corps conceived the idea of 'aerial target', a remote controlled pilotless aircraft. The concept was to develop a small aircraft, load it with explosives and guide it to the target using radio signals. Though the project was unsuccessful, with three launch attempts in 1917, Professor Low was successful in the development of wireless control apparatus for steering the unmanned aircraft. During the same period, the concept of an aerial torpedo was floated in the United States by the team of Elmer Sperry (the inventor of the gyroscope), Dr. Peter Cooper Hewitt (contributions in the fields of radio and vacuum tubes) and Carl Norden (developer of the Norden Bombsight). With Glenn Curtiss (inventor of the flying boat), the team started development of a pilotless aircraft, called the N-9. In the midst of the research, on March 6, 2018, the Curtis-Sperry aerial torpedo made its longest successful flight, travelling a distance of 1,000 yards.[15] The N-9 aircraft was launched on October 17, 1918, and followed its prescribed course but failed to land at the pre-set range of 14,500 yards, and crashed into the sea.[16]

As World War I was coming to a close, Charles Kettering, along with Orville Wright (of the first manned flight), developed an unmanned aerial bomb, the "Kettering Bug". The bomb, weighing around 240 kg could be delivered at a distance of 80 km in a controlled flight using a gyroscope and stabilisation techniques. Though the bomb failed to achieve a high success rate and was not used in its war at that time, the basic guidance system for aerial delivery was achieved.

It was on September 15, 1924, that two sorties of the N-9 pilotless aircraft were flown using automatic stabilisation and radio control techniques. The aircraft flew for 40 minutes duration, manoeuvred remotely and the first pilotless flight in history of aviation was achieved with a successful landing.[17] In this period, the Royal Air Force (RAF) worked towards the development of a remote controlled aircraft which could be used for reconnaissance, weapons delivery and act as an aerial target. The RAF developed the Fairy Queen in 1931 and followed it up by successful induction of the Queen Bee Remotely Piloted Vehicle (RPV) in 1935. The Queen Bee was derived from the de Havilland Tiger Moth biplane trainer and was the first reusable target. Constructed from wood, it could attain speeds of over 160 km/hour and fly a distance of 482 km.[18] Subsequently, drones were developed and produced in the US as aerial targets in substantial numbers. Successful employment of the drone led to the concept of arming it with depth charge or a torpedo and using it for offensive operations. The first radio controlled assault drone, the "Curtiss TG-2" was used by the US Navy in March 1942. The prototype drone was controlled remotely from a mother aircraft and with its dummy torpedo, it scored a direct hit on the destroyer's raft target. The successful test led to further refinement, development and production of these assault drones. The US Navy then, in 1944, went on to develop the TDR-1 drone which was effectively used in World War II. As per records, during the war, many of the unmanned drones, loaded with explosives, were used as expendable guided missiles.

The technology demonstrated in guidance techniques, radio control and navigation used in the early guided bombs and pilotles aircraft contributed immensely in improving the trajectory and accuracy of rockets. The techniques used for radio control, stabilisation and steering were advanced further and this probably facilitated the scientific community to conceive the launch vehicles in the years to come.

The Evolution of Guided Missiles

World War I created an environment of distrust and instability in Europe which paved the way for World War II in the year 1939. World War II was the largest conflict in history with more than 30 countries involved in the conflict and an equal number of countries being drawn into the war at some time, on one pretext or the other. This war saw the introduction of new weapons and also it was during the period of the war that newer technologies were developed and tested. Developments and innovations included jet aircraft, missiles, guided weapons, tanks, guns, artillery and battleships with advanced weaponry. Electronic warfare surfaced with the deployment of radar and sonar, and played an important role in communication and interception. The introduction, innovation and use of modernised systems during the course of the war by a country helped tilt the balance in its favour. During World War II, inspired by Oberth's work, a German student, Werhner von Braun, started work on rockets and, along with Oberth, developed the famous V-2 rocket for Germany. The 46-ft rocket, with a wing span of 11.7 ft and a diameter of 5.4 ft, weighed 12,250 kg.[19] This rocket, with a warhead of 1,000 kg, was able to achieve speeds of over 3,400 miles per hour (mph)[20] and cover a range of 200 miles, with a ceiling of 55 miles.[21] The first of many attacks using the V-2s from a mobile platform was carried out by the Germans on September 8, 1944, on the cities of London and Paris.[22] The Germans had the capability of launching up to 100 missiles in a day, and adopting a method of 'shoot and scoot', the launchers evaded detection from the allied aircraft. Over the next eight months, 3,172 V-2s were launched by Germany on allied cities. The death toll owing to these rockets in Britain and Belgium alone stood at 2,700 and 4,483 respectively.[23] The configuration and design of the V-2s intrigued the scientific community and military leaders of the US and USSR, and kept them busy trying to grasp the intricacies of the system in the years to come. As will become evident, it was the V-2s which pioneered the shaping of Research and Development (R&D) of the modern-day launchers and long range missile systems.

Another prominent development during this period was the testing of the atomic bomb on July 16, 1945, at Alamogordo, New Mexico. Soon thereafter, post atomic bombs use by the United States on Hiroshima and Nagasaki, World War II culminated in the year 1945. The use of atomic weapons changed the very strategy and outlook of all nations towards war. Conventional warfare against an atomic power was ruled out as a single bomb dropped from an aircraft was sufficient to devastate cities.

Dawn of the Space Age

Post World War II, the USA and USSR rose as the two superpowers. Though the USA and USSR had fought in the war as allies, the equation between them was of mutual distrust and enmity. The strained political and military relations, coupled with economic differences, resulted in a stalemate and gave rise to a long enduring Cold War era. Militarily, the strategic equation was skewed toward the USA owing to its monopolistic possession of atomic weapons. However, the US domination in the field of atomic weapons ceased in the year 1949 when the Soviet Union tested its first nuclear weapon. The USSR's gaining possession of nuclear weapons struck a strategic balance between the two superpowers.

The Cold War saw a race between the two superpowers for supremacy in varied fields, including economic growth, political clout, military regimes and technological advances. Both superpowers were in competition for gaining supremacy in psychological, nuclear and proxy warfare. Both entered a race to develop Inter-Continental Ballistic Missiles (ICBMs) capable of delivering nuclear warheads and this propelled advancement in rocket propulsion and technology. Developments and improvements in rocket technology opened up the idea of launching objects into space.

In the aftermath of World War II, the Americans and Russians had captured scores of rockets for reproduction and a number of personnel working for the German Rocket Factory surrendered to both sides. Werhner von Braun surrendered to the American forces and carried on his work to improve the existing design of the V-2. It was the effort put into the improvement of the V-2 rockets that paved the way to build the Saturn–V rocket for the Apollo programme and made possible the first manned exploration of the Moon. The basic design of the V-2 rockets also contributed to the development of ICBMs.

In the year 1946, project MX-774 was initiated by the United States for the development of an ICBM with a range in excess of 8,000 km. The design and development of this project by Consolidated Vultee Aircraft Corporation (Convair) would later culminate in development of ATLAS, the first American ICBM.[24] In the same year, under project Bumper, detailed studies were undertaken to study and modify the German V-2s for larger rockets. In the same period, the Soviets, with the help of German scientists and military personnel under contractual obligations, furthered the development of the confiscated German missiles and weapon systems. The Soviets initiated the development of the R-series of missiles with an aim to improve the accuracy and range of the V-2 rockets while reducing the complexity and costs.[25] Sergei Korolev[26] led the research work in long range missile systems and worked on the R-7 Semyorka missile with the aim to develop it as the world's first space rocket. It was on August 3, 1957, that the world's first ICBM was successfully launched, using the R-7 missile (also documented as the SS-6 Sapwood). With this launch, the Soviets declared a monopoly in possessing an ICBM and the sheer size of the missile created ripples in the United States on the capability of the Soviets to deliver a nuclear warhead. The second ICBM launch followed on September 7, 1957. The successful tests of the R-7 were soon to fulfil the dream of Korolev and stun the world.

Use of space and space-based assets finally evolved with the launch of the Sputnik aboard an improvised R-7 rocket by the USSR on October 4, 1957, from Baikonur cosmodrome in Kazakhstan, Russia's launch of the Sputnik marked the beginning of the space age with the world's very first artificial satellite settling in an orbit and mystifying the world. This was followed by the launch of another satellite, Sputnik 2, on November 3, 1957, which also carried a dog for experimental evaluations into space.

The Race to Space

Russia's advances in the space field in the midst of the Cold War did not go down well with the Americans. Russia's space venture forced the Americans to focus on research and development in space technology, with substantial funds being earmarked and spent on scientific research. The USA had already started work on project Vanguard in the year 1955 and the urge of achieving and showcasing own capability to launch satellites was fast-tracked by advancing the satellite's launch on December 6, 1957. The much hyped live telecast attempt of launching the satellite failed as the rocket exploded on take-off and dented the USA's reputation further. American efforts finally culminated in the successful launch of its first satellite, the Explorer-1 on February 1, 1958. This was followed by the successful launching of a solar powered satellite called Vanguard 1 on March 17, 1958. These satellites were mainly designed for scientific experiments to gather information in regard to the Earth. Then, on December 18, 1958, the USA covered substantial ground in space technology with the launch of the first communication satellite SCORE (Signal Communication by Orbiting Relay Equipment). Gauging the futuristic scenario of space in support of military might, John F Kennedy, in 1960, had stated, "Control of space will be decided in the next century. If the Soviets control space, they can control Earth, as in the past...the nations that controlled the seas dominated the continents".[27]

The Sputnik's launch ignited the spark in the early space race with a new vision to shape political, military and technological developments in the years to follow. Enormous amount of resources were deployed by both the superpowers in scientific R&D. The conflict and competition in the arena of space between the USA and USSR spearheaded the technological revolution and one spectacular event followed another. Human exploration of space began with Soviet cosmonaut Yuri Gagarin orbiting the Earth on April 12, 1961, aboard the Russian spacecraft Vostok. The Soviet space programme went on to achieve a series of other space firsts in the late 1950s and early 1960s: first man in space, first woman, first three men, first space walk, first spacecraft to impact the Moon, first to orbit the Moon, first to impact Venus, and first craft to soft-land on the Moon. The United States, during this period, took a lead in the launching of a weather satellite, spy satellite, geostationary satellite, satellite navigation system, and spacecraft docking. The United States' greatest success came on July 20, 1969, with the successful landing of two astronauts on the surface of the Moon with the Apollo-11 lunar-landing programme.[28] This was where the USA regained the prestige lost post-Sputnik, by surpassing the USSR in manned space exploration. During the period 1970 to 1990, various missions for planetary explorations and scientific experiments were undertaken by the USSR and USA. Missions were accomplished by landing unmanned probes, flying in close vicinity, taking close-up pictures and sensing the environmental conditions of Venus, Mars, Jupiter, Saturn, Neptune and Sun. Competition, healthy or unhealthy, drove one event after another and the pursuit for attaining space supremacy was unremitting.

Space Assets and Societal Fallout

The advances in scientific research and technology made by both the USA and USSR in the space field prompted other nations the world over to initiate and accelerate their own space programmes. As the technological and economic barriers for entry into the space arena got lowered, the number of countries setting their sights on space continued to grow every year, by hiring of services from established space-faring nations or by outsourcing of complete projects. With newer countries progressively developing their own space capability, space emerged as a domain with far-reaching economic, political and social implications.

The information and networking infrastructure with real-time inputs from satellites gives an impetus to the growth of the industry, accruing a vast set of benefits from space assets in our day-to-day lives. These services (over 30,000) have become so all-pervading that we simply take them for granted but any disruption of these services would dramatically affect our daily lives.[29] The day has come when the world has become increasingly dependent on space assets for social and environmental needs. Extensive use of satellites in beaming television programmes, telephone connectivity across the globe coupled with data transmission, weather forecasting and monitoring of natural resources laid the foundation for the commercial space market. Technological R&D drove the commercial market with communications, mobile telephony, direct-to-home television to the remotest areas earlier accessible with difficulty. A few more examples are transport optimisation, mapping of crops, crisis management, environment monitoring, healthcare facilities using remote access, and last mile connectivity to rural areas.

The use of the Global Satellite Navigation Systems (GSNS) has increased almost four-fold in the past four years, due to the dramatic increase in its accurate, real-time, positioning data and the steep drop in the prices of equipment. GSNS services are expected to become a standard feature integrated into a variety of multi-functional products such as low priced wireless personal communication devices. Space technology now represents an immensely valuable bank of knowhow that is used worldwide to bring new products, systems and services to the global market at competitive prices.[30] Though the space market is regulated by the respective governments, the entry of private players has been solicited for the exponential growth and development of the sector. While this creates ample opportunities for both established and emerging space-faring nations, it raises new security concerns in terms of space congestion.

Evolution of Space Power in Military Operations

In 1991, Operation Desert Storm ushered in a new era of warfare commonly referred to as "the first space war". Prior to Desert Storm, the utility of space capabilities in actual war had not been demonstrated on such a large scale, and the US did not lose the opportunity to showcase its might to the world. This was the time when the world got a glimpse of the concept of Network-Centric Warfare (NCW), albeit in its nascent stage of development. Out of Iraq and Kuwait came clues for conjuring up future scenarios, where the US military could strike anywhere with force, precision, and relative safety, its enemies electronically confused into submission, with little of warfare's normal collateral destruction.[31] The United States, in the shadow of the conflict, made heavy use of satellite applications of the Global Positioning System (GPS), early warning satellites, high resolution satellite imagery and satellite communications. Desert Storm changed everything; in the words of Gen Kutyna, commander-in-chief for space during the operation, it was "the first space applications war".[32] This conflict was one of the test-beds for evaluating and validating the effectiveness of newer developed weapon systems and military applications using space-based assets. The efficacy of space power on a large scale in tactical warfare capability was witnessed for the very first time in addition to the conventional strategic ability. In terms of shortfalls, the GPS contained an incomplete satellite constellation affecting accurate Positioning, Navigation, and Timing (PNT). The tactical units in a theatre were constrained by small lightweight GPS receivers. Also reported were weather obstructions obscuring real-time imagery, time lags in communication, and delays in information sharing. Shortcomings also existed in the availability of satellite communications, intelligence and surveillance information, and meteorological data.[33]

In the aftermath of the Persian Gulf War, the shortcomings and limitations of space assets and services were addressed by the United States. The lessons learnt in terms of training, requirement of joint planning and force application were incorporated to minimise the efforts and optimise the resources. They also planned for ensuring minimal collateral damage and fratricide in combat. Before the war began, Maj Gen Franklin J. Blaisdell, the USA Air Force's (USAF's) director of space operations and integration, stated, "We are so dominant in space that I pity a country that would come up against us" [34]. This became visible in Operation Iraqi Freedom, where the space forces displayed awesome power and flexibility. As per Robert Dudney, editor-in-chief of the *Air Force Magazine*, "They put the 'precision' in precision attack, found tanks in howling sandstorms, relayed commands to unmanned air vehicles, tracked troops on the move, listened in on Iraqi communications, and drenched the battle space with usable decision information".[35] The innovations in satellite technology, satellite launch platforms, communication and coding, computer technology, optics, imagery, and Intelligence, Surveillance, Reconnaissance (ISR) systems complemented each other, bringing about a revolution in modern conflict, opening new windows of opportunity for further developments. The NCW concept was realised to its near full potential by innovations and transformation in the field of information technology, coupled with introduction of a robust network for communication. NCW capability provided an unparalleled edge to American combat effectiveness and amazed observers around the world. Many of these improvements were brought about by the active participation of commercial players on a global scale owing to the vast economic incentives and encouragement by the respective governments.

Military-Civil and Civil-Military-Spinoffs

Throughout history, war and conflicts have driven technology and, in turn, technology has evolved to shape future conflicts. If we look back at the technology developed in pursuit of better weapons and arsenals over the past centuries, analysis reveals that a majority of military innovations, stemming from the branch of physics (the argument may not hold good for chemical and biological weapon systems, barring a few exceptions) have contributed in a very big way in support of commercial applications and economic well-being. These commercial spinoffs are being used by people worldwide in their normal day-to-day routine, and dependence on these has grown to an extent that non-availability of a particular service renders humans virtually handicapped. Similarly, technology which had been developed solely for the benefit of mankind and for commercial purposes, has found extensive applications in the military domain. The idea of rockets floated in the 18th century crystallised in creating a credible weapon system and weapon delivery platform during the World Wars. The advances in rocket technology during the Cold War period made the transport of humans into space and to other celestial bodies possible. The developments made for peaceful utilisation of rockets were also militarily used for development of ballistic missiles. Similarly, one can argue that development and testing of nuclear weapons has contributed to peaceful use of nuclear power such as the overarching aim to attain total energy security. Satellites developed with a military mindset have gone through a realm of technological improvements and are now ruled by commercial markets. Unmanned Aerial Vehicles (UAVs), currently used to spy on, and confront, extremist elements, are now being eyed by commercial players in a wide range of civilian activities in agriculture, archaeology and the service sectors.

As seen from the preceding examples, it emerges that most of the developments in the space sector have contributed immensely to the growth of military and commercial programmes. As these programmes progressed, the convergence of various applications of communications, navigation, imaging and data services mutually complemented each other. We have witnessed that the developments and innovations in the field of semi-conductors, microwaves, information technology, nano-technology and optics have contributed in the advancement of both commercial and military technology.

Other Space-Faring Nations

The use of space technology has helped in unravelling the mysteries of the universe and transformed space into a strategically important domain for nations the world over. The rivalry between the two superpowers led to the development of space related technologies ranging from expended rockets to reusable launch vehicles and state-of-the-art satellites for varied applications in the commercial as well as military sector. In the 1960s, Britain, Italy and Canada used American rockets to launch their satellites, while Australia used Russian rockets. France became the third country, on November 26, 1965, to launch its own satellite, 'Asterix'. The decade of the 1970s witnessed Japan, China, the United Kingdom, West Germany and India developing autonomous capability to launch satellites on their own. Space-faring nations are increasingly recognising the indispensable role and benefits of space-based services to the civil populace, national economy, security and global competition. The space policy drivers of the world's major space-faring nations revolve around national prestige, scientific progress, discovery, economic growth, security, international relations, education and varied applications linked within. The space domain, earlier dominated by just two countries, now involves more than 50 national space agencies.

China

Employment of space technology in the first Gulf War attracted Chinese defence analysts in recognising the significance and effect of space control in contemporary warfare. Judging the perception and importance of space assets, Chinese political leaders and military planners initiated a series of policy changes to counter futuristic US dominance in space. Since then, backed by a robust economy and flourishing academia, China is seen to be fast growing as a space power and developmental activities in space are advancing at a rapid pace, supported by indigenous expansion of the space industry. Following the souring of Sino-Soviet ties in the 1960s, China started to develop a series of indigenous rockets mainly based on the primitive R-series missile procured from the USSR. This led to the development of the Long March launch vehicle family and the first successful satellite launch in 1972.[36] Since then, Long March rockets have been used with reliable consistency. Entering the commercial launch market in the year 1990, China successfully launched satellites for varied applications spanning communication, navigation, reconnaissance, meteorology, and has achieved strides with the successful launching of its Shenzhou series of manned and unmanned spacecraft since November 1999. In 2003, a Long March booster put the first Chinese astronaut into space, making China only the third state to launch humans into space[37]. On January 11, 2007, China tested its ground-to-space weapon system, an Anti-Satellite (ASAT) missile which successfully destroyed its own old weather satellite, the 'Feng Yun 1-C'. This was followed by the launch of the Chang'e 1 lunar probe on October 24 in the same year, placing China in the club of nations with the capability to orbit around the Moon. Successful launching of the Tiangong-1 space station on September 29, 2011, to be followed with the subsequent rendezvous and docking of the Shenzhou spacecraft has consolidated China's international standing in space. In its latest efforts, on December 26, 2013, China successfully achieved a soft landing on the Moon with its robotic rover 'Yutu', also known as 'Jade Rabbit'. China, of late, is seen as advocating the concept of weaponisation of space. "The weaponization of space," say the Chinese, "is an inevitable developmental trend" and the "commanding height" of strategic competition in the 21st century "will not be on Earth, but in space"[38].

European Union

The European Space Agency (ESA) was officially established in 1975 with the merging of the European Launcher Development Organisation (ELDO) and European Space Research Organisation (ESRO).[39] ESA has achieved prominence in the commercial space launch services market and contributed in varied satellite applications covering the fields of Earth Observation (EO), communications, meteorology, and materials processing. From an initial membership of 11 nations, by the end of the year 2013, ESA had 20 member states: Austria, Belgium, Czech Republic, Denmark, Finland, France,

Germany, Greece, Ireland, Italy, Luxembourg, The Netherlands, Norway, Poland, Portugal, Romania, Spain, Sweden, Switzerland and the United Kingdom.

Amongst the notable achievements of ESA is the Ariane project, a highly successful rocket from Arianespace. The Mars Express was launched in 2003 by ESA and is playing a key role in an international exploration programme. In 2005, ESA achieved success in the landing of the Huygens probe on the surface of Titan, Saturn's largest moon—the first ever to land on a world in the outer solar system. ESA also launched the Columbus laboratory on the Space Shuttle Atlantis to the International Space Station (ISS). Most of ESA's projects revolve around scientific expeditions and commercial applications, however, the European Defence Agency (EDA) is quietly moving toward involvement in the military-space sector by providing Europe's civil space authorities with a list of military requirements for future civilian-financed Earth Observation (EO) and space-situational awareness projects, according to EDA and other European officials[40]. In February 2013, the European Commission proposed to establish the EU Space Surveillance and Tracking (SST) programme to monitor space objects and debris in order to prevent damage to spacecraft or to objects or persons on the ground[41].

Japan

In the backdrop of the 1969 resolution of "Space Development exclusively for Peaceful Purposes", Japan's space activities, under transfer of technology agreements with the USA in the 1970s, progressed at a slow pace. Japan has state-of-the-art rocket and satellite capabilities for both civilian and military uses. The Japanese outlook towards utilisation of space exclusively for economic and social benefits changed in 1998 when North Korea's Taepodong missile test intruded into its territory. This led to the development and testing of the 'intelligence gathering satellite programme' for early warning, detection and tracking of missiles. Japan has conducted manned space activities and space science missions and is now planning human space flight. Importantly, its developments on all fronts have taken place in plain sight of the public and under constitutional mandates, stressing the peaceful uses of space.[42] Japanese policy-makers perceive a requirement to try to catch up with China's burgeoning military space capabilities, and even maintain parity with South Korea's and India's military interests in space. Japan further requires enhanced capabilities to keep in step with, and improve, interoperability with its US ally, and also to try to lessen dependence on the US for key early-warning satellites for Ballistic Missile Defence (BMD).[43] This is evident with the Upper House of Japan's Diet passing legislation on June 20, 2012, paving the way for military space development programmes, with an emphasis on space-based missile early warning.

India

India has established itself as technologically capable amongst the space-faring nations with the launch of successful space missions and more than 70 satellites for various scientific and technological applications. With the launch of the Chandrayaan-1 spacecraft to the Moon on October 22, 2008, India became the fourth individual country to send a probe to the lunar surface and gained considerable international standing by discovering evidence of water on the Moon. With the successful launch of the Mars Orbiter Mission on November 5, 2013, followed by the success of its indigenous rocket Geosynchronous Satellite Launch Vehicle-Development 5 (GSLV-D5) on January 5, 2014, the Indian space industry is witnessing unprecedented growth, with a vast array of achievements in satellite manufacturing and launching.

While its space programme is perceived as being for peaceful purposes, the ballistic missile development programme has raised some concerns amongst the international community. In the year 1999, the Indian government initiated development of its own BMD system. After a series of successful tests, the ballistic missile defence shield has demonstrated the capability to counter missiles with range close to 2,000 km, travelling at speeds ranging from Mach 3 to

Mach 8.[44] India became the fourth country possessing the capability of developing an anti-ballistic missile system after the United States, Russia and Israel[45]. Phase-2 of the project aims to handle ballistic missiles with a range of 5,000 km and is expected to be completed by 2016.[46]

Israel

Israel stepped into the space age in 1988 when it launched its first indigenous LEO satellite, the 'Ofek-1' aboard the 'Shavit' launcher. Israel has launched a number of satellites to meet its reconnaisance, communication, EO and experimental aims. It sent its first geostationary telecommunications satellite into orbit on May 16, 1996. The Afro-Mediterranean Orbital System (AMOS) was built by Israel Aircraft Industries (IAI) in partnership with Alcatel Espace of France and Daimler-Benz Aerospace of Germany. Launched by the French-built Ariane-4 launch vehicle, the AMOS communications satellite continues to provide high quality broadcasting and communication services for the growing markets of Eastern Europe and the Middle East.[47]

Security and Vulnerability of Space Assets

Militarily, use of space-based assets, when integrated with operations, emerges as one of the many force multipliers. As on date, outer space is extensively used by the armed forces for varied services which include navigation, intelligence, surveillance, reconnaissance, environmental monitoring and advance warning. Command and control in today's net-centric environment also depends on space resources. Thus, we have been using outer space as the medium, with space-based assets, in support of military operations, leading to the deduction that space stands militarised.

The context in which outer space is viewed and used by international actors is evolving rapidly, and in potentially divergent directions. As nations continue to depend on space-based resources for economic prosperity and national security, these assets are increasingly becoming vulnerable. Space dependence also increases the vulnerability quotient due to the possibility of attacks on these systems during future conflicts. Thus, of late, it is seen that many of the advanced nations have developed or are expanding existing capabilities of attacking space-based assets to disrupt command and control links. Nations like the USA, followed by China, are contesting for space supremacy and are working towards developing space-based weapons that can be delivered directly from space based platforms. This, in turn, is infusing insecurity amongst other nations, including India, and has raised concerns worldwide. The development of space-based weapons by any state will instigate a new race for arms in space as many countries possess the wherewithal for launching space-based assets capable of carrying the required payloads. Thus, from the present capability of militarisation of space, we seem to be graduating towards weaponisation of space.

At present, a number of international treaties and agreements on peaceful uses of outer space are in place. However, the international law on prohibiting weaponisation of outer space is yet to reach a consensus. Advanced nations like the USA and China continue to tow the line that research and development in this field is restricted to peaceful purposes but as per available reports and studies, these countries covertly continue research on developing space weapons and associated platforms. As space is owned by all, any sort of deployment or employment of space weapons raises concerns and any use of space-based weapons will have unpleasant cascading affects. In the absence of any international curb or law on space weaponisation, the inevitability of weaponisation of space cannot be overlooked.

Conclusion

Most advanced nations have robust research and development programmes in space and space-based applications, from the commercial as well as military angle. Space assets are integral to combat operations and, presently, have become indispensable in the concept of operations to provide real-time intelligence, reach across the globe, and contribute in building a nation's power. Applications of GPS, and satellite communications are ever increasingly being used by states in all facets of modern warfare and continue to evolve for enhancing the paradigm of national security and economic well-being with the growing dependence on space assets. The advances in space technology drive the changing tactical scenario and this, in turn, necessitates realignment of strategic planning. The US, in this space age, exploits its dominance and possesses an asymmetric advantage in space-based applications; nonetheless, its security challenges are deepening. Any disruption or destruction of space assets will not only have economic and societal fallouts, but will also confer an asymmetric advantage to the opponent. The new evolving powers are preparing to, and posing a, challenge the hegemony of the US.

The advanced nations possess the technology for developing and deploying space-based weapons. Weaponisation of space is increasingly gaining the support of political and military leaders. In the absence of an international law governing weaponisation of outer space, the inevitability of the deployment of space weapons is a most point. The weaponisation of space will result in a space race and put forth challenges that will necessitate steps in arms control, space-based asset management, security policies and societal fallout post use of space weapons.

Notes

1. Available at http://www.nmspacemuseum.org/halloffame/detail.php?id=27. Accessed on March 26, 2014.
2. Gregory Vogt, Carla B. Rosenberg and Deborah A. Shearer, "Rockets: An Educator's Guide with Activities in Science, Mathematics, and Technology" at quest.arc.nasa.gov/space/teachers/rockets/58269main_Rockets.Guide.pdf. Accessed on March 26, 2014.
3. David Soo, "Asian Space", *IIAS Newsletter* | #30 | March 2003, p. 46.
4. "Rocket History", at www.grc.nasa.gov/www/k-12/rocket/BottleRocket/13thru16.htm. Accessed on March 25, 2014.
5. Available at http://www.uroc.org/phocadownload/Books/Dean_Black_Rocket_Evolution/CHAPTER_1.pdf. Accessed on March 10, 2014.

6. "History of Rocketry: 18th and 19th Centuries", at http://www.spaceline.org/history/2.html. Accessed on March 10, 2014.
7. "New Mexico Museum of Space History"; at http://www.nmspacemuseum.org/halloffame/detail.php?id=44. Accessed on March 10, 2014.
8. Vogt, et. al., n.2.
9. n.7.
10. "Brief History of Rockets", at http://www.grc.nasa.gov/WWW/k-12/TRC/Rockets/history_of_rockets.html. Accessed on March 10, 2014.
11. Robert H Goddard "A Method of Reaching Extreme Altitudes," at http://www.clarku.edu/research/archives/pdf/ext_altitudes.pdf. Accessed on March 7, 2014.
12. Available at http://www.space.com/20063-hermann-oberth.html. Accessed on March 10, 2014.
13. Ibid.
14. Zehra Ceren and Erdinc Altug, "Image Based and and Hybrid Visual Servo Control of an Unmanned Aerial Vehicle", Springer online publication dated September 6, 2011.
15. John F. Keane and Stephen S. Carr, "A Brief History of Early Unmanned Aircraft", *Johns Hopkins APL Technical Digest*, vol. 32, no 3, 2013, p.560.
16. Ibid.
17. Capt Linwood S. Howeth, USN (Retd), *History of Communications-Electronics in the United States Navy* (1963), pp. 337-351.
18. "UAV Universe", available at sites.google.com/site/uavuni/1920s-1930s. Accessed on March 11, 2014.
19. Available at http://militaryhistory.about.com/od/artillerysiegeweapons/p/v2rocket.htm. Accessed on March 10, 2014.
20. "Factsheet V2 Rockets", available at http://www.nationalmuseum.af.mil/factsheets/factsheet.asp?id=894. Accessed on March 10, 2014.
21. Available at http://militaryhistory.about.com/od/artillerysiegeweapons/p/v2rocket.htm. Accessed on March 10, 2014.
22. Ibid.
23. Available at http://www.history.com/this-day-in-history/germans-launch-last-of-their-v-2s. Accessed on March 10, 2014.
24. David N. Spires, "On Alert: An Operational History of the United States Air Force Intercontinental Ballistic Missile Program", 1945-2011, Air Force Space Command, United States Air Force, Colorado Springs, Colorado, available at http://afmissileers.com/onalert.pdf. Accessed on March 10, 2014.
25. "The Soviet Land-Based Ballistic Missile Program 1945-1972, An Historical Overview", at www.archives.gov/declassification/iscap/pdf/2010-005-doc2.pdf. Accessed on March 11, 2014.
26. "The Man Behind Sputnik", *Astronotes,* October 2007, available at http://www.armaghplanet.com/pdf/AstroTopics/History%20and%20Biographies/korolev.pdf. Accessed on March 11, 2014.
27. Quoted in Major Elek J. Szkalak, "Military Implications of the Soviet Space Program (1988)", at http://www.globalsecurity.org/space/library/report/1988/SEJ.htm. Accessed on January 22, 2014.

28. Valery Babintsev, "The Peaceful and Military Development of Space: A Historical Perspective", in Alexei Arbatov and Vladimir Dwarkin, eds., *Outer Space Weapons, Diplomacy, and Security* (Washington DC: Carnegie Endowment for International Peace, NW, 2010), ch. 2, p.19.
29. Available at http://ec.europa.eu/enterprise/policies/space/files/policy/space_policy_leaflet_en.pdf. Accessed on March 27, 2014.
30. "Commercial Benefits and Spin-offs from Space", at http://www.un.org/events/unispace3/bginfo/spin.htm. Accessed on January 24, 2014.
31. Steven Metz and James Kievit, "Strategy and the Revolution In Military Affairs: From Theory to Policy", June 27, 1995, available at http://www.au.af.mil/au/awc/awcgate/ssi/stratrma.pdf. Accessed on March 11, 2014.
32. Benjamin D. Forest, "An Analysis of Military Use of Commercial Satellite Communications", September 2008, available at www.dtic.mil/dtic/tr/fulltext/u2/a488621.pdf. Accessed on March 11, 2014.
33. Rick W. Sturdevant and Haithe Anderson, "Space Effects in Operation Iraqi Freedom", available at www.spacebusiness.com/sample2.pdf. Accessed on January 23, 2014.
34. Dr. Rebecca Grant, "Gulf War II: Air and Space Power Led the Way", as quoted in *An Air Force Association Special Report*, published September 2003 available at www.dtic.mil/dtic/tr/fulltext/u2/a466395.pdf. Accessed on January 24, 2014.
35. Robert S Dudney, "Space Power in the Gulf", June 2003, *Air Force Magazine*, vol. 86, no.6, at http://www.airforcemag.com/MagazineArchive/Pages/2003/June%20 2003/0603edit.aspx. Accessed on January 21, 2014.
36. Prof Keith Hayward, "The Chinese Aerospace Industry — A Background Paper", Royal Aeronautical Society, at http://aerosociety.com/Assets/Docs/Publications/DiscussionPapers/ChineseAerospaceIndustryDiscussionPaper.pdf. Accessed on January 27, 2014.
37. Ibid.
38. Mary C. FitzGerald, "China's Military Modernization and its Impact on the United States and the Asia-Pacific", Statement on "China's Military Strategy for Space", before the US-China Economic and Security Review Commission, March 30, 2007, available at http://origin.www.uscc.gov/sites/default/files/transcripts/3.29-30.07HearingTranscript.pdf. Accessed on November 22, 2013.
39. Andrew Wilson, "More Than Thirty Years of Pioneering Space Activity", European Space Agency, at http://www.esa.int/esapub/br/br250/br250.pdf. Accessed on January 23, 2014.
40. Peter B. de Selding, "European Defence Agency Has Growing Interest in Military Space", published October 6, 2008, at http://www.space.com/4261-european-defence-agency-growing-interest-military-space.html. Accessed on January 29, 2014.
41. Ron Davies, "Towards an EU Industrial Policy for Space", Library of the European Parliament, dated July 31, 2013, at http://www.europarl.europa.eu/RegData/bibliotheque/briefing/2013/130613/LDM_BRI(2013)130613_REV1_EN.pdf. Accessed on January 21, 2014.

42. Saadia Pekkanen, "Japan's Evolving Space Programme", excerpts of interview with Kate Wilkinson on September 9, 2011, published on the NBR website: www.nbr.org.
43. Christopher W. Hughes, "Japan's Military Modernisation: A Quiet Japan-China Arms Race and Global Power Projection", *Asia-Pacific Review*,16:1, pp.84-99 at http://www2.warwick.ac.uk/fac/soc/pais/people/hughes/researchandpublications/articles/japans_military_modernisation_arms_race.pdf. Accessed on February 3, 2014.
44. Frank O' Donnell and Yogesh Joshi, "India's Missile Defense: Is the Game Worth the Candle?" August 2, 2013, at http://thediplomat.com/2013/08/indias-missile-defense-is-the-game-worth-the-candle/?. Accessed on February 13, 2014.
45. "A Look at the Indian Ballistic Missile Defence Programme", at http://www.indiatvnews.com/news/india/a-look-at-the-indian-ballistic-missile-defence-programme. Accessed on February 27, 2014.
46. "Missile Defence Shield Ready: DRDO Chief", at http://www.thehindu.com/news/national/article3390404.ece. Accessed on February 13, 2014.
47. Wendy Elliman; "Israeli Space Research", at http://www.jewishvirtuallibrary.org/jsource/Economy/spaceres.html. Accessed on March 13, 2014.

2

The Quest for Space Weapons

It is difficult to say what is impossible, for the dream of yesterday is the hope of today and reality of tomorrow.[1]

— Robert Goddard

Human activity and presence in outer space, a global commons, is growing incessantly. Since the launch of the very first satellite, mankind has witnessed unremitting advances in space systems, with design and development of multi-stage rockets, satellites and payloads for varied applications. The civil-military-civil spinoff cycle has changed a multitude of commercial and military capabilities. During the last six decades, human presence and interest in space have grown exponentially in frequency and duration, driven with a purpose and focussed approach. This can be corroborated by the fact that more than 6,000 satellites have been launched of which more than 1,167 (UCS Satellite database, January 2014) are active. An unbiased analysis would reveal that the competition in the space domain between the two superpowers in the Cold War era and the resulting spinoffs in support of space applications have resulted in more good than bad and have improved the overall comfort and prosperity of the common man.

Militarisation of Space

Militarily, use of space-based assets when integrated with operations, assumes importance as one of the many force multipliers. The militarisation of space started in 1958 when the United States launched a communication satellite, SCORE (Signal Communication by Orbiting Relay Equipment) in support of military operations. Today, satellites are consistently used in support at all levels and domains (land, sea and air) of warfare. With the improvement and advancement in technology, utilisation of space services now finds a place in almost all facets of modern-day military functions. As on date, outer space is extensively used by the armed forces for varied services like navigation, intelligence, surveillance, reconnaissance, targeting, advance warning and environmental monitoring. The command and control in today's net-centric environment also depends on the space resources. All across the globe, nation-states are increasingly utilising space systems and working towards building up, and improving, the existing space support infrastructure. As the reliance on space services grows, the military might all over the globe has become increasingly dependent on space assets in terms of strategic reach and tactical potential.

From the above argument, it can be deduced that use of outer space as a medium and space-based assets as means in support of military operations has led to 'militarisation' of space. The rationale of 'militarisation of space' stems from the fact that space assets are used in support of military operations in a non-aggressive manner not resulting in direct destruction of any space-based, aerial or land-based target. In that, the space-based assets are increasingly used in support of combat operation (force enhancement) enabling combat forces to utilise their war-waging apparatus (force application).

Vulnerability of Space Assets

With advances and proliferation in space technology, space ventures are now affordable and accessible not only to many governments but to private players as well. The myriad services offered by satellites have become integral to the growth of the commercial sector and play an indispensable role in military operations. The growing reliance on satellites is rapidly increasing every year, leading to a deficit in the demand-supply cycle of satellite services. The direct impact of space resources on the economy and security of nations has made it imperative for them to indulge in a contest for acquisition and utilisation of space resources that could potentially snowball into geopolitical standoffs. As the number of nations advance and flourish in entirety, the demand on satellites and satellite-based services will swell out of proportion and the consequential contest for control of space resources will result in tense geopolitical rivalries.

The framework for use of outer space is evolving rapidly with potentially divergent directions. As nations continue to depend on space-based resources for economic prosperity and national security, these assets are increasingly becoming vulnerable. The military usages of space assets have given rise to a situation where the space-based assets are susceptible to attacks, forcing nation-states to adopt defensive measures. Thus, the attacking and defending capabilities in the context of space-based assets comprise an ontological basis for space weaponisation.

Raison d 'Etre for Weaponisation of Space

The weaponisation of space has been a topic of intense and acrimonious debate over the years. Scores of arguments and counter-arguments have come forth in respect of 'space stands weaponised'. The issue of weaponisation of space is fraught with differing perceptions. The proponents argue that space stands weaponised from the very time the first nuclear tipped ballistic missile was deployed. Many advocate that as no weapons are deployed in space, space cannot be assumed to be weaponised. The overriding concern at this juncture is the safety of space assets in the eventuality of a conflict, and the assurance that none of the space assets will be compromised. To come to a conclusion, a detailed understanding and analysis of the weapon system and capabilities in relation to space will be needed.

From the dawn of the space age, both the erstwhile USSR and the United States worked diligently to develop capabilities to attack their adversary's orbiting assets.[2] The Soviets were driven to develop ASAT capabilities to neutralise the threat of US reconnaissance satellites and the Americans conceived ASAT capabilities to ensure parity during the Cold War. Space dependence also instilled a continual fear that adversaries might attack these systems during future conflicts. Thus, of late, it is seen that many of the advanced nations have developed, or are expanding, the capabilities of attacking space-based assets to disrupt and deny critical services supporting the commercial and military services. State players like, the USA, followed by China, are contesting for space supremacy and are working towards developing space-based weapons that can be delivered directly from space-based platforms. Counter-space developments by potential adversaries are varied and include everything from jamming to kinetic kill anti-satellite weapons.[3] This, in turn, is infusing insecurity amongst other space-faring nations, including India, and has raised concerns worldwide. Development of space-based weapons by any state will instigate a new race for arms in space as many more countries possess the wherewithal for launching space-based assets capable of carrying the required payloads. Thus, from the present capability of militarisation of space, and the possession of the wherewithal to attack space assets, we seem to be graduating towards unequivocal weaponisation of space. As will be assessed, weaponisation of space is not something new, being conceptualised for futuristic scenarios. Development and testing of space weapons has been taking place sporadically since the very first space venture (Sputnik).

Power Projection from Space in 20th Century

It was on August 9, 1961, that Premier Khrushchev articulated, "You (US) do not have 50 and 100 megaton bombs. We (USSR) have bombs stronger than 100 megatons. We placed Gagarin and Titov in space and we can replace them with other loads that can be directed to any place on Earth".[4] Openly challenged by the Soviet disclosure, and in the midst of the prevailing mistrust and uncertainty, the US initiated the multi-pronged development of the anti-satellite programmes, releasing funds to the army, navy and air force. The US Army, much before this revelation, had initiated the Nike Zeus project in 1955 as an Anti-Ballistic Missile System (ABMS).[5] The Nike Zeus, under programme 505, codenamed 'Mud Flap', was essentially an attempt to develop an ASAT capability that delivered mixed results in the 12 tests carried out till 1966. The US Air Force in the same period developed the ASAT system called Satellite Interceptor (SAINT) which was supposed to search, track and, if warranted, destroy an orbiting satellite by launching small spin stabilised rockets or by self-destruction in the vicinity of the target satellite. This was the period when Bell Aircraft floated the idea of the manned space vehicle, Dyna-Soar (X-20), capable of delivering Bomber Missiles (BoMi) to a specified point on the Earth from orbit; however, owing to budget constraints, the project was scrapped in the post evaluation stage. The US Navy in this period, explored the possibility of an ASAT weapon in the name of 'Early Spring', a submarine launched, non-nuclear, high altitude hovering missile with a proximity fuse. The development of ASAT weapon systems continued, and in June 1964, under programme 437, the Thor Intermediate Range Ballistic Missile (IRBM), with an intercept range of 700 miles, was tested and made operational.

In the year 1967, the USSR, working on the concept of the Fractional Orbit Bombardment System (FOBS), developed the capability of delivering the megaton class of thermonuclear warhead into a steeply inclined low altitude polar orbit and, following a programmed braking manoeuvre, reentering from a direction skirting detection by Ballistic Missile Early Warning (BMEW) radars.[6] This was followed up closely in 1968 by the development of the co-orbital ASAT system which was declared operational in February 1973 for an orbital altitude of 230 to 1,000 km. In all, 20 tests[7] of a Soviet co-orbital ASAT system were conducted from 1968 to 1982. In each test, the weapon was discharged, fragmenting the interceptor.[8]

The ASAT capability was not just limited to kinetic attacks. ASAT capabilities were worked out using high altitude Electro-Magnetic Pulse (EMP) and jamming of satellites as well. On July 8, 1962, a high-altitude nuclear test was conducted by the US at an altitude of

400 km in the Pacific Ocean under the code name "Starfish Prime". The resulting EMP destroyed a number of satellites and also created artificial radiation belts. It also led to the failure of electrical grids in parts of the US.[9] The Soviets achieved success in jamming and blinding of two US satellites in the later part of 1975.

Inspired by President Ronald Reagan's "Star Wars" speech[10] on March 18, 1983, and based on Central Intelligence Agency (CIA) inputs[11] (refer boxed text) on the Soviet space programme as of July 19, 1983, the US focussed its attention on developing weapons based on new technology. Working diligently in this direction, the Air Launched Mini Vehicle (ALMV) was conceived for delivering the ASAT weapon using aircraft. The missile, delivered from an aircraft, would ascend to a target satellite in Low Earth Orbit (LEO) and destroy the satellite in a high speed collision, with a kinetic kill.[12] On September 13, 1985, the US employed the F-15A aircraft for launching a two-stage missile, the ASM-135, and destroyed an obsolete military observation satellite at an orbital altitude of 345 miles.[13]

CIA's Key Judgments and Summary of the Soviet Space Programme

One of the principle goals of the USSR was to deny use of space to the enemy in war-time. The report brought out the following salient points in respect of Soviet ASAT development for the 20th century:

- Significant improvements in non-nuclear ASAT and high altitude conventional orbital capability are not expected.
- The most serious threat to the US space system is active Electronic Warfare (EW); the most likely method adopted would be brute force jamming.
- Though the potential exists, ICBMs and direct ascent ABMs are unlikely to be used in the ASAT role.
- There is high probability for testing of the high energy laser ASAT weapon in LEO by the early 1990s. This would be preceded by prototype testing of the 1 Mega Watt (MW) class of the laser weapon in the later part of the 1980s, and, if successful, could result in an operational laser ASAT system in the mid-1980s.

In response, the USSR floated its own version of the ALMV under project 'Kontakt', using a 3-stage missile aboard the MiG-31 variant. The system was supposed to attack 24 satellites in a 36-hour period. However, post disintegration of the erstwhile USSR, the project was put on hold. The project was revived in 2010 and prototype tests are in progress.[14]

As the Outer Space Treaty (OST) prohibits placement and detonation of nuclear weapons in space, and use of nuclear weapons in space would destroy the assets of friend and foe alike, the focus shifted to development of an ASAT system within the bounds of international law. By this time, world lobbies were opposed to the destruction of satellites in orbit as it created a phenomenal amount of debris, posing a challenge for future satellite operations. Thus, while experiments and testing of kinetic kill vehicles continued, development of Directed Energy Weapons (DEWs) gained momentum with advances in technology. Use of DEWs would not result in the creation of debris as in a kinetic kill. The prominence of high powered microwave devices and high power lasers grew in the context of ASAT weapon development. Another advantage was the clandestine cover provided by such weapon systems. Moreover, it would not be necessary to destroy the space asset, rather degradation could be infused into its functioning with differing levels of intensity.

The US, in the period of the 1980s, worked on the development of the Mid-Infrared Advanced Chemical Laser (MIRACL), a mega watt class chemical laser. The programme was terminated following a temporary ban by Congress, but post termination of the ban period, MIRACL was used in conjunction with the 'Sea Lite' beam director to illuminate a satellite orbiting at an altitude of 420 km. As per available reports, the laser succeeded in tracking and illuminating the satellite and temporarily degrading it.[15] Another striking example was the employment of a high energy laser by the USSR against the US Space Shuttle Challenger in October 1984. Lased in low power mode, the Challenger was illuminated and tracked, resulting in the malfunctioning of the onboard system and discomfort to the crew.[16] The USAF had initiated the project on an Airborne Laser Lab (ALL) in 1976 which boosted their confidence to develop the AL-1A Airborne Laser (ABL) on a Boeing 747-400 aircraft in the year 1996. Operating in the ASAT role, the AL-1A would fly an intercept profile to intersect the ground track of a low orbit reconnaissance or surveillance satellite, or manned space vehicle, and damage or destroy it.[17] In response, the Soviets initiated the 'Almaz/Beriev A-60', High Energy Laser Directed Energy Weapon Test-bed aboard an IL-76 Candid aircraft.[18]

The concluding period of the 20th century had already laid the foundation for the development of new age weapon systems with experimental evaluation, testing and demonstration of laser weapons. The potential use of microwaves to damage equipment was discernible, but generating the required power and frequency in the right direction posed a challenge. Another major disadvantage was the mammoth size of the equipment (weapon) for generating optical or microwave energy due to technology constraints. The progress in space related technological advances witnessed a slowdown due to the diminishing competition post disintegration of the USSR and due to the concerns voiced in support of maintaining a weapon-free space.

Securing Outer Space

As power projection from space was making headway with the evolution of new concepts taking shape from fictional artefacts, it was but natural for the international community to take cognisance of securing space for peaceful purposes and forbidding the use of weapons in outer space. A number of agreements and treaties have been floated to prevent weaponisation of outer space. The response to these treaties has been a mixed one, with resilient acceptance or outright rejection. The Partial Test Ban Treaty (PTBT) bans nuclear weapon tests in the atmosphere, in outer space and under water. The OST provides the basic framework on international space law, and states, *"States shall not place nuclear weapons or other weapons of mass* *destruction in orbit or on celestial bodies or **station them in outer space** in any other manner"*. Taking a hint from this, it is construed that as long as weapons are not placed in orbit or on celestial bodies, the ground rules conform to the policy of avoiding space weaponisation. Further, in the shadow of "the use of military personnel for scientific research or for any other peaceful purposes shall not be prohibited" (refer boxed text), nation-states continue to exploit and test weapons in space. Another important treaty proposed was the "Prevention of Arms Race in Outer Space (PAROS)".

Article IV of "Treaty on Principles Governing the Activities of States in the Exploration and Use of Outer Space, including the Moon and Other Celestial Bodies"

States Parties to the Treaty undertake not to place in orbit around the Earth any objects carrying nuclear weapons or any other kinds of weapons of mass destruction, install such weapons on celestial bodies, or station such weapons in outer space in any other manner.

The Moon and other celestial bodies shall be used by all States Parties to the Treaty exclusively for peaceful purposes. The establishment of military bases, installations and fortifications, the testing of any type of weapons and the conduct of military manoeuvres on celestial bodies shall be forbidden. The use of military personnel for scientific research or for any other peaceful purposes shall not be prohibited. The use of any equipment or facility necessary for peaceful exploration of the Moon and other celestial bodies shall also not be prohibited.

Under the draft treaty submitted by Russia in 2008 to the Conference on Disarmament (CD), *"State Parties would commit to refrain from placing objects carrying any type of weapon into orbit, installing weapons on celestial bodies, and **threatening to use force against objects in outer space**."*[19] The draft denies the freedom to attack space assets using conventional ground-to-space weapons. The treaty was opposed by the US in its own interest, stating that there was no military race in space. Russia and China are strong supporters of the treaty and have been negotiating with the US to reach a consensus, and acceptance. The various mechanisms in the draft proposal of the treaty have been contested by nation-states to safeguard their own security interest. In the absence of credible and legally binding regulations on space security, the design, development and testing of new and advanced space systems, with an inherent capability to be used as weapon platforms will continue unabated. More on this is elaborated in the chapter titled "Space Weaponisation and Legal Framework".

The Rationale Behind Development of Space Weapons

Both the USA and USSR started launching satellites in the 1960s in support of reconnaissance, navigation, military communication and intelligence gathering. As part of the strategic design, the development of ASAT weapons was pursued to counter the use of rockets, artificial satellites and long range missiles capable of carrying a nuclear arsenal. Space assets in general and artificial satellite systems in particular are vulnerable to the wide variety of threats from the intentional or unintentional creations of the human race. While in orbit, satellites travel in a predictable trajectory and can be easily tracked. As satellites generally do not possess extensive *counter-measures for self-protection*, they are susceptible to wide ranging types of attacks. The ASAT weapon programme was conceptualised and developed in an environment of mutual distrust and enmity, with the strategic imperative of safeguarding and countering perceived nuclear threats from, or passing through, the realms of space. A number of ASAT projects[20] were initiated by both powers, followed by experimental evaluation and testing. The advancing technology and assessed outcomes of these tests were furthered by improvising the delivery capabilities and payloads. The development of ASAT capabilities progressed with alacrity during the Cold War in the name of space deterrence and space superiority. As any technology advancement is associated or followed with a counter technology, the same is true with space systems. As has been brought out earlier, with the increasing dependence on them, the space assets are progressively becoming more vulnerable. As technology is exploited to neutralise space assets, measures are being initiated for their protection. Neutralising would involve disruption, degradation or destruction of space assets, on the one hand, and on the other, protection from such attacks would entail hardening of space systems to absorb any attack and/or to neutralise the source of attack. Neutralising the targets in support of both defence and attack would require the use of weapons against space-based assets.

The alarming trend of competing for space weapons was arrested with the disintegration of the USSR. As a result, a majority of the projects conceived by the US were reevaluated for their viability and strategic necessity in the years to come and were put on hold or abandoned in totality, either due to the exorbitant costs or the loss of strategic relevance. However, the United States vigorously pursued the militarisation of space, visualising the importance of support from space assets. The overdependence on the use of space-based sensor systems and integrating the communication infrastructure using satellite services increased the vulnerability issues. These vulnerability issues came into sharp focus with the advances made by other space-faring nations, bringing to the fore a sense of insecurity from a futuristic perspective. Thus, under the umbrella of space security and protecting its space-based assets, the United States started funding research and development in the field of soft and hard kill technology and development of space-based platforms and orbital vehicles. These new developments elevated the concerns amongst the international community. On the one hand, while new strides were made in the exploration of space, the inherent dual use technology, on the other, paved the way for the possibility of use of technology to place weapons in outer space. The interest in design and development of space weapons was spawned for the following reasons:

- To ensure unrestricted freedom of operation of space assets.
- For safeguarding of own and friendly space assets against likely attacks.

- To deny the use of space assets to ensure sovereignty and maintain dominance in the space field.
- For demonstrating credible deterrence capability to subjugate dominance.
- For innovations and inventiveness to reinforce future space missions.
- Research and development in space weapons technology would serve the dual purpose of using the technology in the commercial service sector to boost the economy.

21st Century: Challenging US Hegemony in Space

The use of kinetic kill vehicles as ASAT weapons began only in the later two decades post the disintegration of the USSR. However, in the interim, the emerging powers had been contemplating development and testing of ASAT weapons using indigenised launch vehicles. On January 11, 2007, China, using the multi-stage rocket, successfully conducted its first ASAT test, destroying its own inactive polar orbit satellite 'FengYun-1C', at an altitude of 865 km. China, in an era of a unipolar world, has emerged as an aspirational power and posed a challenge to US hegemony in space. The disintegration of the satellite created one of the largest clouds of debris, polluting outer space and endangering space assets and future space activities. Michael Krepon, president emeritus of the Henry L. Stimson Centre, while terming the Chinese test predictable and unfortunate, said, "The Chinese are telling the Pentagon that they don't own space, we can play this game, too, and we can play it dirtier than you".[21] This was soon followed by the US demonstration of an agile, sea-based ASAT capability in 2008, by the shooting down of a non-functioning intelligence satellite, in a manner that minimised debris consequences.[22]

In January 2010, China conducted another test, this time on ground-based mid-course missile interception technology. With the two tests, in 2007 and 2010, it can be construed that China has bridged the gap of linking anti-satellite and missile defence systems and made headway in "hit-to-kill" technologies.[23] There have been reports suggesting that China may be planning to conduct another ASAT test in Medium Earth Orbit (MEO).[24] China is reported to have developed parasitic satellites as an additional method to deploy an ASAT weapon.[25] Unconfirmed reports suggest that China has also developed satellite jamming technologies to temporarily disrupt satellites. The Chinese are also believed to be investing in small (nano) satellites technologies which could be used as space mines.[26]

China has been pursuing development of DEWs since 1990. It has made considerable progress in the field of ground-based laser systems and radio frequency weapons for degradation of satellites and, as pointed out, is likely to be involved in the design of parasitic satellites. As per the 1998 Pentagon report to Congress, "China already may possess the capability to damage, under specific conditions, optical sensors on satellites that are very vulnerable to damage by lasers", and that "given China's current interest in laser technology, it is reasonable to assume that Beijing would develop a weapon that could destroy satellites in the future". The assumption gained credibility when in August and September of 2006, China reportedly used high-powered, ground-based lasers to illuminate US reconnaissance satellites. Reports stated that these were either ASAT tests or relatively "low-power" laser ranging devices intended to precisely determine satellite orbits for ASAT targeting purposes.[27] According to one account, the "Chinese routinely turn powerful lasers skywards, demonstrating their potential to dazzle or permanently blind spy satellites".[28] This report went on to quote Gary Payton, a senior Pentagon official, who said "They let us see their lasers. It is as if they are trying to intimidate us."[29]

In its annual reports to Congress in 2003 and 2004, the Pentagon asserted that China has "developed and tested an ASAT system described [in a Hong Kong newspaper article in January 2001] as a parasitic microsatellite", i.e., a small satellite that attaches itself to a target satellite to disrupt or destroy that satellite on command. Though this report is unconfirmed, the progress made by China in launching a number of recoverable satellites and mastering docking practices do give strong indications of such development.

In terms of co-orbital ASAT development, China's recent BX-1 microsatellite test, which was carried out as a part of the manned Shenzhou-7 mission, demonstrated technology that can be used as a base for future covert satellite inspection missions, as well as co-orbital ASAT attacks.[30] The BX-1 was actually a simulated run to test capabilities required for a co-orbital ASAT attack as the satellite passed in close quarters of the International Space Station.[31]

The People's Liberation Army (PLA) writings emphasise the necessity of destroying, damaging, and interfering with the enemy's reconnaissance and communication satellites with the aim of blinding and deafening the enemy.[32] The same PLA analysis of US and coalition military operations also states that "destroying or capturing satellites and other sensors will deprive an opponent of initiative on the battlefield and [make it difficult] for them to bring their precision guided weapons into full play."[33]

Advances in laser technology and techniques of laser generation have witnessed innovation in weapon systems development. The ideas professed in early writings and motion pictures only a few years ago have started taking shape and are fast becoming reality. In all probability, the laser generation systems will shrink in size, allowing weapon systems to be carried on small platforms enabling a high degree of mobility. Accordingly, given the continued R&D, war-fighters in the near-term will have additional weapon options for dealing with a spectrum of threats and contingencies.[34] While ground-based systems appear to offer the most immediate near-term laser threat, such systems may be supplemented by air-based laser weapons. Development and employment of laser weapon systems by the regional powers is expected in the middle of the 21st century and will pose a credible challenge to major space-faring nations. States embroiled in regional conflicts may develop these weapons to suit their design, and proliferation of the technology cannot be ruled out. Platforms similar to the US Air Force's YAL-1 Airborne Laser

(ABL), which has clear potential against satellites, may emerge in the inventories of future adversaries in the next century.[35] Another important weapon in the category of radio frequency weapons is the Electro-Magnetic Pulse (EMP) bomb. The weapon, yet to be demonstrated (if already realised), will usher in a new dimension to existing warfare strategy and tactics.

Types of Space Weapons

The classification and categorisation of space weapons can be done in a variety of ways, depending on the basing, characteristics and technicalities. Space weapons can be designed to neutralise the targets as a result of direct collision, explosion in the vicinity of space assets or by means of electronic attack. Based on the type of weapons, space weapons can be treated in two general categories of mass-to-target and energy-to-target weapons. While the former type encompasses weapons with destructive capability using kinetic attacks, the latter make use of directed energy, capable of physical destruction, disruption, degradation and denial of space assets. Strictly speaking, space weapons can be based either on the Earth or in its surroundings, or they may be positioned in the outer atmosphere to target any point in the universe. Space weapons can be classified in four categories depending on their own and target basing.

- Earth-to-space weapons.
- Space-to-Earth weapons.
- Space-to-space weapons.
- Earth-to-Earth weapons transiting from the realm of space.

While all the above types of weapon systems will qualify as space weapons, the weapons which fall in the second and third categories would exclusively fall in the gamut of outer space weapons. At this juncture, the international community is more worried about the aspect of space security, safeguarding of space assets, and any attack on its territory directed from, or towards, space. Space weapons can also be classified depending on the mode of attack adopted for neutralising targetted space assets. The different types of space weapons based on the mode or method of attack in vogue are:

- Kinetic kill weapons.
- Directed energy weapons.
- Cyber attacks on space assets.

United States' Approach Towards Space Weapons

The United States has been involved in a series of conflicts after the end of the Cold War and has dominated its adversaries in conventional conflicts. Of late, this dominance is largely attributed to the integration of space support and inputs which enables its forces to have a strike capability at a tactical level across the globe. The United States, in the last 20 years, has been involved in major conflicts like Operation Desert Storm, Operation Allied Force, Operation Enduring Freedom and Operation Iraqi Freedom. In addition, it has carried out special covert operations on a number of occasions as part of the global war on terror. If we analyse these conflicts, one of the common things that emerges is the superior war-fighting ability that the US forces accrue from space-based services. The services are wide-ranging, from seamless communication to remote locations, exchange of information, weather prediction, ISR inputs, weapon guidance, navigation, and many more. Such an overarching dependence on space services in varied facets of warfare has put forth newer problems in the context of security of these space assets, wherein they become increasingly indispensable and vulnerable to attacks. In a number of studies carried out in the US on the subject of space security, it has, time and again, been brought out that US space assets are vulnerable to attacks and face an enormous risk of being attacked in future conflicts. As per one RAND report, "With a growing number of states acquiring the ability to degrade or destroy US space capabilities, the probability that space systems will come under attack in a future crisis or conflict is ever increasing".[36]

China's Approach Towards Space Weapons

While China continues to stride on its space advances in support of societal and commercial services, it has consistently worked towards integrating and improvising space services in the military domain. China, of late, is also seen as advocating the concept of 'weaponisation of space' and is actively pursuing ambitious, incremental and multi-pronged activities in this field. The secrecy associated with Chinese space projects has kept the space powers on tenterhooks and it now poses a challenge to the dominance that the US has enjoyed post break-up of the Soviet Union. China has reportedly also been experimenting with DEWs to attack satellites. PLA writings emphasise the necessity of "destroying, damaging, and interfering with the enemy's reconnaissance ... and communications satellites," suggesting that such systems, as well as navigation and early warning satellites, could be among the targets of attacks designed to "blind and deafen the enemy".[37] The same PLA analysis of US and coalition military operations also states that "destroying or capturing satellites and other sensors will deprive opponents of initiative on the battlefield and make it difficult for them to bring their precision guided weapons into full play".[38] In international forums, China has advocated that outer space should be kept free of weapons and has earnestly made efforts under the UN umbrella to push for an international Code of Conduct to avoid weaponisation of space. It is also in favour of signing the treaty on Prevention of Arms Race in Outer Space (PAROS). The United States, in spite of having a well-established ballistic missile defence system, and possessing technical advantages in potential space weaponry, has consistently refused to negotiate PAROS in the Conference of Disarmament (CD).[39] The US' failure to ratify this treaty has left little choice for China but to continue research and development in space weapons.

Conclusion

The quest for developing and deploying weapons against space-based assets has witnessed a continuum in growth since the time man-made objects made way into the cosmos. The US, as the sole superpower in the unipolar world, is in a position to exploit its dominance in space-based applications. This inequitable expansion of military space potential, while conferring asymmetric advantage over its contenders, has increased the vulnerability of space assets. Aspiring powers like China and Russia, while grudgingly accepting the present hegemonic order, would not desist in contesting for their prominent place in the current world order. Any disruption or destruction of space assets will not only have an economic and societal fallout, but will also confer an asymmetric advantage to the opponent.

The use of weapons in space has been demonstrated using missiles launched from the ground or delivered by aerial platforms resulting in a kinetic kill. The resulting debris has raised concerns in the international community, which have been well taken by the defaulting parties as it would hurt their own futuristic designs also. However, sporadic incidences of destroying space assets and creating space debris have cast a shadow and call for an immediate moratorium in this regard.

ASAT technology, in making use of DEWs, has progressed considerably; however, the emergent technology is expected to evolve further and improve the capability of such weapons. The development of laser and radio frequency weapons may well be within the reach of developing nations and could tilt the strategic balance of the current unipolar world.

While the development of kinetic and DEW ASAT weapons continues, new inroads have been made to target satellites or their services by means of Information Warfare (IW). With cyber attacks, the disruption or degradation of satellites, leading to their complete failure is very much feasible. ASAT attacks using cyber means are not restricted to the advanced nations but can be carried out by an individual or a group in a clandestine manner. Cyber attacks on commercial satellite services can hinder essential services and take a toll of a nation's economy, breaking its will to fight a war.

At present, no weapon has been positioned in outer space. However, the capability of placing weapons in outer space exists, in that nation-states have developed space platforms that can carry the required payloads and can use these platforms for delivering weapons. A majority of the space-faring nations, with indigenised capability of launching satellites, would be in position to launch small or micro-satellites and with growing technical acumen, co-orbit them with target satellites as ASAT weapons.

Notes

1. Available at http://www.nasa.gov/centers/goddard/about/history/dr_goddard.html. Accessed on March 26, 2014.
2. Peter Grier; "The Flying Tomato", *Air Force Magazine*, February 2009, at http://www.airforcemag.com/MagazineArchive/Documents/2009/February%20 2009/0209tomato.pdf. Accessed on March 17, 2014.
3. Gen William L. Shelton, commander, Air Force Space Command, March 12, 2014, at www.armed-services.senate.gov/download/shelton_03-12-14. Accessed on March 19, 2014.
4. Matthew Gillard, "The Evolution of the Space Weaponization Regime During the Cold War: A Test of Hegemonic Stability Theory", Centre of International Relations, 2007, UBC Conference Paper Series, University of British Columbia, Vancouver, BC, Canada.
5. Maj Michael J. Muolo, "Space Handbook - A War-Fighter's Guide to Space", Vol I, at http://cryptome.info/shall.htm. Accessed on February 20, 2014.
6. R. James Woolsey, former director of the CIA, "Testimony Before the House Committee on Energy and Commerce", May 21, 2013, available at http://highfrontier.org/r-james-woolsey-testimony-before-the-house-committee-on-energy-and-commerce-may-21-2013/#sthash.PsBE9is7.tEvgDnnU.dpbs. Accessed on February 20, 2014.
7. David Steele, "The Weaponisation of Space: Next Arms Race?" Centre for Defence and Strategic Studies, Australian Defence College, 2007, at http://www.defence.gov.au/adc/docs/publications2010/Publctns_ShedPaper_050310_TheWeaponisationofSpaceNextArmsRace.pdf. Accessed on October 29, 2013.
8. Nicholas L. Johnson, , "Deliberate Satellite Fragmentations and their Effects on the Long-Term Space Environment", NASA Johnson Space Centre, Houston, TX, United States, at http://ntrs.nasa.gov/archive/nasa/casi.ntrs.nasa.gov/20100008966.pdf. Accessed on October 29, 2013.
9. Necati Ertekin, "E-Bomb: The Key Element of the Contemporary Military-Technical Revolution", September 2008.
10. President Ronald Reagan called on the scientific community for research and development of new technology that could help eliminate threats posed by strategic nuclear missiles

11. Available at http://www.foia.cia.gov/sites/default/files/document_conversions/89801/DOC_0000284020.pdf. Accessed on March 18, 2014.
12. Laura Grego, senior scientist, UCS Global Security Program, " A History of Anti-Satellite Programs", January 2012, at http://www.ucsusa.org/assets/documents/nwgs/a-history-of-ASAT-programs_lo-res.pdf. Accessed on March 7, 2014.
13. Grier, n. 2.
14. "Resuscitated Soviet Crown will Shoot Down Satellites or Ground-Based air Missiles", at http://izvestia.ru/news/543550. Accessed on March 18, 2014.
15. Grego, n. 12.
16. David R Tanks; "Future Challenges to US Space Systems", Institute of Foreign Policy Analysis Inc., Washington DC, June 1998, at http://www.ifpa.org/pdf/chalFull.pdf. Accessed on March 18, 2014.
17. Dr Carlo Kopp, "High Energy Laser Directed Energy Weapons", *Air Power Australia*, May 2008, at http://www.ausairpower.net/APA-DEW-HEL-Analysis.html. Accessed on March 18, 2014.
18. Ibid.
19. "Proposed Prevention of An Arms Race in Outer Space (Paros) Treaty", at http://www.nti.org/learn/treaties-and-regimes/proposed-prevention-arms-race-space-paros-treaty/. Accessed on March 18, 2014.
20. Refer chapter 1, " Quest for Space Weapons".
21. Marc Kaufman and Dafna Linzer, "China Criticized for Anti-Satellite Missile Test", *The Washington Post*, at http://www.washingtonpost.com/wp-dyn/content/article/2007/01/18/AR2007011801029_2.html. Accessed on August 22, 2014.
22. Michael Kreponm, "Anti-Satellite Weapons, Deterrence and Sino-American Space Relations", September 2013, at http://www.stimson.org/images/uploads/Anti-satellite_Weapons.pdf. Accessed on November 29, 2013, p.28.
23. Rosita Dellios, "China and Outer Space", *Humanities & Social Sciences Papers*, Paper 571, 2012, at http://epublications.bond.edu.au/hss_pubs/571. Accessed on October 29, 2013.
24. Ajey Lele and Gunjan Singh; "China's Space Strategy and Modernisation", *ORF Issue Brief*, February 2013, Observer Research Foundation, New Delhi at www.orfonline.org. Accessed on January 27, 2014.
25. M.V. Smith, "Ten Propositions Regarding Space Power", School of Advanced Airpower Studies, Maxwell Air Force Base, Alabama, June 2001, available at http://www.au.af.mil/au/awc/awcgate/saas/smith.pdf. Accessed on February 20, 2014.
26. Lele and Singh, n. 24.
27. Desmond Ball; "Assessing China's ASAT Program", APSNet Special Reports, June 14, 2007, at http://nautilus.org/apsnet/assessing-chinas-asat-program/. Accessed on November 29, 2013.
28. "The Militarisation of Space: Disharmony in the Spheres", January 17, 2008, at www.economist.com/node/10533205. Accessed on March 20, 2014.
29. Ibid.

30. Ian Easton, "China's Evolving ASAT Weapons Programs and Their Implications for Future U.S. Strategy", Project 2049 Institute, at http://project2049.net/documents/china_asat_weapons_the_great_game_in_space.pdf. Accessed on December 2, 2013.
31. Brian Weeden, "China's BX-1 Microsatellite: A Litmus Test for Space Weaponization," *The Space Review*, October 20, 2008, http://www.thespacereview.com/article/1235/1, Accessed March 20, 2014.
32. Ibid.
33. Ibid.
34. Melissa Olson, Report on "History of Laser Weapon Research", Naval Surface Warfare Centre, Dahlgren, VA, 2012 at www.dtic.mil/cgi-bin/GetTRDoc?AD=ADA557756. Accessed on July 11, 2014.
35. Tanks, n. 16.
36. Forrest E. Morgan, "Deterrence and First-Strike Stability in Space : A Preliminary Assessment", available at http://www.rand.org/content/dam/rand/pubs/monographs/2010/RAND_MG916.pdf. Accessed on October 31, 2013.
37. Office of the Secretary of Defence, "Annual Report to Congress: Military and Security Developments Involving the People's Republic of China 2014," April 24, 2014 , http://www.defense.gov/pubs/2014_DoD_China_Report.pdf. Accessed on July 11, 2014.
38. Ibid.
39. "Proposed Prevention of an Arms Race in Outer Space (PAROS) Treaty", Centre for Non-Proliferation Studies, Washington DC, available at http://cns.miis.edu/inventory/pdfs/paros.pdf. Accessed on March 18, 2014.

3

Kinetic Kill Space Weapons

The only way of discovering the limits of the possible is to venture a little way past them into the impossible.[1]

— Arthur C. Clarke

The ability to attack and kill remotely rather than proximally has played a major role in human evolution. In the not so distant past, this capability increased human survivability and gave the ability to bring down predatory and ferocious animals. Other than humans, all species have to be in close proximity of their prey to achieve a kill. Lanchester's Square Law for Mechanised Warfare, in its generalised form, states that the capacity to kill or injure from a distance by any means has an unexpectedly large consequence. *Concomitant with this evolutionary* phenomenon is the development of kinetic kill weapons. These weapons use the principle of kinetic energy for physical destruction of a target. Kinetic energy is acquired by any object by virtue of its motion and depends on the mass and velocity of the object. A kinetic kill weapon is launched towards the target with the aim to crash into the target and disintegrate it. This weapon system may be designed to intercept the target all by itself or may be armed with sub-munitions which could be initiated and directed towards the target to achieve a physical kill. Another method for achieving a kinetic kill is self-destruction of the kill vehicle in the near vicinity of the target. A kinetic kill weapon system can be used irrespective of its own as well as target basing. When such a weapon is used to destroy or impair the operational capability of an orbital asset, it is categorised as a kinetic kill space weapon.

Kinetic kill space weapons are capable of being directed from Earth to space, space to Earth, space to space and Earth to Earth, transiting through the realms of space. This chapter brings out the different types and capabilities of kinetic kill weapons in use or that can be developed with the present and evolving technologies. In the absence of a consensus on the definition of a space weapon, the categorisation of weapons as space weapons is subject to interpretations and considerable disagreements. However, weaponisation of space, in essence, should involve any weapon being directed to, or from, space, on a target, irrespective of its basing. This chapter aims to broadly cover the types of weapon used against space-based assets or being directed from space to attack targets on the Earth, in the Earth's atmosphere, and in space, irrespective of the international moratoria against the use of such weapons. Further, in this chapter, Earth-to-Earth weapons transiting through space have been omitted, as in a strict sense, these do not qualify for the definition of space weapons.

Orbital Mechanics

For appreciating and analysing the types and capabilities of space weapons, the understanding of orbital mechanics becomes obligatory. If any kinetic weapon is launched into space, either for a kinetic engagement or for insertion of the weapon in an orbit, the launch mechanism and technology adopted are similar to those adopted for satellites. A kinetic kill weapon can use a rocket or a simple long range ballistic missile to attack space assets in orbital altitudes. In case the weapon is being launched so as to place it in orbit, the rocket used for the launch should be capable of providing a higher degree of thrust to take the payload to the required altitude and release this payload at the accurate speed so that the weapon falls into the predestined orbit. The main difference between a conventional ballistic missile used to attack a space asset in a direct ascent mode and a rocket placing a weapon in orbit is the speed of the launch vehicle. The ballistic missile, owing to its less speed, falls back towards the Earth. Though this may be the case with rocket launchers as well, they release the payload with a thrust that balances the tangential speed of the payload to the Earth's gravitational pull. At this point, the centrifugal force comes into play, maintaining the object in orbit.

Putting satellites into orbits is a complex affair and involves techniques that factor in the capability of launch systems, satellite payload in terms of equipment, fuel to sustain it for its planned life-cycle and interactive forces like gravitational forces acting between the heavenly bodies of the universe. Additional factors like the elliptical shape of the Earth, the gravitational forces not being constant at fixed distances from the Earth's centre, the Earth's spinning around an oblique axis, etc. also have a considerable effect on orbital mechanics. However, for basic elucidation of orbital mechanics, the Earth is considered as a spherical entity and orbits as circular, unless otherwise stated. While the endeavour of this chapter is not to go into the technicalities of satellites and their orbital mechanics, a few of the ground rules derived from the orbital behaviour of rockets and their payloads seem to be in order to understand the complexities of launching weapons towards space assets or positioning weapons in space. For a detailed description, it is recommended to refer to the book *Physics of Space Security*.[2]

- **Sustaining Objects in Orbit:** Once an object is released by the launch vehicle at a particular altitude with a predetermined speed to maintain an orbit, it will continue to orbit the Earth by the relation between balancing the centrifugal force and the Earth's gravity and would not require any further power to sustain in this orbit.
- **Relation Between Satellite Speed and Altitude:** The speed of a satellite is closely related to its altitude and is not dependent on its size or mass. However, the Earth's gravitational force is balanced by the direction and speed with which the satellite is released into the orbit. . The altitude and speed of the satellite are related by the equation[3]:

$$Satellite\ Speed\ (V) = \sqrt{\frac{G_p}{(R_E + h)}}\ Km/s$$

Where, Gp = Earth's gravitational parameter in km^3/s^2 = 398,600 Km^3/s^2

R_E = Radius of Earth in km (6,378 km)

h = Altitude of satellite above the Earth

Fig 3.1: Circular Orbital Speed as a Function of Altitude for LEO Satellites[4]

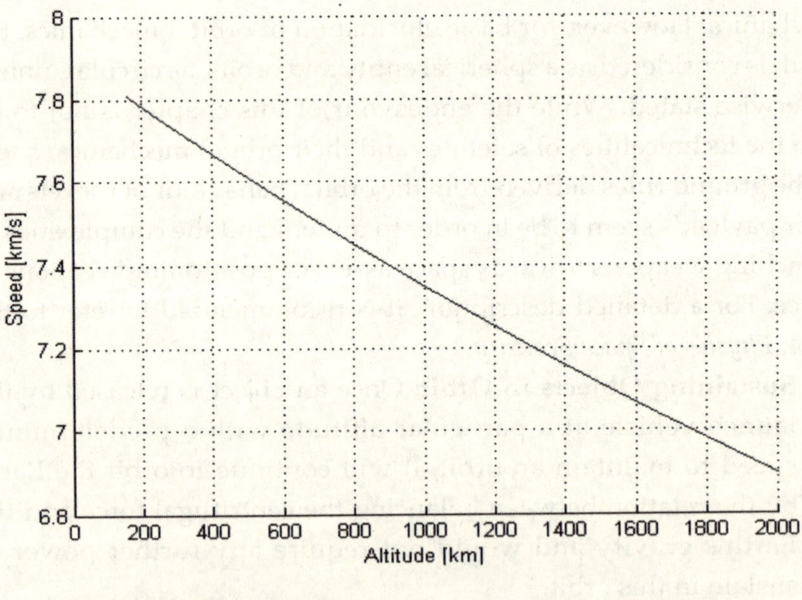

From the above equation, it is clear that the higher the satellite orbit, the lower is the speed[5]. Thus, satellites in LEO will travel at a higher speed than satellites in Medium Earth Orbit (MEO) and High Earth Orbit (HEO). The graph of circular orbital speed as a function of altitude is shown in Fig 3.1. Thus, a satellite, irrespective of its mass orbiting at an altitude of 200 km, will travel at a fixed speed of

7.78 km/s. Increasing the altitude to 500 km would result in a lower orbital speed of 7.61 km/s. Thus, if we attempt to increase the speed using external force (rocket thrusters), it will result in lowering of the orbital altitude. Similarly, if we use the external force to increase the altitude, the speed of the satellite will reduce. Thus, the relation between satellite speed and its altitude is governed by the centrifugal force which balances the satellite's speed with the Earth's gravity.

- **Relation Between Satellite Altitude and Orbital Period:** Any object in orbital space, irrespective of its mass, is governed in that orbit by centrifugal force and will travel in the same orbit with a constant orbital period. Thus, any satellite, big or small, or for that matter, even a small pebble, will travel at the same speed in a particular orbit. Any deviation in speed or altitude resulting from additional thrust imparted to this satellite would result in transition of the orbit. The orbital period (T) in seconds is governed by the Earth's gravitational parameter and altitude by the following equation[6]:

$$Orbital\ period\ (T) = \frac{2\pi(R_E + h)^{1.5}}{\sqrt{G_p}}$$

Where,

Gp = Earth's gravitational parameter in km^3/s^2 = 398,600 km^3/s^2

R_E = Radius of Earth in km (6,378 km)

h = Altitude of satellite above the Earth

Once any object is released in space with a velocity so that it falls into an orbit, it will continue to orbit the Earth at a fixed speed and fixed altitude indefinitely, without using any propelling means. Objects in lower orbits travel faster. As we increase the orbital altitude, the speed of the satellite reduces and the time taken to orbit around the Earth (orbital period) also increases. Satellites in LEO travel at the speed of 7 to 8 km/s.[7] Thus, satellites in medium and higher orbits would have slower speeds. While the orbital periods of satellites in LEO are in the range of 1 to 2 hours, the time to complete one orbit increases with the altitude of the orbit. The plot of a circular orbital period as a function of altitude for LEO satellites is given at Fig 3.2. Thus, a satellite at an altitude of 200 km will complete one orbit in 88.5 min and a satellite at an altitude of 500 km will complete one orbit in 94.6 min. Thus, for a satellite to orbit the Earth exactly in one day, we can substitute the time and arrive at the orbital altitude. Thus, taking 24 hours (86,400 seconds), we get the orbital altitude 'h' of 35,863 km. This type of orbit is termed as a geosynchronous orbit. A geosynchronous satellite can assume any plane around the Earth and it will revisit that point on the Earth exactly after 24 hours or one orbital rotation. This is because the Earth's axis is tilted and rotation of the Earth on this axis, would cause a mismatch in lateral displacement of the Earth's plane with that of the satellite's orbital plane.

Fig 3.2: Circular Orbital Period as a Function of Altitude for LEO Satellites[8]

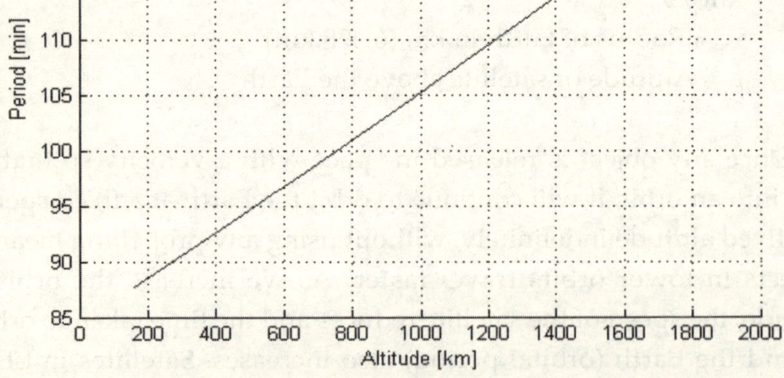

However, if a geosynchronous satellite is placed exactly on a point above the equator, and the orbital plane and equatorial plane coincide, we have a unique situation when the satellite irrespective of any time in the day is on the same point of the Earth. Such geosynchronous satellites orbiting above the fixed point on the equator are called geostationary satellites and the orbit is called the equatorial orbit. The geostationary orbit is unique in nature and the only orbit which gives round-the-clock coverage for the vast geographical area under its footprint on the Earth. Thus, countries which lie on the equator can accrue immense benefits from satellite services.

- If the object launched from the Earth exceeds or equals the speed of 11.2 km/s, it will break away from the gravitational force exerted by the Earth and will be lost into the infinity of the deep space. This speed is called escape velocity.[9]
- As a rule of thumb, a ballistic missile that can launch a given payload weighing 2 tons to a distance of, say, 1,000 km on a flat Earth, will be able to launch the given payload vertically for half the distance i.e. 500 km.[10] Modern rockets can launch in LEO a payload of the order of 2-4 per cent of the initial launch mass, and to place a payload of 1 ton in orbit, roughly 45 tons of fuel is consumed.[11]
- Satellites can follow different types of orbits and an external force can change the nature of the orbit. In general, as the Earth is more elliptical than circular in nature, most of the satellite orbits are elliptically shaped.
- As almost all the satellites, barring the geostationary satellites, have a relative motion to the Earth point directly below (the point on the Earth's surface made by the line joining the satellite and the centre of the Earth), a constellation of satellites would be needed for continuous coverage of the Earth. This constellation would entail a higher number of satellites in lower orbits.
- If a specific target, for example, an ICBM launch site is to be provided round the clock coverage, a large constellation of LEO

satellites would be required. The number of satellites required in this constellation is called the absentee ratio which reduces with increasing the altitude of the satellite constellation. Deploying Space Based Interceptors (SBI) for attacking ground targets would have a high figure of absentee ratio and this absentee ratio will further increase if the reaction time to target a point on Earth is to be reduced[12]. Further, to reduce the reaction time, multiple satellites will be required in the same orbital trajectory (orbital plane), and there will be many such orbital planes[13].

- The SBIs would be vulnerable to attack from the ground as they can be tracked, being in LEO, and their positions can be predicted.

Kinetic Kill Earth-to-Space Weapons

Whenever an object is launched from the Earth or from its surrounding atmosphere with an aim to crash into a space target or is used as a platform for the release of a projectile to intercept a space target, it will be categorised as an Earth-to-space kinetic kill weapon. The attack using kinetic kill capability envisages physical damage and destruction of the asset in space by subjecting it to a deliberate high speed collision. Such a weapon system will fall in the category of a direct ascent weapon system as it is not designed to stay in outer space.[14] A direct ascent space weapon would constitute a rocket or missile launched directly from the Earth or could use a launch platform like a ship or an aircraft. This missile itself could be designed to intercept a target satellite or may carry a projectile which could be guided to the target. The interceptor weapon uses its own mass and, generally, would be equipped with a homing sensor to guide it to the target. Such a rocket or missile is generally fired after calculating target coordinates and predicting its position for a successful intercept. The weapon system may be delivered in the proximity of the target satellite and could be designed to carry an explosive payload that initiates in the vicinity of the target. Alternately, the payload could constitute multiple warheads or pellets which could be released as a high velocity cloud for the destruction of the satellite. Conceptually, these weapon systems are *simple in their functionality* but complex and cumbersome in their implementation. The associated complexity becomes increasingly challenging with the increasing accuracy, range and intercept timing. The technology to target a satellite using a ballistic missile is much less complex than carrying the payload on the launcher and positioning it in the precise orbit. Satellites travel in predictable orbits and can be tracked to correlate their future position at a reasonably foreseeable time. This would give the attacker sufficient time to assemble its rocket or missile, and would allow multiple attempts for target destruction.

Working Principle

The kinetic kill vehicle used for intercepting and destroying a satellite will have the same basic design parameters as a ballistic missile. It would have a power source, would be armed with a warhead and have a guidance system comprising controls and homing sensors on a rocket motor or a booster. On initiating the launch sequence, the rocket motor would provide for the initial boost, propelling the missile in a vertical trajectory at very high speed in the region of 7 km/s and this would carry the warhead out of the realms of the Earth's atmosphere towards the predicted intercept point. For control and guidance in the initial phase, the missile may use techniques like inertial navigation system, and for correction of the trajectory, it may be fitted with the Divert and Attitude Control System (DACS) which forces the missile to correct its trajectory by the firing of thrusters. As the fuel of the rocket motor is exhausted, the warhead is jettisoned and travels towards the target unpowered in a ballistic profile by virtue of its kinetic energy. This warhead would be equipped with onboard sensors which would provide the inputs to guide it to the target for a successful intercept.

Outer space begins at an altitude of approximately 100 km above the mean sea level. Satellites in LEO travel at a speed in the range of 7 km/s and complete the orbit around the Earth in one to two hours. A kinetic kill vehicle using a ballistic missile in a direct ascent configuration will generally be limited to target satellites or space vehicles in LEO. This is because if a missile with a payload of, for example, 'x' kg can be designed for launch at a range of 'y' km, then the same missile, if fired vertically, would be capable of reaching an altitude of approximately 'y/2' km. Any decrease in payload 'x' will enhance the altitude to some extent. All space-faring nations that have developed an indigenous capability to launch rockets or possess credible ballistic missile technology, will be in a position to develop such a weapon system. This means that any country possessing the capability of manufacturing ballistic missiles operating over a range in excess of 400 km to target a point on the Earth can venture into development and experimentation of a weapon directed at targets in LEO. The only requirement for the kill vehicle would be to institute a system to track and home onto the desired target.

Sub-Orbital ASAT Weapon

All countries that have a Ballistic Missile Defence (BMD) programme or are pursuing such a programme are inherently capable of developing and employing ASAT weapons. Generally, the BMD system will rely on intercepting a rogue ballistic missile in the mid-course phase as intercepting in the boost phase is limited by the reaction time available. In comparison, interception of a satellite is much easier as the satellites can be easily tracked and monitored; and their exact position can be predicted in advance. The ASAT tests carried out by both China and the United States used ballistic missiles to destroy the satellites. The details of the ASAT tests and their comparison clearly highlights that this kind of capability is within the reach of a majority of nations equipped with long range ballistic missiles.

- **Chinese ASAT Tests:** On January 11, 2007, China destroyed its Fengyun series weather satellite, the FY 1-C. The 750 kg satellite was destroyed at an altitude of 865 km by the intercept missile travelling at a speed of 8 km/s in a head-on configuration. China's direct-ascent, kinetic-kill ASAT launch vehicle is the derivative of the technology used in its Kaituozhe-1 (KT-1) (Pioneer or Explorer) solid-fuelled launch vehicle[15] which itself is a four-stage variant of the Dong Feng-21 (DF-21) Medium Range Ballistic Missile (MRBM).[16] The KT-1 has been developed by the China Aerospace Solid Launch Vehicle Company (CASLV), a subsidiary of the China Aerospace Science and Industry Corporation (CASIC) with the aim of launching small satellites weighing in the range of 300 kg into LEO. The KT-1 vehicle is designed to launch in a mobile configuration, truck-based platform from anywhere in the country.[17] A series of launches was attempted in January and September 2002, and in September 2003. All these launches, aimed at placing of small satellites in LEO and polar orbits, were unsuccessful. Learning from the failures and aiming to develop the launch vehicle into a kinetic kill interceptor, the Chinese 9th Academy (also known as the Sanjiang Group or Base 066) was awarded the contract in 2002 for developing a four-stage kinetic kill vehicle capable of delivering 100 kg payload into a 700 km Sun Synchronous Orbit (SSO). The missile was modified to be launched as part of an integrated system capable of being readied at a short notice of less than 12 hours. The homing system for the missile warhead could have made use of Imaging Infra-Red (IIR) and active radar sensors.[18] The Inertial Navigation System (INS) and Global Positioning System (GPS) updates could have been used for steering it towards the target.[19] The experimental evaluations of the ASAT tests were conducted on July 7, 2005, and February 6, 2006. Though no target was hit, it was not clear if they missed the target or target destruction was not planned. However, these experimental evaluations seem to have contributed to the successful interception of the FY-1C satellite on January 11, 2007. China followed up this ASAT with a successful exo-atmospheric test of a ballistic missile at the altitude of 120 km. On September 25, 2013, the KT-1 launch system was used to place a small remote sensing satellite in orbit. It appears that China is developing both offensive and defensive capabilities using the KT-1, the defensive capabilities for replacement of downed/malfunctioning satellites in a short period of time, and providing for redundancy in operations.

Thus, by integrating a suitable homing sensor used with inertial navigation methods and provision of radar correlation data, a simple ballistic missile or rocket can be modified to intercept a space target in LEO. On May 13, 2013, China launched a rocket from the Xichang Satellite Launch Centre in Sichuan province. The rocket reached an altitude of 10,000 km and the ceiling covered was one of the highest suborbital launches worldwide since 1976. The rocket apparently did not place any satellite or object in orbit and as per the Pentagon, this launch could be the first interceptor test aimed at destroying a satellite in higher orbit.[20] While admitting that the launch did take place, China maintains that the rocket carried a science payload to study the Earth's magnetosphere[21]. The system appears to be designed to place a kinetic kill vehicle on a trajectory to deep space that could reach Medium Earth Orbit (MEO), Highly Elliptical Orbit (HEO), and Geostationary Earth Orbit (GEO).[22] If true, this would represent a significant development in China's ASAT capabilities as no other nation has tested such a system.[23]

- **US ASAT Test of 2008:** The United States, on February 20, 2008, targeted and destroyed its own National Reconnaissance Office satellite, the USA-193. The weapon used was a standard missile SM-3 from the Aegis BMD system, fired from a sea-based platform. The SM-3 missile warhead is equipped with a high resolution long wave infrared sensor and has an advanced divert and altitude control system to steer its course towards the target[24]. The warhead incorporates a large aperture field of view that enables target acquisition at 300 km. The data streaming is encrypted for secured transmission. The sea-based platform was the USS *Lake Erie* with the onboard Aegis radar sensors to detect and track the satellite and identify the intercept points for engaging the satellite. Additional inputs were contributed to the success of mission by the US Space Surveillance Network and from the tracking facilities at various sites. The intercept was carried out at an altitude of 247 km.

- **Comparison of US and Chinese ASAT Tests:** As the comparison given below will reveal, almost all the nations engaged in production, development and testing of long range ballistic missiles can indulge in the development of ASAT weapons. The ballistic missiles would need only minor modifications and if the facility of detecting and tracking satellites is available, the modified missile can be directed to intercept a target using homing sensors.

Table 3.1: Comparison of US and Chinese ASAT Tests[25]

	United States Sm-3	Chinese Deng Fong-21
Length	6.55 m	10.7 m
Diameter	0.34 m	1.4 m
Launch Mass	708 kg	14,700 kg
Estimated Kinetic Vehicle Mass	102 kg	600 kg
Configuration	3-stage solid propellant	2-stage solid propellant
Guidance	GPS/INS radar guidance	Inertial plus terminal radar guidance
Interceptor/ Target closing speed	28,000 km/hr	32,400 km/hr
Interceptor Launch (Ground/ Sea)	Shipborne	Ground-based
Interceptor Launch Facility	USS *Lake Erie*	Xichang Space Centre
Interceptor type	Modified Standard Missile-3	Modified DF-21/ KT-1
Intercept Altitude	247 km	864 km
Estimated Debris Pieces in Orbit	None after 40 days	2,200 (for 20-100 years)

Kinetic Kill Weapons with Explosive Warhead and Projectiles

The capability of launching satellites with indigenised launch vehicles rests with a handful of nations which include the USA, Russia, China, France, Japan, India, and a few more. While the first three countries have been engaged in development and testing of ASAT vehicles, the other space-faring nations possess the inherent capability to develop ASAT technology in a short period of time. For a space-faring nation, having an indigenous capability to launch satellites and release them in the exact orbit with the required velocity is a much more complex and formidable task than the technology required to intercept a space asset. A primitive kinetic kill weapon system may incorporate an explosive (including nuclear) or fragmenting warhead capable of initiating itself in the vicinity of the target satellite. Even a high speed collision of a single fragment or pellet can lead to complete or partial neutralisation of the target. Rocket launch vehicles and ballistic missiles can be designed to carry projectiles and multiple warheads. Just like the concept of the Multiple Independent Reentry Vehicle (MIRV) designed for reducing the effectiveness of a BMD programme, countries with a credible ballistic missile programme can develop a rocket or a ballistic missile, armed with multiple projectiles or submunitions with homing sensors that can be used to target multiple space assets. A rocket or a ballistic missile can also be used to deliver a loitering warhead (with a single or multiple warheads) in the vicinity of the target satellite. It can be equipped with sensors that can locate, identify and destroy multiple space assets in a hunter killer configuration. This loitering warhead will be an expendable 'fire and forget' weapon system, having the capability to recognise and attack selected satellites.

Air-Launched Kinetic Kill Weapon

The air-launched kinetic kill capability will use an airborne platform for launching a missile to attack a space asset. In contrast to a ground-launched ASAT weapon, use of an airborne platform to launch a missile to attack a satellite has its advantage, wherein, due to the flexibility and mobility of the launch vehicle, the need for the satellite to overfly in the near vicinity of the launch region is obviated. The second advantage that accrues to a missile is that it needs to traverse less altitude and distance to intercept the target. These advantages will also allow for rapid launches which would be cost-effective compared to the ground or sea-based launch systems. The example of the Air

Launch Mini Vehicle (ALMV) using the two-stage ASM-135 missile fired aboard the F-15A aircraft as brought out in Chapter 1, falls in this category. The 1985 test of the ALMV was successful in intercepting a defunct US satellite at an altitude of 555 km but further development was stalled in view of the ban imposed on ASAT testing under the Defence Authorisation Act.[26] The United States Air Force (USAF) research laboratory is pursuing development of a MicroSatellite Launch Vehicle (MSLV) that will use the F-15E aircraft as the mother platform and, in turn, will be capable of launching small satellites into LEO.[27] In addition to the USA, China and Russia have shown keen interest in developing this technology. China is reported to be developing a Satellite Launch Vehicle (SLV) called Shenlong (Divine Dragon), capable of being carried under the fuselage of the Xian H-6 bomber and launch aircraft.[28] The SLV, designed to be launched at an altitude of 11 km, can place a payload of 50 kg in LEO up to 600 km altitude.[29] Russia, on the other hand, has attempted a similar system, using MiG-31 aircraft armed with the R-33 variant of the air-to-air missile in the ASAT role to target satellites in LEO.[30]

Kinetic Kill Space-to-Earth Weapons

The kinetic kill space-to-Earth weapon can be used for physical destruction of terrestrial targets or targets like aircraft and missiles in the Earth's atmosphere. Such a weapon system would provide the capability of attacking any point on the Earth. For the weapons to qualify under this category, they have to be launched and positioned into space well in advance, before the weapon is initiated. Once in space, the weapon platform will be governed by the laws of orbital mechanics. Thus, for a weapon to be placed in space, the first and foremost requirement is to launch the weapon into space and stabilise it in the requisite profile by means of controlled manoeuvring. The second requirement would be to sustain it in this profile or orbit for the planned duration till it is put to use. The technology used for placing a weapon platform in a particular orbit will be the same as being used for insertion of a satellite in that place and at that point of time. Thus, only countries with developed indigenous rocket launching capability will be in a position to exploit this kind of weapon technology.

Once initiated, the kinetic kill weapon, directed from space to the Earth, will rely more on the kinetic energy gained by virtue of acceleration of its own mass assisted by gravity. Now, any object travelling towards the Earth from space is subjected to intense friction caused by the atmosphere. The physics which governs the laws of reentry of an object towards the Earth from space is a complex subject. The Earth's atmosphere dons a protective shield for mankind from the unearthly wields of the space-based natural projectiles hurled towards the Earth. The meteors attracted towards the Earth travel towards it at a speed of 10 to 70 km/s.[31] Due to the friction experienced from the Earth's atmosphere, they slow down considerably and in the process, heat up to an extent that they burn out well before they can impact the Earth's surface. Hardly any of these meteors make it to the Earth's surface. The ones that make contact, lose a majority of their mass in the burnout process and impact the Earth's surface at the speed of a few hundred km/hour.[32]

Similar to naturally occurring meteors, a kinetic weapon directed from space to physically attack a target on the Earth or its atmosphere, will be required to survive the reentry procedure into the Earth's atmosphere by means of protective shielding. This protective shielding will entail additional weight to be factored in when placing it in orbit. Increase in the mass of a space weapon system results in cost escalation and increased launch complexities. Additionally, the weapon system will have to be catered with the fuel requirement to de-orbit and propel towards the target on the Earth. Also, once orbiting in space, the intended target has to fall in the shadow of its attack footprint, putting restrictions on firing the weapon at the time and place of choosing. To overcome this, a constellation of weapon systems will be required, the cost of which will be prohibitively high. Thus, such a kinetic kill weapon system though technologically feasible and operationally viable, will be effort and design intensive. Further, to target any infrastructural assets on the ground, the kill radius will be constrained as destruction of the selected target will be based on the penetration effect of the weapon.

Thus, as far as efficacy is concerned, such a weapon will be more suited for direct impact on a target for greater devastating effect derived from mass and velocity. Incorporating a warhead would not be beneficial as, in all likelihood, the warhead will disintegrate owing to the excessive heating. Even with adequate protective shielding to the warhead, the atmospheric drag will cause a lateral shift in the intended trajectory, leading to unacceptable inaccuracies. This degradation in accuracy will be further compounded due to the distortions in the aerodynamic structure from the heat and possible peeling off of the outer protective sheath during the terminal homing phase of the weapon's flight. Thus, fielding of kinetic kill space-to-Earth weapons will not only be complex, but also cost prohibitive. Moreover, except for the penetration capability, it won't have any distinct advantage over conventional weapons.

However, if a space-based kinetic energy interceptor is used against ballistic missiles so as to intercept it in the outer periphery of the atmosphere, either during the terminal part of the boost phase, the mid-course phase or the early part of the terminal phase, then such weapon systems will be workable albeit at a high cost. Such weapons would be placed in LEO, where they would remain until a hostile missile launch was detected. To intercept a ballistic missile in the boost or terminal phase, the space-based weapon will de-orbit and accelerate towards the target missile to destroy it by means of direct impact. Mid-course intercepts would occur in space. [33]

Space-Based Missile Defence System

A space-based BMD system would be the most suited to intercept any missile across the globe with its widespread coverage provided that the system is feasible, cost-effective and efficient. The idea of a space-based BMD system was strengthened by the Strategic Defence Initiative (SDI)[34] proposed by President Ronald Reagan in a nationwide television address on March 23, 1983. While the SDI concept was floated by the US to tackle and nullify ICBM attacks by the Soviets using ground, sea-based and space-based BMD systems, one of the major components of this initiative was utilisation of Space-Based Interceptors (SBIs).

Brilliant Pebbles

Amongst the various ground-based and spaced-based weapon systems, one of the weapon systems conceived and developed was the SBI. It was aimed at intercepting ballistic missiles in their boost phase using satellites orbiting in LEO. Called "Brilliant Pebbles", a space-based, kinetic kill interceptor that was part of President Ronald Reagan's SDI programme[35], the system was a non-nuclear, space-based, 'detect and intercept to kill' weapon, conceived to achieve effects akin to those of a meteoroid impact. Each SBI satellite would constitute a tungsten metal ball weighing in the range of 45 kg[36] and orbiting the Earth at an altitude of 400 km.[37] This SBI concept was built around placing a constellation of football sized 1,000 metal ball satellites in LEO which would cater for complete coverage over the globe. Each pebble satellite in LEO would have an advanced sensor system capable of providing early warning to detect the missile launches and would be in a position to track, and home on to, the target. Further, each brilliant pebble would be interlinked with other brilliant pebbles in an interactive network. Additionally, the brilliant pebbles would be supported with the inputs of any missile launch in the early boost phase from a parallel space surveillance network called "Brilliant Eyes". The pebbles capable of tracking the missile from the boost phase could intercept it then, in its mid-course phase or in the early part of the terminal phase. On detection of any missile launch, the most suited brilliant pebble would be selected for intercept. The selected brilliant pebble's onboard propulsion system would be initiated and the metal ball would then de-orbit to intercept the missile, preferably in the boost phase of the launch in such a fashion that it would be intercepted at an altitude of above 80 to 100 km[38] so as to avoid the extreme temperatures experienced during the reentry manoeuvre. The brilliant pebble concept was an efficient, workable and cost-effective option for a credible space-based missile programme using a kinetic kill capability. As the space military and commercial sectors at the time had the experience of placing small commercial and military satellites like the Iridium constellation, increasing availability of off-the-shelf technology would have bolstered the production, launch and operational costs of this system.[39] However, after a series of budget cuts, the Brilliant Pebbles demonstration-validation programme was scaled down to a technology demonstration programme, presumably because of concerns about the Anti-Ballistic Missile (ABM) Treaty, which subsequently was cancelled in entirety during the Clinton Administration in early 1993.[40] The stalled programme once again stood a chance of revival when in 2002 , the US withdrew from the ABM Treaty of 1972 . The revival of the SBI programme has been advocated by many eminent strategic organisations in the United States.

Hypervelocity Rods

One of the spinoffs of the 'Brilliant Pebbles' programme that created considerable interest was the feasibility of the use of tungsten rod bundles aboard a space-based platform. Called "Rod from Gods", this weapon, based entirely on kinetic capability, was proposed by the Sandia National Laboratory and involved use of high-mass, high-density tungsten or uranium rods that could be fired from space, similar to bullets. The only difference with the conventional ammunition being that each of these tungsten rods would be 20 ft long and one foot in diameter, capable of travelling at almost meteoritic speeds once fired from space.[41] Such rods would have to sustain extreme temperatures experienced during the reentry manoeuvre and would cause extensive damage to the target by virtue of their penetration capability and heat effects. As the damage to the target would be due to the direct impact with transfer of intense kinetic energy, each of these rods would be suited to attack a point target buried in depth. Further, such a weapon system would be ineffective against mobile targets. Thus, for multiple targets, a number of rods would be required to be housed in the space weapon platform. Moreover, a global attack capability would require a constellation of such weapon platforms. According to a 2003 RAND report, a constellation of roughly 35–65 space-based long-rod penetrators in orbit at 4,000-8,000 km could achieve global coverage and a maximum response time of about one hour.[42] Thus, making use of these long-rod penetrators against singular selected targets was not found to be economically viable. Secondly, the technical complexities in bringing on the weapon to the target, the installation of compatible sensors, tracking and homing devices on the interceptor and the associated logistics problems for a global coverage were found to be cost exorbitant. The life-cycle of these platforms would be governed by the amount of fuel carried and necessitate replicating/ replacing the complete system, leading to phenomenal dead assets (and, thereby, contributing to the space debris problem). In fact, such a weapon system using a finite set of rods would be more suitable on a space plane, as discussed later.

Manoeuvring Asteroids to Earth

We have been witnessing the natural impacts of asteroids on the Earth's surface every year. A question that has often been contemplated is: can these asteroids be diverted from their orbit using external force, and directed towards a target of choice towards the Earth? In today's scenario, the diversion of an asteroid could seem a prudent feasibility; however, the means and the capability to direct it to the specified point of impact on Earth do not seem to be possible. In 1999, the US National Aeronautics and Space Administration (NASA) had conceived the project "Deep Impact"[43], which was launched on January 12, 2005, to study the outcomes of a comet impact mission and record any minor changes in trajectory. After a series of manoeuvres, the Deep Impact spacecraft, on July 3, 2005, separated the passive interceptor weighing 370 kg to intercept the comet Tempel-1, a comet weighing approximately 7.9×10^{13} kg and with surface dimensions of approximately 38 km^2. The kinetic collision took place on July 4, 2005, resulting in a crater of 150 m on this asteroid. While splitting of smaller or larger asteroids could be attempted, predicting the path of, or exercising control on, the resulting fragments is highly unlikely. Thus, while using interceptors against a near Earth asteroid is possible, the capability to change its course for directing it to a specified target is not possible.

Kinetic Kill Space-to-Space Weapons

This category would comprise weapon systems based in space to act against any satellites or assets based in, or transiting, the realm of space. These weapons would characterise future war and would comprise manoeuvrable space planes, co-orbital satellites, satellites armed with projectiles or space mines. Positioning of weapons in space would require them to be launched aboard rocket launchers in the same manner as satellites. Once the weapon platform is inserted with the required velocity in the planned orbit, it would not require any propulsive power and the only power requirements would be for correcting the altitude or orbit, if deemed necessary. The weapon will fall in two categories based on the time period it spends in orbit. Firstly, the weapon could be launched to stay in orbit for an indefinite period before its initiation to attack another space asset. Such a space weapon will follow a particular fixed orbit and if so designed, can be manoeuvred using onboard propulsion. After being placed in an orbit, the weapon system would require a considerable payload of propellant to carry out the attack. Secondly, the weapon platform could be launched just a few hours prior to a planned attack. For such a payload to qualify as a space weapon, it has to spend a finite time in orbit. To distinguish it from the projectiles or rockets which fall back towards the Earth and burn out in the process, it would qualify as a space weapon if, and only if, it continues to orbit in the released altitude at the speed governed by the Earth's centrifugal force (or it could be designed to orbit other heavenly bodies) and is capable of staying in such orbit for at least one orbital period.

Space Plane

A space plane consists of a manoeuvrable reentry space vehicle which would be launched into space on a rocket vehicle emulating a satellite launch. Once the plane is released into space, it will assume an orbit, and continue in this orbit. A space plane, just like an aircraft, is designed for manoeuvrability in space and, thus, would be capable of changing speeds and the altitude or orbits. The manoeuvrability in space would entail spending of onboard fuel and, thus, the major part of the payload would constitute vast amounts of propellant fuel for it to qualify as a credible space weapon. In addition to carrying propellant fuel, the space plane will have additional payloads of weapons, sensors and communication. At any given time in space, it would be require preserving a high reserve of this fuel to cater for the reentry manoeuvre requiring considerable propulsive force to slow down the speed in order to self-guard itself from atmospheric burn-out, and for a safe landing. A space plane can undertake a variety of tasks and as a weapon platform can carry conventional as well as non-conventional weapons. It can be used to launch multiple projectiles, small satellites and space mines with onboard equipment for executing electronic attacks. Thus, a space plane can be used to attack terrestrial as well as space-based targets.

The X-37B Orbital Test Vehicle (OTV): The X-37 spacecraft operated by the US Air Force, was conceived by NASA in the year 1999 and developed by Boeing. This unmanned reusable spacecraft is an OTV that is launched into space using a rocket and then reenters the Earth's atmosphere to land as a space plane. Designed in a fashion similar to the US Space Shuttle, the OTV is much smaller and more compact, fielding advanced technologies. The initial version, the X-37A was an Approach and Landing Test Vehicle (ALTV). The X-37 B is a modified version of the X-37 A and is a technology demonstrator for a reusable unmanned space plane designed to stay in LEO and manoeuvre in space for a prolonged duration spread over months. The X-37B is 29 ft in length, spans 14 ft in width, and stands 9 ½ ft tall, weighing 11,000 pounds[45]. As on date, three missions have been completed, with the first mission launched on April 22, 2010, and spending a total of 224 days in space. The second mission was launched aboard the Atlas-V rocket on March 5, 2011, and spent 469 days in orbit. The third mission of the X-37B was launched on October 25, 2012, and landed back after completing 1,041 days in space. The fourth mission, launched on May 20, 2015, is presently in orbit. The official version describes all these launch projects to be purely experimental for evaluating and consolidating the reusable space vehicle technology. A space plane can be planned for a myriad tasks that would include maintenance of space assets, extension of logistics support for improving the life-cycle, carrying out ISR missions, acting as a platform for insertion of satellites or acting as a space weapon platform. As a weapon platform in orbit, it can be used to launch rogue satellites, scatter space mines, act as a projectile firing platform and carry equipment to interfere with the functioning of space assets. However, as the size of the X-37 B OTV is small, the payload capability and the cargo hold may not be sufficient to use it as a credible weapon platform. Thus, in all probability, the United States uses the X-37B OTV as a space-based sensor and an experimental test platform for its future projects like the Space Manoeuvre Vehicle (SMV) which could be better suited to carry heavy weapon payloads.

Responsive Access, Small Cargo, Affordable Launch (RASCAL): In March 2002, the Defence Advanced Research Projects Agency (DARPA) of the United States started development work on the RASCAL project, aimed at launching small payloads in a rapid and responsive manner. The project envisaged routine launches of the order of 50 to 130 kg in sun-synchronous orbit at an altitude of 500 to 1,250 km at a significantly reduced cost[46]. The RASCAL system was planned with a reusable launch platform using two major components: the first was an aircraft employing the Mass Injection Pre-Compressor Cooling (MIPCC) for enhancing the speed and altitude; the second was a two-stage Expendable Rocket Vehicle (ERV) for accelerating payloads to orbital velocities. The system was planned to incorporate flexibility in terms of a 250 nautical miles (nm) range, response time of one hour, could loiter for 30 minutes and the turnaround time would be as low as 24 hours.[47] The project was cancelled in the year 2005; however, the United States continues to evaluate the feasibility of a reusable space plane launch vehicle by improving upon the airframe structures, higher temperature tolerance and retaining the advantages of aircraft-like operations[48]. On the lines of RASCAL, DARPA is now in the process of carrying out trials on the Experimental Space plane (XS-1) to demonstrate technology for an operational system capable of launching payloads in the range of 1 to 3 tonnes to LEO for less than US $ 5 million per flight, at a launch rate of 10 or more flights a year.[49] If the project proceeds as per plan, the orbital flight demonstrations could be undertaken by the year 2018.

"Buran" the Russian Snowstorm: The Buran space plane was conceived by the Russians as a response to the US Space Shuttle in the 1980s. One of the likely objectives of this space plane was delivery of nuclear warheads. The purpose included deterring the enemy from military use of space and acting as an experimental platform for manned space missions.[50] The spacecraft was launched on November 15, 1988, aboard an Energiya booster, to an altitude of 250 km. The de-orbiting was carried out after two orbits due to technological constraints. The project was shelved in 1993 owing to shortage of funds.

"Shenlong" the Divine Dragon: In addition to the USA and Russia, China has also pursued development of its space plane, the "Shenlong". Academic models displayed in the year 2000 revealed a delta winged space plane with a single vertical stabiliser, equipped with three high-expansion engines.[51] Chinese media outlets have reported a test flight of the Shenlong space plane that apparently included its airdrop from an H-6 bomber[52]. As per information garnered through reports from the Chinese local government website in the early part of 2014, a highly secretive "automated high-speed approach and landing test" had been successfully conducted[53] and this, in all probability, could be a related to the Shenlong.

Co-orbital Weapons

Co-orbital weapon satellites are space-to-space weapons launched in the vicinity of a target satellite. These weapons in the ASAT role can target other assets in space by means of direct collision, firing of onboard projectiles, self-destruction in the target's vicinity, and neutralising the target by means of fragmentation. The concept of a co-orbital ASAT was first floated by the USSR in the 1960s and the system was declared operational in 1973. Loaded with conventional explosives, these killer satellites, each weighing 1,400 kg, would be launched, and parked into a LEO, would eventually manoeuvre to a transfer orbit within 2 to 3 hours to close in with the target satellite. Once the target satellite was in range, it would initiate the explosive payload to damage the target satellite with shrapnel.[54] In all, 20 tests were conducted from 1968 to 1982 over altitudes varying from 230 km to 1,600 km.[55] The system remained in operation till it was decommissioned in the year 1993. The technology needed for this category of ASAT weapon is quite primitive by present-day standards and, hypothetically, all nations capable of launching satellites using indigenous rockets are capable of deploying co-orbital ASAT weapons. While Russia has experimented with, and deployed, co-orbital ASATs over two decades, the present-day technology will permit better sensor systems for homing and tracking, and onboard explosive charges can now be replaced with single shot kill probability kinetic projectiles. While the United States has monitored the USSR's programme closely, it has not shown any specific inclination to pursue the co-orbital ASAT system. China, on other hand, has shown keen interest in co-orbital technology, and in a recent evaluation, is said to have experimented with the co-orbital satellite capability with its BX-1 micro-satellite. The experiment was carried out as a part of the manned Shenzhou-7 mission and demonstrated technology that could aid in co-orbital ASAT attacks.[56] The evaluation involved the release of the microsatellite BX-1 by using the mother platform as a springboard. The BX-1 is said to have ventured out into space to a distance of more than 100 km and then by self-manoeuvring, rejoined the Shenzhou-7. During its space manoeuvre, the microsatellite, at one given time, was in the range of 25 km from the ISS. Thus, it is widely believed that the BX-1 was actually a simulated run to test capabilities required for a co-orbital ASAT attack as the satellite passed in close quarters of the ISS .[57] While no co-orbital ASAT tests have been conducted since the Russian programme was decommissioned, the advancing technology in launch systems and the miniaturisation of satellites have made possible the development of parasitic satellites and space mines.

Space Mines and Parasitic Satellites: These are another offshoot of the co-orbital ASAT system designed to attack the target satellites, resulting in a kinetic kill. The difference between the two is that a space mine could be placed in the vicinity of a target satellite, whereas a parasitic satellite would attach itself to the target and detonate itself on command. These would constitute satellites in the class of micro or nanosatellites and could weigh from less than a kilogram to a few kilograms. These space mines can be used to trail the target, can be in very close quarters or could be attached to target satellites, or could be placed in a different orbital plane (with the same altitude as the target satellite).[58] The attack on the adversary's satellite would involve a direct collision or it could self-destruct after closing in with the target satellite. These weapons would be generally configured to take on one of the satellites and, thus, for neutralising a constellation of satellites, multiple space mines would be required. While miniature space mines could be difficult to detect, once detected, they can be tracked effectively and the likely target could be easily assimilated. Multiple space mines can be launched over a single rocket or they could be placed in orbit using a spacecraft. These space mines can be launched and maintained in orbit for a number of years or if called for, could be launched in times of conflict. The Chinese are believed to be investing in small (nano) satellites technologies which could be used as space mines.[59]

Robotic Arm in Space

On July 20, 2013, China, as part of a covert anti-satellite weapons development programme, had launched a set of three satellites called Chuangxin-3 (Innovation-3), Shiyan-7 (Experiment-7), and Shijian-15 (Practice-15).[60] As per available reports, one of the small manoeuvrable satellites was equipped with a robotic arm that was tested to capture another satellite[61]. While reports on the actual mission remain unverified, Pentagon officials believe the small satellite activity is closely associated with China's secret ASAT programme.[62] The report also goes on to state that the robotic arm could have been an experiment to facilitate future maintenance and repair activities in relation to space assets.[63] Experimenting with the robotic arm to physically control space assets or using it for on-station maintenance are assertions of advances made by the Chinese scientific community in a span of one decade. This technology, in the future, could be sought internationally to manipulate the orbits, improve the longevity of satellites, and safeguard satellites from probable collisions with debris. China can also use it as an ASAT system without contravening the legal obligations of placing of weapons in space.

Conclusion

Kinetic kill Earth-to-space weapon systems are *simple in their functionality* but complex and cumbersome in their implementation. The associated complexity becomes increasingly challenging with the increasing accuracy, range and intercept timing.

The technology to target a satellite using a ballistic missile is relatively much less complex than carrying the payload on the launcher and positioning it in the precise orbit. A satellite's predictable orbit and its future position at a foreseeable time give the attacker an opportunity, with sufficient available time, to assemble and position its rocket or missile, and would also allow multiple attempts for target destruction. Several types of weapon systems like ballistic missile have an inherent ASAT capability. The technology to target a satellite using a ballistic missile is rather simple in its implementation, and states with proven capabilities in the field of long range ballistic missiles will have a 'head start' in the development of ASAT weapons. While fielding of air-launched kinetic kill weapons has considerable advantages, a majority of nation states are hesitant to make exploratory attempts in the territory of space weaponisation, fearful of a backlash of international sanctions and of being accused of escalating the arms race in space. Further, the general outlook of the developing countries is tilted towards accruing the benefits of satellite services and overall prosperity rather than on space-based weapons.

The kinetic kill space-to-Earth weapon will be used target aircraft and missiles in the Earth's atmosphere and provide for the capability of attacking any point on the Earth. For the weapons falling in this category, they have to be launched and positioned into space well in advance, before the weapon is initiated. Thus, while space-to-Earth kinetic kill weapons offer global reach, with prompt attack capability, they are, however, poorly suited for attacking ground targets using kinetic energy or explosive weapons. A kinetic kill weapon, when used from space to attack a ground installation, would not offer any distinct advantage over a conventional weapon except for the deep penetration capability. Space basing of kinetic weapons in the ballistic missile defence configuration would provide for rapid response, however, the infrastructural requirements and placing of an unwieldy constellation make the cost exorbitant.

Kinetic kill space-to-space weapons would constitute weapon systems based in space to act against satellites or assets based in, or transiting, the realm of space. These weapons would employ platforms like manoeuvrable space planes, co-orbital satellites, satellites armed with projectiles or space mines. Such a space weapon will be following a particular fixed orbit and if so designed, could be manoeuvred using onboard propulsion. Amongst these weapon systems, the concept of space planes is an attractive concept and would be sought in multiple activities, including fielding it as a credible weapon platform. The other space-to-space weapons like the co-orbital ASAT, space mines and parasitic satellites could be fielded by all nations having an indigenous satellite launch capability. With modern technology, selective targeting of space assets using these weapons is feasible.

Notes

1 "Clarke's Three Laws", at https://en.wikipedia.org/wiki/Clarke%27s_three_laws. Accessed on December 2, 2013.

2. David Wright, Laura Grego, and Lisbeth Gronlund, *The Physics of Space Security*, a reference manual (Cambridge MA: American Academy of Arts and Sciences, 2005), at http://www.ucsusa.org/sites/default/files/legacy/assets/documents/nwgs/physics-space-security.pdf. Accessed on March 6,2014.

3. http://smallsats.org/2013/01/16/circular-orbital-speed-and-period-as-a-function-of-altitude-for-leo/. Accessed on August 5, 2014.

4. Ibid.

5. Where the numerator is the gravitational parameter of the Earth, 6,378 km is the Earth's radius and h is the altitude of the satellite above the Earth.

6. http://smallsats.org/2013/01/16/circular-orbital-speed-and-period-as-a-function-of-altitude-for-leo/. Accessed on August 5, 2014.

7. Wright, et al., n. 2.

8. http://smallsats.org/2013/01/16/circular-orbital-speed-and-period-as-a-function-of-altitude-for-leo/. Accessed on August 5, 2014.

9. "Escape Velocity", at http://home.southernct.edu/~tremblayr1/FurtherThought/Escape%20velocity.pdf. Accessed on August 12, 2014.

10. Wright, et al., n. 2.

11. Ibid.

12. Ibid.

13. Ibid.

14. Should the projectile miss the target for any reason, it will either reenter the Earth's atmosphere or will be lost in space if the velocity exceeds the escape velocity. In layman's terms, "escape velocity" is the speed attained by an object to break free from the gravitational forces of nature and continue movement in a direction without propulsion (not making use of fuel).

15. *IHS Jane's weapons: Strategic 2013-2014.*

16. Ian Easton, "China's Evolving ASAT Weapons Programs and Their Implications for Future US Strategy", Project 2049 Institute, at http://project2049.net/documents/china_asat_weapons_the_great_game_in_space.pdf. Accessed on December 2, 2013.

17. http://www.globalsecurity.org/space/world/china/kt-1.htm. Accessed on August 5, 2014.

18. n. 15, p. 319.

19. Ibid.
20. "US Sees China Launch as Test of Anti-Satellite Muscle: Source", at http://www.reuters.com/article/2013/05/15/us-china-launch-idUSBRE94E07D20130515. Accessed on July 17, 2014.
21. Ibid.
22. Brian Weeden, "Through a Glass, Darkly Chinese, American, and Russian Anti-satellite Testing in Space", March 17, 2014, at http://swfound.org/media/167224/Through_a_Glass_Darkly_March2014.pdf. Accessed on July 09, 2014.
23. Ibid.
24. Lt Col James Mackey, USAF, "Recent US and Chinese Antisatellite Activities", *Air and Space Power Journal*, US Air Force Research Institute, Fall 2009, at http://www.airpower.maxwell.af.mil/airchronicles/apj/apj09/fal09/mackey.html. Accessed on Aug 14, 2014.
25. Geoff Forden, "A Preliminary Analysis of the Chinese ASAT Test," and Geoffrey Forden, "A Preliminary Analysis of the Proposed USA-193 Shoot-down," March 12, 2008, cited by Lt Col James Mackey, USAF, "Recent US and Chinese Antisatellite Activities", *Air and Space Power Journal*, Fall 2009, at http://www.airpower.maxwell.af.mil/airchronicles/apj/apj09/fal09/mackey.html. Accessed on August 14, 2014 .
26. Steven M. Kosiak, "Arming the Heavens: A Preliminary Assessment of the Potential Cost and Cost-Effectiveness of Space-Based Weapons", Centre for Strategic and Budgetary Assessments, Washington DC, 2007, p. 79, at http://csbaonline.org/publications/2007/10/arming-the-heavens-a-preliminary-assessment-of-the-potential-cost-and-cost-effectiveness-of-space-based-weapons/. Accessed on July 11, 2014.
27. Wright, et al., n. 2.
28. "Shenlong Space Plane Advances China's Military Space Potential", at http://www.strategycenter.net/research/pubid.174/pub_detail.asp. Accessed on August 7, 2014.
29. n. 15, p. 319.
30. Ibid.
31. "Meteorite Impacts", accessed August 8, 2014, at http://csep10.phys.utk.edu/astr161/lect/meteors/impacts.html. Accessed on August 08,2014.
32. Ibid.
33. "Missile Defense, the Space Relationship and the Twenty-First Century", 2009 Report, The Institute for Foreign Policy Analysis, Cambridge MA, at www.ifpa.org/pdf/IWG2009.pdf accessed on January 23, 2014.
34. "Strategic Defense Initiative (SDI)", at http://www.britannica.com/EBchecked/topic/568214/Strategic-Defense-Initiative-SDI. Accessed on August 9, 2014.
35. Donald R. Baucom, "The Rise and Fall of Brilliant Pebbles", *The Journal of Social, Political and Economic Studies*, vol. 29, no. 2, Summer 2004, p. 145, at http://highfrontier.org/oldarchive/Archive/hf/The%20Rise%20and%20Fall%20of%20Brilliant%20Pebbles%20-Baucom.pdf. Accessed on August 9, 2014.
36. n. 33.

37. " Strategic Defense Initiative: Estimates of Brilliant Pebbles' Effectiveness Are Based on Many Unproven Assumptions", Report to Chairman, Committee on Armed Services, US Senate submitted by US General Accounting Office in March 1992, at http://www.gao.gov/assets/160/151636.pdf. Accessed on January 23, 2014.
38. Wright, et al., n. 2.
39. n. 33.
40. Ibid.
41. Theresa Hitchens, Michael Katz-Hyman and Jeffrey Lewis, "US Space Weapons: Big Intentions, Little Focus", *Nonproliferation Review*, vol. 13, no 1, March 2006, Centre for Nonproliferation Studies, Washington DC.
42. Steven M. Kosiak, "Arming the Heavens: A Preliminary Assessment of the Potential Cost and Cost-Effectiveness of Space-Based Weapons", Centre for Strategic and Budgetary Assessments, Washington DC, 2007, p. 39, at http://csbaonline.org/publications/2007/10/arming-the-heavens-a-preliminary-assessment-of-the-potential-cost-and-cost-effectiveness-of-space-based-weapons/. Accessed on July 11, 2014.
43. Available at http://en.wikipedia.org/wiki/Deep_Impact_(spacecraft). Accessed on August 15, 2014.
44. Brian Weeden, "X-37B Orbital Test Vehicle Fact Sheet", at www.SecureWorldFoundation.org. Accessed on April 7, 2014.
45. Available at http://www.456fis.org/RASCAL_-_PROJECT.htm. Accessed on August 14, 2014.
46. Jason M. Tardy, "Responsive Access, Small Cargo, Affordable Launch", at https://www.google.co.in/url?sa=t&rct=j&q=&esrc=s&source=web&cd=1&ved=0ahUKEwiJw-rmt6vKAhVEuhQKHYe_B_EQFggbMAA&url=http%3A%2F%2Fdigitalcommons.usu.edu%2Fcgi%2Fviewcontent.cgi%3Ffilename%3D0%26article%3D1744%26context%3Dsmallsat%26type%3Dadditional&usg=AFQjCNH1t7NuenZ9_cXQyAbEf6I6H378yQ&sig2=8XDQ3c9ySQgm3ltd23cjrw&bvm=bv.112064104,d.d24&cad=rja. Accessed on August 14, 2014.
47. "Darpa Targets Lower Launch Costs With XS-1 Spaceplane", *Aviation Week & Space Technology*, December 2, 2013, at http://aviationweek.com/awin/darpa-targets-lower-launch-costs-xs-1-spaceplane. Accessed on August 14, 2014.
48. Ibid.
49. "Buran", http://indianspacestation.com/space-alphabet/84-buran.pdf. Accessed on August 18, 2014.
50. "Shenlong Space Plane: China's Answer To US X-37B Drone?", at http://www.huffingtonpost.com/2012/11/10/shenlong-space-plane-china_n_2110084.html. Accessed on August 17, 2014.
51. Ibid.
52. http://sinodefence.com/2014/02/22/chinas-spaceplane-programme/. Accessed on August 17, 2014.
53. Laura Grego, "A History of Anti-Satellite Programs" , Union of Concerned Scientists, January 2012, at http://www.ucsusa.org/nuclear_weapons_and_global_security/

solutions/space-weapons/a-history-of-anti-satellite.html. Accessed on August 13, 2014.

54. "Co-orbital ASAT" at http://www.globalsecurity.org/space/world/russia/coorb.htm. Accessed on August 13, 2014.
55. Easton, n. 16.
56. Brian Weeden, "China's BX-1 Microsatellite: A Litmus Test for Space Weaponization," *The Space Review*, October 20, 2008, at http://www.thespacereview.com/article/1235/1. Accessed on March 20, 2014.
57. Wright, et al., n. 2.
58. Ajey Lele and Gunjan Singh; "China's Space Strategy and Modernisation", *ORF Issue Brief*, Observer Research Foundation, New Delhi, February 2013, issue brief#49, p.3
59. "China Testing New Satellite-Hijacking Space Weapons", October 4, 2013, at http://www.china-defense-mashup.com/china-testing-new-satellite-hijacking-space-weapons.html. Accessed on July 9, 2014.
60. Ibid.
61. Ibid.
62. Ibid.

4
Directed Energy Weapons

Directed energy weapon systems encompass a wide array of technologies that will bequeath unique capabilities in all domains of future warfare.

The genres of science fiction and fantasy are filled with depictions of lethal rays in the wars against extraterrestrial creatures trying to annihilate life on the Earth. This fictional narrative has started transforming into reality and opened up the possibility of delivering lethal power over considerable distances with the invention of high powered directed energy. Directed Energy Weapons (DEWs) have sporadically featured in conflicts albeit on a very low scale, for neutralising mines, for crowd control, and for denial and disruption of electronic systems. The evaluation, testing and occasional demonstration of these weapons using varied technology and concepts are still under progress and efforts are underway to bridge the gap between theoretical potential and practical implementation. Directed energy weapon systems encompass a wide array of technologies that will bequeath unique capabilities in all domains of future warfare. The potential of DEWs to become the preferred weapons of choice will be largely attributable to the advantages they will provide over the conventional weapon systems. DEWs can provide capability to deliver scalable destructive power over varied distances in support of tactical and strategic operations. As the technology associated with directed energy evolves, we will start witnessing a measured shift from the current weapon systems to more and more use of DEW systems. While DEW systems hold innovative promises for future warfare in all the domains (land, sea and air), the Research and Development (R&D) will witness a slew of activities to use DEWs from the context of weapons directed from, and towards, space. As and when the concept of directed energy matures to the required levels, where it could be effectively used for space-based platforms, the technology will be exploited in developing a new grade of space weapons. The realisation of advanced techniques and capabilities will rest on the ongoing R&D which, in turn, will bring in a new Revolution in Military Affairs.

The use of DEWs for destruction of space-based targets in conflict situations is yet to be demonstrated. As per available reports till 2015, space basing of such weapon platforms is yet to take place. In spite of this, one should not overlook the fact that there have been some instances when testing and evaluation of prototype weapons that could well be placed on space-based platforms have been carried out over the past decades. The R&D in the field of generation and deliverance of directed energy using newer and efficient techniques is an ongoing process and these R & D efforts will fructify in realisation of the new category of space weapons. As and when such weapons come to the fore, the resistance or moratorium on maintaining a weapon free outer space would weaken on many grounds. In this context, DEWs visualise a unique capability in tackling different threats, with a precise and real-time response for every situation to unleash the lethality in a pinpointed manner. Further, the attack using DEWs will provide for long range attack capability and will also obviate the possibilities of collateral damage. The required damage could be contained as per choice and one may opt for a temporary or permanent nature of damage to personnel and equipment, or use it for terminating services integral to the operations. Thus, DEWs would present a vivid opportunity to indulge in a direct or indirect attack capability. Further, such an attack using directed energy will not be catastrophic in nature when compared with the effects of kinetic weapons. Thus, one can predict with a certain degree of confidence, that space will be free from being weaponised only till the time directed energy evolves as an effective space weapon. In fact, it would not be out of place to mention that these space-based weapons could be effectively used for the service of humanity. For example, one can visualise a situation where weapons of mass destruction unleashed by a rogue state or non-state actor could be neutralised at the launch itself, taking into account the availability of prior intelligence inputs.

How are Directed Energy Weapons Different?

As we have seen in the preceding chapter, a kinetic kill conventional weapon system destroys the target with physical transfer of energy by means of a direct impact. For the physical intercept, the weapon platform or a projectile fired from it has to traverse over a credible distance at high speeds. This entails limitations in terms of time and payload delivered to the target. In comparison to kinetic weapon systems, DEWs make use of Electro-Magnetic (EM) energy to deny, disrupt, deceive, damage or destroy the target or its capabilities. The EM spectrum includes EM energy spanning frequencies of radio waves, microwave, infrared, visible light, ultraviolet and gamma rays. In the context of DEWs, the focus has been on technology to generate lasers (which fall in the infrared and visible light portions of the EM spectrum) and High Power Microwave (HPM) systems. The directed energy weapons would be tailored for Effects-Based Operations (EBO) with lethal as well as non-lethal outcomes ranging from denial of services to permanent damage to infrastructure, equipment and personnel. Depending on the frequency and potency of the attack against an identified target, the level of incapacitation and damage can be controlled. DEWs can be used to attack targets on Earth, objects in the atmosphere and space assets. Despite the fact that a number of DEW weapons have been conceived and tested, the technology is still in its nascent stage. While DEW weapons have penetrated the realms of tactical warfare to some extent, the destructive capability of these weapon systems in a strategic sense is yet to be exploited owing to technological limitations. The progress in refining these weapon types for weapon grade results is an ongoing process. With the wide-ranging research and development in generating weapon grade directed energy, the DEW systems would soon mature to be fielded as war-fighting machinery and provide for capabilities over a comprehensive spectrum of warfare.

Importance of DEWs in Present Day Context

As compared to previous decades, military operations in the present set-up are marked with unforeseen challenges due to the evolving asymmetric nature of warfare. In addition to conventional conflicts, military operations are being increasingly used against non-state actors, with restricted rules of engagement. In conventional warfare, even with the kinetic kill weapon system, the tacit norm of the day is to avoid collateral damage so as not to have a hostile world opinion. With the proliferation of terror groups and cells, the responsibility of governments and military leaders has increased manifold. Military operations are now not limited to the homeland but expand overseas across international borders to target groups and individuals who seek safe havens in inaccessible pockets and in urban areas. Asymmetric warfare tactics against non-state actors have witnessed a spurt in the past decade and are being *mainstreamed into military operations* at the national as well as international level. With the advances in technology and credible intelligence inputs, it is now possible to target any point on, or in, the Earth's atmosphere. However, such operations still face complexities in terms of weapon to target matching and time management. In such scenarios, the advent of directed energy weapon systems would offer significant advantages and overcome the limitations posed by the use of kinetic kill weapon systems. Technological breakthroughs in laser and HPM are expected to reduce the size of the weapon equipment and increase its lethality for an offensive as well as defensive role in space.

DEW systems could be used to take on targets, irrespective of their own and target basing in real-time. Visualising this would be akin to a radar system, wherein the radar beam continuously illuminates a target and tracks it. A directed energy beam, in a similar fashion, will illuminate the target albeit with the beam intensity in excess of hundreds of Mega Watts (MW) for a measured destructive effect on the target.

Advantages of DEWs

The importance of directed energy in futuristic weapon platforms stems from the distinct advantage such weapons promise to provide in strategic, tactical and operational capabilities. These advantages will be discussed in the respective sub-sections; however, before proceeding with the intricacies, it would be in order to bring out the general advantages of DEWs.

- Directed energy, travelling at the speed of light, possesses the unique capability of transmitting lethal power by concentrating and directing high powered energy for destruction, incapacitation or maiming of targets.
- The lethal attack on the target would be in near real-time allowing targeting of all categories of mobile and immobile targets.
- DEWs can be employed for varying degrees of lethality ranging from temporary to permanent degradation and, if need be, for complete destruction. DEWs cater for both soft and hard kill capability.
- Further, such weapon platforms would be activated far off from the target and, thus, would fall in the category of 'standoff' weapons.
- Any attack from a DEW would be stealthy in nature as it would be extremely difficult for the opponent to pinpoint the direction from which the attack originated.
- It can act as an area or point weapon, with the ability to simultaneously engage multiple targets in all domains of land, sea and space.
- Directed energy is not affected by gravity.
- Collateral damage is avoided due to the precision attack and measured power of destruction.
- DEWs can attack targets at far-flung ranges with pinpoint accuracy.

- The weapon platform carrying out the attack would be difficult to identify by the adversary and provides for stealthy operation. The degree of degradation could be premeditated to be prominent at a later stage, making it difficult to pinpoint the source and time of attack.
- The power of the directed energy beam can be amplified with multiple sources emitting beams of similar characteristics in the same direction.

The electro-magnetic field potency from the weapon system at a given range can be calculated accurately in specified conditions and can be controlled, but its effectiveness on the target is constrained by a range of factors. These factors like atmospheric losses, target ability to resist damage and intensity of the directed energy focused on the target over the required duration, all will play an important role in ascertaining the effectiveness of the weapon system.

Types of Directed Energy Weapons

The technology used in directed energy is diverse, using different principles, each possessing unique characteristics with exclusive applications in distinct fields. The technology specialising in the field of optics and microwave has raised considerable interest with regard to DEWs. Directed energy weapon systems encompass the field of lasers producing powerful bursts of coherent waves in the optical wavelengths, generation and transmission of high power high frequency microwaves and bombardment of high density charged atomic and sub-atomic particles travelling in the form of narrow beams at exorbitantly high speeds. The weapon platform discharging a high density Electro-Magnetic (EM) beam can be broadly categorised as High Power Laser (HPL), High Power Microwave (HPM) or a charged particle beam. As the capabilities of charged particle beam weapons have not been practically demonstrated and in a strict sense would be falling in the category of kinetic kill weapons, the endeavour in this chapter would be focussed on the former two types. While jamming techniques making use of radio frequency and lasers have been effective forms of DEW attacks, the lethality required to destroy targets by concentrating high power energy at large distances exhibits its own complexities and technical challenges. Research and development in the diverse field of EM technology has allowed introduction of innovative products and services, leading to a stiff competition to exploit this technology to the hilt in support of peaceful and military benefits.

Laser Weapons in Space

Laser is an acronym which stands for "Light Amplification by Stimulated Emission of Radiation". As the name suggests, generation of a laser involves stimulated radiation produced in the form of light of a specific wavelength in the infrared, ultraviolet and visible ranges of the EM spectrum. An incandescent or normal light bulb produces light waves or dissipates the photons[1] equally in all directions. The light waves emanating from a light bulb are characterised by random generation of frequencies, resulting in out of phase transmission of multiple wavelengths which inherently spread out in all directions. In contrast, a laser source would emit concentrated coherent light characterised by constant frequency or wavelength dispersed in a precise direction in the form of a condensed, narrow beam.[2] In other words, identical waves from the monochromatic source add up and so will be the energy they carry.

Since the discovery of lasers by Albert Einstein in the year 1917, a lot of innovation has taken place in the field of lasers and it is being used by mankind in a wide variety of civil, commercial and industrial applications like medical equipment, surgery, law enforcement, communication, laser cutting machines, pointers, data engraving, gyroscopes, welding, ranging and sighting devices, etc. On the military front, the applications include communications, range finding, target designation, radar and different categories of weapon systems.

Advantages and Limitations of Employing Lasers as Weapon Systems

The advantages of employing lasers as means for a weapon system have already been brought out earlier in the general advantages of DEWs. The use of the laser as a weapon provides for pinpoint accuracy and avoids the collateral damage caused by conventional weapon systems. Further, laser weapons have attracted the military planners as they come with a promise of stealthy application of force over a measured scale of lethality and allow near simultaneous multiple targeting from a single weapon platform. Lasers in an optical spectrum offered the deliverance of an intense source of energy at the speed of light (3×10^8 m/s) and, in the bargain, opened up the possibility of creating and employing an all purpose weapon that could be used for instantaneous effects ranging from degradation to complete destruction of the target category to include humans, equipment, aircraft, ships and armoured vehicles. From the weapon development point of view, the ability of the laser to focus on a precise point and cut through thick metal, over hundreds of kilometres, away has fascinated and kept alive the interest of the military R&D community.

Though the laser beam is directed towards the target with the speed of light, the generation of a high power laser is constrained by various factors. Firstly, if directed from Earth to space or space to Earth, the laser beam is subjected to atmospheric attenuation, absorption and scattering effects. Secondly, the laser beam has to track and illuminate the target over a finite time and, in the process, has to discharge the required amount of energy necessary for the degradation or destruction of the target. Thirdly, with the increase in the power and intensity of the laser beam, the size of the laser generation equipment becomes gigantic, with increasing complexities, and demanding a higher payload capacity for the launch vehicle. Ground-based lasers to attack space or air assets would also require massive infrastructure to include huge reflectors, tracking system, laser generators, a cooling system and associated peripheral equipment which, when integrated as an entity, would entail a sizeable devoted facility for operation.

Lastly, high power lasers are limited by phenomenal power and cooling requirements. While high grade lasers have been produced and used in diverse applications worldwide, the use of high energy lasers in space is constrained in terms of integrating the requirements of the power plant and ancillary cooling systems suitable to be launched aboard a rocket and then sustained in space with ease. If the research towards generating an efficient laser beam with the required lethality, using a compact apparatus, succeeds, the much visualised Star Wars concept may fructify.

Laser Weapon Developments

Invention and generation of laser energy *opened up a plethora of potential advantages* that could be exploited. Since its inception, laser technology has made big headway in support of military operations and has evolved considerably in the last few decades in various facets of warfare applications like communication, target designation, target ranging, precision guidance of smart munitions, blinding and dazzling. Use of lasers as a means of delivering lethal power in support of military operations has been recognised from the time the laser was first realised. The initial achievements in laser development coerced the military mindset of the advanced nations to steer, and spearhead, the research in technology to beget decisive military advantage over adversaries. The utilisation of lasers as a weapon system would contribute equally in offensive and defensive roles and is being viewed for projecting credible deterrence. Laser weapons are now part and parcel of the military inventories of the advanced nations for enhancing the operational capability of conventional forces in tactical warfare. As on date, while a number of nation-states are investing in the research and development of laser technology, the United States is the forerunner in its approach with a number of laser weapon projects. The other nations believed to possess a credible laser weapon programme include Russia and China; however, due to the clandestine nature of their projects, very little has been revealed about the advances made in R&D.

The continued efforts and substantial investment in laser generation techniques by the United States from 1960 to 2000 resulted in the generation of weapon grade lasers; however, these much hyped projects could not advance beyond the point of being showcased as technology demonstrators. Generation of a high power weapon grade laser faced a multitude of challenges in terms of high power consumption, low power output, atmospheric attenuation, colossal size of equipment and economic viability.

Since the beginning of the 21st century, the United States has invested considerably in the R&D in the field of high powered solid state laser weapons. Solid state laser weapon platforms come with the promise of higher power output with reduced dimension and weight of the weapon equipment. Furthermore, the solid state laser system can be configured in a modular concept where output from multiple sources can be utilised for generation of scalable high power, paving the way for a controlled measured output. The testing and evaluation of lasers against surface, maritime and aerial targets have contributed to advanced laser programmes and are now opening up the possibility to field credible weapon systems against space-based assets. The following examples indicate how technology has gained prominence with demonstrations of prototype weapon platforms in the 21st century.

- **Maritime Laser Demonstrator (MLD):**[3] MLD was developed as a high-energy laser demonstrator to validate laser weapon system technology as a near-term solution to counter emerging threats from Unmanned Aerial Vehicles (UAVs), small boats, rockets, artillery and mortar. In April 2011, the solid state laser system, developed by Northrop Grumman, and mounted on the ex-USS *Paul F. Foster*, was integrated with the ship's radar and navigation system successfully. The laser beam destroyed a small boat, validating the engagement models to include propagation, lethality, tracking and fire control.
- **Gamma[4] (FIRESTRIKE series of laser):** In April 2012, Northrop Grumman, at its Redondo Beach laboratory, demonstrated the

solid state lasers' capability to burn through the skin and critical components of a target drone which was used to simulate anti-ship cruise missile threats to US Navy ships.

- **Tactical High Energy Laser (THEL) demonstrator:**[5] Located at the High Energy Laser Test Facility, White Sands Missile Range, THEL is a fixed site system using a high-energy Deuterium Fluoride Chemical Laser (DFCL) which is integrated with an acquisition, pointing, and tracking system and an organic fire control radar. In the field tests from 2000 to 2005, it destroyed 46 rockets, artillery and mortar rounds in flight. Based on THEL, the US has conceived a project called 'Skyguard', a laser-based counter- MANPADS / C-RAM system[6] to provide limited area defence in a radius of 10 km against short-range ballistic missiles, rockets, artillery shells, mortars, UAVs and cruise missiles.
- **Joint High Power Solid State Laser (JHPSSL) programme:**[7] In 2009, JHPSSL achieved an output of over 100 Kilo Watt (KW) with a chain of modules, in that each module provided a 15 KW output. Thus, it was established that laser output from multiple sources can be utilised for the generation of scalable high power using a modular concept. JHPSSL and THEL are being integrated to provide the US Army with the world's first high-power, Solid State Laser Testbed Experiment (SSLTE).
- **MATRIX and Laser Avenger:**[8] In May 2009, Boeing demonstrated the tracking and targeting capability of the Mobile Active Targeting Resource for Integrated Experiment (MATRIX) using a single laser beam to shoot down five UAVs at various ranges. The US Air Force (USAF) sponsored tests at theNaval Air War Centre also used a Laser Avenger, another Boeing funded initiative to shoot down another UAV.
- **Laser Area Defence System (LADS):**[9] LADS is an integrated system of radar, infrared and video trackers with a solid-state laser to destroy incoming mortars, rockets and missiles. The project involves a shipboard as well as a truck mounted version which would use the turret of the existing Phalanx shipboard close-in

weapon system. The prototype weapon was demonstrated to detonate 60 mm mortars at a range of 550 yards.[10]

- **High Energy Liquid Laser Area Defence System (HELLADS):** Monitored and funded by the Defence Advanced Research Projects Agency (DARPA) and the Air Force Research Laboratory (AFRL), the project has been under development since 2003 by the General Atomics Aeronautical Systems. As per latest reports, HELLADS has successfully completed the beam quality and power output test and is now ready to undergo field trials.[11] HELLADS is a light weight and compact third generation solid state laser which is ten times smaller than the existing laser systems envisaged to deliver a similar output. With a high power to weight ratio, the liquid cooled thermally efficient system is expected to provide a power output in the range of 150 KW using a multi-modular concept. On completion of field trials on a ground-based platform, the system will be further developed for integration with airborne platforms to include tactical aircraft and drones. The system aims to counter the threats from Rockets, Artillery, Mortar (RAM) and airborne targets.[12]
- **Laser Dazzlers:** Directed against personnel, these are non-lethal laser weapons meant to dazzle rather than inflict injury and have been tested by the US forces in the Iraq and Afghanistan Wars.[13]
- **Chinese Low Altitude Air Defence System:** The China Academy of Engineering Physics (CAEP) has developed an indigenous Low-Altitude Air Defence System to intercept low flying aircraft. The laser-based system with a range of 1.2 miles can bring down small-bodied aircraft within five seconds of locating targets. As per trial reports, more than 30 drones have been shot down.[14]
- **Soviet Laser projects: the** USSR has had its own share of projects involving laser weapons. It had invested considerably in the shipboard laser projects "Dikson" and "Foros" to counter missiles and a tank-based laser weapon "Sjatie", using a multi-channel laser.[15] The projects, not being efficient, were shelved post break-up of the Soviet Union.

As the testing and evaluations continued and newer techniques evolved, it has now become possible to generate million billion (10^{15}) watts of laser power. The use of high powered lasers to take on space targets has been on the anvil ever since it became possible to launch satellites. Compared to conventional weapons in use, the potential advantages of laser weapons also make them an ideal choice for use in the space domain and propel the prospective world powers towards weaponisation of space. Laser weapons can be based on Earth or in space and take on targets irrespective of their basing as long as the target is in the line of sight. The option of using various types of lasers with controlled intensity has enabled development of a non-destructive weapon system capable of interfering with target equipment to degrade its functioning over a period of time.

Testing and Evaluation of High Energy Laser Weapons in Space

Due to the unique characteristics offered in terms of capability, speed and reach, laser technology has increasingly fascinated the likes of military researchers and planners for the use of weapon grade lasers for strategic advantage. This, coupled with the capability to control the lethality and avoid collateral damage with its precision and unlimited range, has raised widespread interest in the design, development, deployment and employment of the laser weapon directed towards, and from, space. Of particular interest is the distinct advantage proffered by high energy lasers in tackling threats against ballistic missiles.

Lasers are categorised on the basis of the lasing medium used and the techniques employed for generation. Today, we have solid state lasers, chemical lasers, gas lasers, free electron lasers, semi-conductor lasers, and many more different types of lasers.[16] Of these, the chemical laser has generated considerable interest in research and development of space weapons. As on date, three types of chemical laser generating techniques have been considered for laser weapon systems directed towards, or from, space.[17] The leading laser generating techniques are Deuterium Fluoride Laser (DFL),

Chemical Oxygen Iodine Laser (COIL) and Hydrogen Fluoride Laser (HFL).[18] Chemical lasers use chemical reactions to generate high power laser beams in the range of mega watt levels and, thus, are well suited for strategic applications.[19] The chemicals fed in the reaction chamber would react to form a gas stream which would act as a lasing medium and the old reactants are vented out of the lasing chamber. In the field of laser weapons directed towards or from, space-based assets and aerial mounted laser weapon platforms, only three countries i.e. the USA, Russia and China, have demonstrated the technological capability.

United States

Similar to land and sea-based laser platforms, the United States has also pursued development and testing of laser technology to target space assets. The US has evaluated a number of space weapon projects like Zenith Star, MIRACL, Airborne Laser (ABL), Tactical High Energy Laser and Advanced Tactical Laser (ATL) projects. While all these projects have now been scrapped, they have enriched the US research and scientific community with the advances in laser technology and the achieved benchmarks have become stepping stones in support of developing space-based laser systems.

MIRACL

The Mid-Infrared Advanced Chemical Laser (MIRACL) was the first megawatt class, continuous wave, deuterium fluoride chemical laser developed and tested by the United States.[20] As part of the US Navy project, the laser system was conceived to track and destroy anti-ship cruise missiles; it was first tested in the year 1980. However, as an afterthought, the viability of the system was considered for anti-ballistic missile defence and as an anti-satellite weapon system.[21] This chemical laser was demonstrated in the year 1980 by TRW Inc. (Thompson Ramo Wooldridge Inc.) by generating laser power in excess of one megawatt. Integrated with the SEALITE Beam Director (a large pointing telescope for HELs), MIRACL successfully shot down a rocket at the United States High Energy Laser Systems Test Facility in the year 1996.[22] MIRACL was also tested in the Anti-Satellite (ASAT) capability on October 17, 1997, when it illuminated an ageing US Air Force satellite called Miniature Sensor Technology Insertion (MTSI-3).[23] The Pentagon revealed that neither the satellite nor its sensors suffered any permanent damage, and the objective of evaluating the vulnerability of satellites against such weapon system was successfully achieved.[24] As per some reports, the test was successful only partially as MIRACL suffered damage in the form of internal melting during the lasing phase conducted over a duration of ten seconds.[25] The MIRACL was evaluated and tested in its lifespan for a total duration of 3,000 seconds, at an estimated cost of $6,000 per second.[26]

Zenith Star[27]

As part of the Strategic Defence Initiative (SDI), the Zenith Star project was conceived for demonstration of essential elements of space-based laser missile defence before the end of 1988. The two major elements of the Zenith Star constituted a Large Advanced Mirror Programme (LAMP) and the Alpha chemical laser (derived from MIRACL), both of which were evaluated in laboratory experiments. The idea of LAMP was to utilise many small mirrors ganged together in a phased array structure to act like a single large mirror. On the other hand, Alpha envisaged utilising small individual laser units to operate as a phased array laser. However, the project was closed owing to technological constraints, delays and cost overruns. The generation of a full scale laser beam as well as systems for acquisition, tracking and pointing were way behind the original schedule, even after the committing of the allotted funds.

Airborne Laser Lab (ABL) and Advanced Tactical Laser (ATL) Projects

The use of lasers on aerial platforms as a weapon system started to take shape from the time the mega watt power levels were achieved in laser generation. The possibility of having a laser weapon aboard an aircraft dawned when the US Army in the 1970s consistently employed electrically pumped lasers to destroy winged aircraft and drones.[28] In 1976, the US Air Force launched its Airborne Laser Lab (ALL) as a technology demonstrator aboard Boeing's NKC-135 Stratotanker which was successfully used to track and destroy airborne targets using a gas dynamic laser.[29] A number of technical challenges like power losses in the optical feed and beam distortion at various stages surfaced and continued to plague the project. The project culminated after a total of 11 years in 1984 and during its testing and evaluation, one BQM-34A Firebee drone and a total of five AIM-9 Sidewinder missiles were destroyed.[30]

The concept of an airborne laser platform got a boost with the development of the Chemical Oxygen Iodine Laser (COIL) by the United States Air Force in the year 1977. This infrared chemical laser, pioneered in the field of advanced laser techniques with power output in the megawatts range, opened up the possibility for developing a long range laser weapon platform. COIL became the leading candidate for a space-based laser system and was successfully evaluated in the Airborne Laser (ABL) project (on Boeing 747-400 platform). Using a mega watt class of COIL system, a single ABL platform was conceived for the destruction of 20 to 40 missiles in their boost phase during a 12 to 18 hour sortie. The ABL, employed in the area of interest would be supported by air defence and surveillance systems to include satellites, Airborne Early Warning and Control (AEW&C), UAVs exchanging feeds on the data link (link-16). The ABL programme, after few successful intercepts of test targets, was shelved in the year 2011, after 16 years of experimentation due to budget constraints and techno-logistic issues. A staggering amount of US $5 billion was spent on the project. While experimenting with the ABL project, the United States also initiated the Advanced Tactical Laser (ATL) [31] project to exploit the technology developed. In the year 2006, a C-130 Hercules aircraft was proposed to carry COIL with megawatt class power generation capability. Going by the advancing trends in the airborne laser programmes, it can be speculated that an aircraft with an operational capability to take on terrestrial targets, should be available in the next ten years. The feasibility of such a system will also open up the possibility of taking on orbital assets, giving the much needed push to the space-based laser programmes.

Space-Based Laser - Integrated Flight Experiment (SBL- IFX)

The Space-Based Laser (SBL) programme was initiated way back in the year 1977 by DARPA. The use of the SBL concept is now more than three decades old and the use of the high energy laser in space is mainly constrained by size and weight. Subsequent to the declaration of the Strategic Defence Initiative (SDI) in the year 1983, the United States has consistently worked on its ballistic missile defence programme (aimed at defending against global strikes by intercepting these ballistic missiles in their boost phase itself). In parallel to the evaluating of space-based kinetic interceptors, as brought out in the previous chapter, the Hydrogen Fluoride Laser (HFL)[32] generated considerable interest and the possibility of exploiting it for space-based lasers was evaluated. In this direction, the Strategic Defence Initiative Organisation (SDIO), in the year 1991, achieved generation of the mega watt class of laser in a simulated space environment, suggesting the feasibility of fielding high powered lasers in the space domain.[33] On March 28, 2000, the Alpha Laser Optimisation (ALO) programme of the United States Air Force and Ballistic Missile Defence Organisation (BMDO) demonstrated the technology for the 'Space-Based Laser - Integrated Flight Experiment (SBL- IFX)' towards maturing its space-based missile defence system.[34] The technology demonstration programme was aimed at launching an experimental laser into space in 2012, followed by targeting of ballistic missiles.[35] However, as of now, the United States is far from meeting the timelines as the requisite laser technology is yet to evolve and become compatible for fielding in space.

Russia

During the Cold War period, when both the USSR and the United States contested for developing and fielding of space weapons, it was the USSR which had almost succeeded in positioning a laser weapon platform in an orbit.

Polyus-Skif

The SDI was announced by President Ronald Reagan in the year 1985. The Soviets opposed the concept and called on the USA to abandon the move. Subsequent to the failure of talks between President Ronald Reagan and Soviet President Mikhail Gorbachev in the 1986 summit in Iceland, the Soviets initiated and prepared for the launch of an ASAT mission, which was already under development. The ASAT mission included two orbital systems: the 'Polyus-Skif' system using lasers to attack satellites and 'Kaskad' system to fire missiles on satellites.[36] The Polyus-Skif satellite was launched covertly on May 15, 1987, from the Baikonur Cosmodrome in Kazakhstan on an Energia booster; however, while the launch of the Energia booster was flawless, the Polyus-Skif satellite failed in its final manoeuvre before igniting its onboard engines.[37] The failure, presumably caused by a bug in the controlling command, resulted in the break-up of the satellite with the onboard laser weapon, and it was completely burned out as it fell back towards the Earth. Had the satellite been placed securely in its destined orbital slot, not only would the notion of an outer space treaty banning the use of space for military purposes been violated, but it would have initiated the race for positioning weapons in space.

Beriev A-60

Like the US airborne laser projects, the USSR had an IL-76 modified aircraft called Beriev A-60 which was used from 1983 to 1987 to test the laser for the Polyus-Skif satellite described above.[38] The project was put on hold post disintegration of the erstwhile USSR; however, as per reports, the project is being revived.

China

China has been pursuing development of DEWs firmly believing that they hold the capability to change the course of future wars. China has emphasised research and development in the fields of ground-based laser systems and radio frequency weapons for degradation of satellites. As per the 1998 Pentagon report to Congress, "China already may possess the capability to damage, under specific conditions, optical sensors on satellites that are very vulnerable to damage by lasers", and that "given China's current interest in laser technology, it is reasonable to assume that Beijing would develop a weapon that could destroy satellites in the future".[39] The assumption gained credibility when in August and September of 2006, China reportedly used high-powered, ground-based lasers to illuminate US reconnaissance satellites. Reports stated that these were either ASAT tests or relatively "low-power" laser ranging devices intended to precisely determine satellite orbits for ASAT targeting purposes.[40]

Radio Frequency Weapons

Radio Frequency (RF) technology is associated with the generation and exploitation of electro-magnetic waves transiting over line of sight in a compatible medium from one point to another over large distances. These waves are manipulated in shape, size and intensity to act as carriers for transfer of information and energy. While the preferred medium would be free space or a vacuum, these waves, characterised by frequencies have penetration capabilities in other mediums to a certain extent. While the radio frequency spectrum, encompassing frequencies in the range of 3Hz to 3,000 Hz, is used for a wide variety of communication and infotainment applications, the microwave frequency range of 3,000 Hz (or 3 GHz) to 300 GHz is better suited for transfer of energy.

The use of microwave applications in support of military operations gained active prominence with the deployment of the Chain Home radar during the Battle of Britain in 1940. First demonstrated effectively in World War II in support of air operations, Electronic

Warfare (EW) measures and counter-measures, capable of changing the course of war, were incrementally used in subsequent conflicts. Today, microwave technology is extensively used in varied civil, commercial and military fields, aiding and assisting communication, navigation, medicine, Intelligence, Surveillance, Reconnissance (ISR) and security implementation applications. While microwave energy on the military front in yesteryears was primarily used in denial and deception configurations (electronic warfare), it has a potent capability of inflicting damage and destruction, when unleashed with enough power and intensity.

This facilitation of concentrating destructive power over large distances has generated considerable interest in the development and application of DEWs. The high powered microwaves have now become a preferred choice to interfere, degrade, deceive or destroy the operational and functional capability of space assets. Depending on the generation techniques and achievable intensity, high power RF weapons can be broadly classified in the two main categories of High Powered Microwave (HPM) weapons and Electro-Magnetic Pulse (EMP) weapons.

High Powered Microwave Weapons

The use of HPM weapons has caught the fantasy of many as they can be used to attack electronic equipment while sparing the human operators with almost no serious effects. HPM devices are electrically powered to generate narrowband frequencies in the Gigahertz range (3-35 GHz) in short bursts of high powered pulses. While high powered microwave signals are commonly used in communication and radar applications, they hold a vast potential in being employed as an effective space weapon. These can be effective in disrupting telecommunication networks, power grids and can significantly damage electronic gadgets and computer systems, leaving the infrastructural set-up intact. While the complete destruction of electronic equipment would entail intrinsic details of target components, the temporary paralysis of the command and control network can be carried out without prior information on the technical characteristics and specifications of the targeted entity. The temporary degradation of the targeted onboard electronic systems would aim to interfere with, and garble, the internal communication set-up by information overload or by feeding in false information. An HPM weapon differs from a normal RF transmission in the sense that the operating frequency of HPM weapons is in the region of GigaHertz while RF equipment uses low frequency.

Distinction between an HPM and Electronic Warfare

The HPM weapon is often put in the same category as electronic warfare equipment as both make use of EM frequency bands in the microwave region. While the principle of microwave generation for both is similar, the EW systems differ in the sense that they are used mainly for jamming and anti-jamming techniques. The EW system is effective only against an active electronic equipment to cause temporary disruption and denial of functionality. The EW attack or counter-attack also entails prior knowledge of the adversaries' system signatures and is generally carried out at power (intensity) levels much lower in comparison to an attack by an HPM weapon. An HPM weapon, on the other hand, transmits power in excess of hundreds of mega watts to damage or destroy a target irrespective of its current operational state and does not necessarily rely on prior knowledge of the adversary's systems signatures to inflict the damage.

Advantages and Disadvantages of HPM

High-power microwave weapons are ideally suited for low-intensity conflicts under politically sensitive environments and non-lethal applications, since the main target of attack is the electronics of the adversary systems rather than munitions or the personnel using them. HPM weapons seek to degrade the functionality or performance of the target rather than to damage its structure or harm its crew.[41] One of the distinct advantages of an HPM weapon over a laser weapon is its all weather capability which does not inhibit its employment even in adverse weather conditions. An HPM weapon can take on multiple targets within its line of sight or the cone of a beam. Such weapons would also be capable of attacking dispersed targets by sequential locking as per the system capability and can be used to track and dispense energy on different targets concurrently. Thus, while a laser weapon can be used to engage one target at a time, an HPM weapon would fall in the category of an area weapon. Another important advantage of the HPM weapon over a laser weapon is that it can penetrate objects and has the capability of affecting targets in covered and sheltered structures. Almost all modern weaponry derives its capabilities from integrated electronics and makes use of microwave signals for operations and functions. An HPM weapon can cause complete failure of an earmarked target's integrated circuitry or could jam the communication and control channels for a finite time. The other advantage over laser weapons is that HPM weapons do not rely on targeting accuracy and need to be directed in the general direction of an attack. However, in doing so, the potency of an attack will be diminished. The counter-measures and defence against HPM weapons would call for better and more sophisticated technology than the weapon system itself.

A HPM weapon, once used will not discern between friend and foe and its causal effect will affect all equipment in the radiation environment. Unlike a kinetic weapon, the quantum and effectiveness of the attack would be difficult to gauge, and the degraded functionality may introduce a time lag. In addition, unlike the obvious damage caused by high energy laser weapons, microwave weapons affect the electronics inside the target systems without the associated lethality, and with difficulty in determining the extent of damage. A prior knowledge of the target characteristics will help in achieving the desired effects. An HPM weapon is limited by range and is dependent on a multitude of factors of the weapon equipment as well as the target characteristics. Microwave radiation, akin to a high burst of energy from a radar system, loses its power or intensity with the range traversed and, thus, is not a lucrative option to attack space-based assets from the ground. The standoff range depends on power and the frequency in use and is also subjected to external factors like attenuation and diffraction in diverse atmospheric conditions. Like laser weapons, the discerning of the direction of the origin of an attack was difficult a few years ago; however, with improved technology, it is now feasible to pinpoint the exact direction of the EM energy emanating source. Another important weakness of high power microwave weapons is that they emit a distinct electronic signature that can be detected from large distances. Thus, high-powered electro-magnetic radiation emitted by microwave weapons makes them susceptible to attacks by anti-radiation missiles, which use the radiation from the source to lock onto the target.

Testing and Evaluation of HPM Weapons

Prior to the disintegration of the USSR, both the USA and the USSR had their share of projects involving HPM weapons. In fact, the interest in the HPM field dates back to the year 1979, when the erstwhile USSR had succeeded in manufacturing a triode capable of producing output in the range of giga watt level.[42] HPM technologies offer an attractive solution to counter a complete range of modern weapons equipment and their platforms. The United States is working towards establishing an HPM-based area defence system termed 'Vigilant Eagle'.[43] Vigilant Eagle was conceived to protect aircraft in the vicinity of civil and military airports from shoulder-fired missiles. Once the missile is detected, it is tracked and this data is then passed on to a Command and Control (C2) System. The C2 system, in turn, initiates an active electronically scanned array to focus a microwave beam on to the missile to disable its circuitry and divert the missile from the target. HPM technology has also been demonstrated in the Active Denial System as a counter-personnel and non-lethal directed energy weapon.[44]

While only a few HPM weapons have been demonstrated and tested, they have been assessed for attacking space assets from the ground. Also, basing of such weapon systems on aerial or space-based platforms to attack space-based assets has been considered as a lucrative and effective option in comparison to kinetic kills. While it is clear that an electronic warfare attack directed at a satellite can be used to interfere with the functioning of the satellite, the use of an HPM attack can damage the satellite permanently. As of now, we assume that no HPM weapons have been based in space, however, such a possibility cannot be ruled out, as the United States, in the year 2012, successfully conceived, consolidated and tested an HPM weapon called CHAMP.

CHAMP[45]

The Counter-electronics High-powered Microwave Advanced Missile Project (CHAMP) is a missile developed by Boeing and the US Air Force Research Laboratory (AFRL) Directed Energy Directorate, Kirtland Air Force Base, New Mexico. The test firing of the missile was carried out successfully on October 16, 2012. During the live demonstration of the flight over the Utah Test and Training Range, the CHAMP missile navigated a pre-programmed flight plan and emitted bursts of high powered energy, effectively knocking out the target's electronic systems. CHAMP allows for selective high-frequency radio wave strikes against numerous targets during a single mission. As per another report, *"CHAMP fired high-power microwave bursts at a multi-store structure containing electronic systems and devices... the drone-like weapon irreparably disabled the computers, electronics and even the cameras recording the operation of seven targets in a one-hour period."*[46] Keith Coleman, the programme manager for this project, stated, "This technology marks a new era in modern-day warfare," and "in the near future, this technology may be used to render an enemy's electronic and data systems useless even before the first troops or aircraft arrive."[47]

While the HPM source in the example quoted was stationed on a missile, it can also be placed on a rocket or a satellite. In fact, the US would be in a position to place it aboard the X-37 series of orbital space planes to target space assets selectively. While the use of HPM as a weapon technology is yet to gain prominence, research and development in this field is shrouded in secrecy, and not released in the public domain. The availability of information is further constrained as assessments of HPM weapons are conducted under laboratory conditions and even if field trials have been carried out, they would go unnoticed unless credible intelligence about the time and place is known in advance. Further, the degree of damage, if any, would not be visible to a third party as the attack would generally not culminate in any external damage on the simulated target. Further, the efficacy of HPM weapons can only be maintained as long as their functional and technical characteristics are closely guarded. If the technical characteristics are known, the counter-measures can be implemented at the fraction of the cost of the attacking weapon.

Electro-Magnetic Pulse

An Electro-Magnetic Pulse (EMP) attack involves generation of an Electro-Magnetic (EM) shock wave characterised by production of a high intensity burst of an EM pulse. This EM pulse is the carrier for exorbitant voltages which, coupled with the modern-day electronic equipment, subject it to transient voltages in the range of thousands of volts. This high energy omni-directional pulse radiates outwardly from the source and affects all the electronic systems and solid state devices in its sphere of influence which may extend up to 400 km or more. EMP, as we all are aware is a by-product of a nuclear explosion. The effect of EMP owing to a nuclear explosion was well documented when the United States conducted the "Starfish Prime" experiment. As has been covered in Chapter 2, the high-altitude nuclear test conducted by the US at an altitude of 400 km resulted in generation of EMP which destroyed a number of satellites, created artificial radiation belts and led to the failure of electrical grids in parts of the US.[48]

EMP is aimed to temporarily or permanently disable or damage electronic equipment and computer systems by coupling with exposed electrical conductive surfaces as well as impregnating the electronic components, inducing high transient voltages by virtue of its potential to penetrate structures. EMP would affect the electronic circuits of computers and communication systems, industrial and commercial applications involving automated production of goods, and signalling and controlling of rail and road traffic. The potential effect on military infrastructure would be visible on the equipment embedded with solid state electronic processors and control systems used in aircraft, ships, air defence equipment and advanced weapon platforms. Receiver systems in all electronic equipment would be vulnerable to EMP, as the modern electronic circuitry makes use of highly sensitive miniature high frequency transistors and diodes that can be easily destroyed by exposure to high voltage electrical transients.[49] Therefore, radar and electronic warfare equipment, satellite, microwave, UHF, VHF, HF and low band communications equipment and television equipment are all potentially vulnerable to the EMP effect. The command and control system would also be affected, with failure of communication links and display systems. One can visualise the effects of complete or partial breakdown of communication in a conflict zone, the computerised artillery and tanks behaving erratically, aircraft and ships getting lost with no means of communication, aircraft controls not working, and failure of power supplies. With technological advances, it is now possible to generate EMP without the help of a nuclear blast.

Non-Nuclear EMP: The Advent of E-Bomb

The devastating effects of the nuclear generated EMP on satellites, electronic components, power grids and like infrastructure fuelled the research in the field of replicating the pulsed characteristic and intensity by non-nuclear means during the Cold War period. Over a period of time, development of non-nuclear HPM sources that could create or exceed nuclear generated EMP levels has taken place, albeit with lower power levels and a short range destructive capability. Such a weapon system, popularly known as the e-bomb could be used to disrupt computer electronics controlling electric power grids, telecommunications networks, financial institution databases, security systems, and aircraft.[50] The e-bomb could be delivered by an aircraft, missile or unmanned aerial vehicle. The bomb could also be positioned in a small package in the target area to initiate at a time of choice. This bomb could be placed aboard a satellite as well. The e-bomb, once initiated, will produce a small burst in excess of thousands of megawatt class chirped pulse capable of coupling with cables, transmission lines and semi-conductor devices. This would affect the functionality of electrical and electronic assets in its sphere of radius. Thus, the aircraft or weapon delivery platform will require a standoff capability and the delivery platform has to ensure skirting out of the effective range of the EMP effect. Use of glide bombs would have an added advantage as the delivery platform can clear the target area well in time before the EMP is produced.

The e-bomb can cover a wideband or a narrowband spectrum of frequencies, and would incorporate a microwave source and a power source. The ultra wideband e-bomb aims to create an electro-magnetic pulse akin to the one produced in a nuclear detonation, except that the nuclear material is replaced with a chemical explosive.[51] The microwave source is fed by giga watts of power. Key technologies which are extant in the area are explosively pumped Flux Compression Generators (FCG), explosive or propellant driven Magneto-Hydrodynamic (MHD) generators and a range of HPM devices, the foremost of which is the Virtual Cathode Oscillator or Vircator.[52] Of these, the explosively pumped FCG is a preferred device capable of producing electrical energies of tens of mega joules in tens to hundreds of microseconds of time with peak power levels of the order of tera watts to tens of tera watts equivalent of 10 to thousand times a lightning strike.[53] The bomb's destructiveness depends on the microwave source and target's vulnerability to an electro-magnetic attack, among other things. A 10-GW, 5-GHz HPM device would have a 'lethal' footprint 400 to 500 m across, producing field strengths of several kilo volts per metre.[54] Such an e-bomb would wreak major havoc if detonated at orbital altitudes. In assessing the odds of such weapons being used against space assets, the key factor will be the maturity of the available hardware and managing the range of EMP for selective targeting. Given that very little information of substance has been publicly disclosed at this time, we can only speculate on whether e-bombs could be used against space assets, and in what numbers. Should a mature e-bomb be directed against space assets, it will represent an important milestone in shifting from a destructive kinetic attack capability to an incapacitating lethal attack without the problem of debris fallout. Because of the simplicity of electro-magnetic bombs in comparison with weapons such as Anti-Radiation Missiles (ARMs), it is not unreasonable to expect that these weapons would be both cheaper to manufacture and allow for substantial weapon stocks.

Conclusion

DEWs are in the process of evolution and are gradually opening up the possibility of delivering lethal power over considerable distances. The realisation of the potential of directed energy will invariably result in exploitation of the technology for a new category of weapon systems offering an opening for dramatic transformation of modern militaries. They would form a class of unparalleled weapon delivery platforms possibly pushing the current state-of-the-art weapon systems to the verge of obsolescence. Encompassing a wide array of technologies that bequeath unique capabilities in all domains of future warfare, they will provide for delivery of scalable destructive power over diverse distances in support of tactical and strategic operations. DEWs would present a potent opportunity to indulge in a direct or indirect attack capability. Further, such an attack using directed energy would not be catastrophic in nature when compared to the effects of kinetic weapons.

When directed towards space assets, DEWs would confer exclusive capability of transmitting lethal power by concentrating and directing prohibitive amounts of energy at the speed of light for destruction, incapacitation or maiming of satellites. DEW weapons can be used to attack targets on the Earth, objects in the atmosphere and space assets. Despite the fact that a number of DEW weapons have been conceived and tested, the innovation in technology for weapon grade results is an ongoing process.

Technological breakthroughs in lasers and HPM are expected to reduce weapon equipment size and increase its lethality for the offensive as well as defensive role in space. Laser technology has evolved considerably and owing to the unique characteristics offered in terms of capability, speed and reach, it has increasingly fascinated the likes of military researchers and planners for use of weapon grade lasers for strategic advantage. Another preferred choice in the directed energy weapons would be employment of high powered microwave to interfere, degrade, deceive or destroy the operational and functional capability of space assets.

The research and development in the field of generation and deliverance of directed energy using newer and efficient techniques is an ongoing process and the realisation of the same would propel design and development of a new category of space weapons. Thus, one can predict with a degree of confidence that space will be free from being weaponised only till the time the directed energy system evolves as an effective space weapon.

Notes

1. Photon is an elementary particle, the quantum of light and the lowest possible physical entity of EM radiation carrying force.
2. Melissa Olson, Report on "History of Laser Weapon Research", Naval Surface Warfare Centre, Dahlgren, VA, 2012 at www.dtic.mil/cgi-bin/GetTRDoc?AD=ADA557756. Accessed on July 11, 2014.
3. Datasheet on "Maritime Laser Demonstration" at www.northropgrumman.com/aerospacesystems and "Maritime Laser Demonstrator" available at http://www.cnet.com/pictures/a-brief-history-of-laser-weapons-pictures/2/. Accessed on February 18, 2015.
4. "Gamma", Northrop Grumman brochure, at http://www.northropgrumman.com/Capabilities/SolidStateHighEnergyLaserSystems/Pages/Gamma.aspx. Accessed on February 18, 2015
5. "Tactical High Energy Laser (THEL)", Northrop Grumman, at http://www.northropgrumman.com/Capabilities/ChemicalHighEnergyLaser/TacticalHighEnergyLaser/Pages/default.aspx. Accessed on February 18, 2015.

6. "Skyguard", Laser Based Counter- MANPADS / C-RAM System, at http://defense-update.com/products/s/skyguard-laser.htm. Accessed on February 18, 2015.
7. "Joint High Power Solid State Laser (JHPSSL)", at http://www.northropgrumman.com/Capabilities/SolidStateHighEnergyLaserSystems/Pages/JointHighPowerSolidStateLaser.aspx. Accessed on February 18, 2015.
8. "Boeing Laser Systems Destroy Unmanned Aerial Vehicles in Tests", Boeing news release, at http://boeing.mediaroom.com/2009-11-18-Boeing-Laser-Systems-Destroy-Unmanned-Aerial-Vehicles-in-Tests. Accessed on February 19, 2015.
9. "Raytheon's Effects Technologies", *Technology Today,* Issue 2, 2008, at http://www.raytheon.com/news/technology_today/archive/2008_issue2.pdf. Accessed on February 19, 2015.
10. "Raytheon Successfully Tests New Solid-State Laser Area Defense System", at http://investor.raytheon.com/phoenix.zhtml?c=84193&p=irol-newsarticle_print&ID=948611. Accessed on May 9, 2016.
11. Graham Warwick, "General Atomics: Third-Gen Electric Laser Weapon Now Ready", *Aviation Week and Space Technology,* April 20, 2015, at http://aviationweek.com/technology/general-atomics-third-gen-electric-laser-weapon-now-ready. Accessed on July 22, 2015.
12. Mark Prigg, "Star Wars Comes a Step Closer: US Military Bosses Reveal Successful Tests of Airborne Death Rays", at http://www.dailymail.co.uk/sciencetech/article-3096369/Star-Wars-comes-step-closer-military-bosses-reveal-success-tests-airborne-death-rays.html. Accessed on July 22, 2015.
13. Debi Dawson, "Army Testing Green Laser Kits in Afghanistan", at http://www.army.mil/article/40214/army-testing-green-laser-kits-in-afghanistan/. Accessed on February 19, 2015.
14. "China Unveils Laser Drone Defence System", at http://www.theguardian.com/world/2014/nov/03/china-unveils-laser-drone-defence-system. Accessed on February 19, 2015.
15. "Secret Laser Devices of the Soviet Union", at http://englishrussia.com/2011/11/08/secret-laser-devices-of-the-soviet-union. Accessed on February 20, 2015.
16. For a comprehensive list of laser types and varied applications, please refer http://en.wikipedia.org/wiki/List_of_laser_types
17. William H., Possel, "Laser Weapons in Space: A Critical Assessment", Air War College Maxwell AFB, Al 36112, April 1, 1998, p. 18.
18. Final report of "Defense Science Board Task Force on Directed Energy Weapons", Office of the Under Secretary of Defence for Acquisition, Technology and Logistics, Defence Science Board, December 2007, at www.acq.osd.mil/dsb/reports/ADA476320.pdf. Accessed on November 10, 2014.
19. Ibid.
20. Robert Sherman, "Mid-Infrared Advanced Chemical Laser (MIRACL)", accessed at http://fas.org/spp/military/program/asat/miracl.htm. Accessed on November 13, 2014.

21. Available at http://en.wikipedia.org/wiki/MIRACL. Accessed on November 13, 2014.
22. Possel, n. 17.
23. "Pentagon Beams Over Military Laser Test", at http://web.archive.org/web/20071230052044/http://www.cnn.com/US/9710/20/pentagon.laser/. Accessed on November 13, 2014.
24. Ibid.
25. Leona C. Bull, "MIRACL Damaged in Experiment", accessed at http://web.archive.org/web/20030805111139/http://www.aerotechnews.com/starc/120897/121197d.html. Accessed on November 13, 2014.
26. Ibid.
27. Charles B. Stevens, "Zenith Star: An SDI Demonstration", *Executive Intelligence Review*, vol. 14, no. 50, December 18, 1987, at http://www.larouchepub.com/eiw/public/1987/eirv14n50-19871218/eirv14n50-19871218_024-zenith_star_an_sdi_demonstration.pdf. Accessed on July 4, 2014.
28. Dr Carlo Kopp, "High Energy Laser Directed Energy Weapons", at http://www.ausairpower.net/APA-DEW-HEL-Analysis.html. Accessed on December 2, 2014.
29. Ibid.
30. Ibid.
31. Ibid.
32. Hydrogen Fluoride Lasers have wavelengths of 2.7 to 2.9 microns which are absorbed readily by earth's atmosphere and, thus, are suitable for space operations.
33. "Space Based Laser", accessed at http://fas.org/spp/starwars/program/sbl.htm on October 29, 2014.
34. "Megawatt Laser Test Brings Space-Based Lasers One Step Closer", accessed at http://www.spacedaily.com/news/laser-00e.html. Accessed on November 10, 2014.
35. "The Space-Based Laser Integrated Flight Experiment: Global Missile Defense in the Boost Phase", Team SBL-IFX at www.wslfweb.org/docs/sblwp.pdf. Accessed on November 10, 2014.
36. Amy Teitel, "The Laser-Toting Soviet Satellite that Almost Sparked a Space Arms Race", at http://www.wired.co.uk/news/archive/2013-05/16/soviet-laser-satellite. Accessed on February 19, 2015.
37. Dwayne A. Day and Robert G. Kennedy III, "Soviet Star Wars", *Air & Space Magazine*, January 2010, at http://www.airspacemag.com/space/soviet-star-wars-8758185/?all. Accessed on February 19, 2015.
38. "A-60 1A Airborne Laser", at http://www.globalsecurity.org/military/world/russia/a-60.htm. Accessed on February 20, 2015.
39. Report to Congress, "Future Military Capabilities and Strategy of the People's Republic of China" (Washington, DC: Department of Defence, November 1998) at http://fas.org/news/china/1998/981100-prc-dod.htm. Accessed on August 22, 2014.
40. Desmond Ball, "Assessing China's ASAT Program", *APSNet Special Reports*, June 14, 2007, at http://nautilus.org/apsnet/assessing-chinas-asat-program/. Accessed on March 20, 2014.

41. Bayram Mert Deveci, "Directed-Energy Weapons: Invisible and Invincible?", September 2007 at www.dtic.mil/dtic/tr/fulltext/u2/a473993.pdf. Accessed on July 4, 2014.
42. Ibid.
43. "Raytheon's Vigilant Eagle Incorporates Fielded Military Technology Adapted to Urban Environments", Raytheon, at http://raytheon.mediaroom.com/index.php?s=43&item=460. Accessed on February 24, 2015.
44. "Active Denial Technology", Factsheet, United States Air Force at http://jnlwp.defense.gov/Portals/50/Documents/Press_Room/Fact_Sheets/ADT_Fact_Sheet_Apr_2015_ver2.pdf. Accessed on July 4, 2014.
45. Randy Jackson, "CHAMPS- Light out", Boeing press release at http://www.boeing.com/Features/2012/10/bds_champ_10_22_12.html. Accessed on February 23, 2015.
46. Brandon Lewis, "Raytheon EMP Weapon Tested by Boeing, USAF Research Lab", at http://mil-embedded.com/news/raytheon-emp-missile-tested-by-boeing-usaf-research-lab/. Accessed on February 24, 2015.
47. Ibid.
48. Necati Ertekin; "E-Bomb: The Key Element of the Contemporary Military-Technical Revolution", September 2008, at www.dtic.mil/dtic/tr/fulltext/u2/a488877.pdf. Accessed on July 11, 2014.
49. Carlo Kopp, "The Electromagnetic Bomb : A Weapon of Electrical Mass Destruction", at http://www.qsl.net/n9zia/apjemp.pdf. Accessed on July 11, 2014.
50. George H. Baker, "High Power Electromagnetic Weapons: A Brief Tutorial", at http://works.bepress.com/george_h_baker/33. Accessed on July, 11, 2014.
51. Michael Abrams, "Dawn of the E-Bomb", October 31, 2003, at spectrum.ieee.org/biomedical/devices/the-dawn-of-the-ebomb. Accessed on November 14, 2014.
52. Kopp, n. 49.
53. Ibid.
54. Abrams, n. 51.

5

Cyber Attacks on Satellites: A Paradigm Shift in ASAT Technology

Cyber attacks are increasingly utilized in all facets of warfare and can hamper the operational capability of a satellite, jeopardizing the economy and security of the nation.

The space-faring nations have consistently worked towards exploitation of space technology to acquire an unequivocal advantage in economic growth and national security. As brought out in the preceding chapters, the pursuit for eminence in the space sector runs parallel to contesting for space supremacy, fuelling R&D in the fields of space weapons. Advances in development of space-based weapons get constrained by the technological wherewithal required for launching and managing of space assets. Whilst no space-based weapons have been deployed, space assets are still vulnerable and subjected to a wide variety of attacks. While kinetic energy attacks are limited to the military powers with established satellite manufacturing and launch capabilities, the testing and evaluation of DEWs is restricted by the techno-logistic potential of a nation. However, for indulging in space negation efforts, as will be established, access to space is neither a prerequisite, nor is it mandatory.

Space negation efforts would include physical attacks on the ground stations or exploitation of the vulnerabilities in the satellites' command, control and communications links. While conventional strikes on the ground segment may not be attempted against a stronger adversary, the more subtle but equally effective way forward would be sabotaging of the satellite's communication links, using cybernetic attacks. A satellite in orbit is small but central to the massive ground-based support infrastructure. Any accidental or deliberate disruption of satellite transmissions can cause catastrophic damage to a nation's economy by affecting the financial institutions, transportation systems, electrical power grids, communication systems and automated services. On the military front, it can hamper or result in considerable breakdown of operational capability. Irrespective of the services provided, breakdown in satellite services directly affects and jeopardises the economy and security of the nation. This growing reliance on satellite services now poses a fundamental threat to nation-states as impediments to satellite services and applications are feasible by covert means of cyber attacks.

Satellites, being integral to modern warfare, are fundamental in providing strategic depth to a nation. On the operational front, they figure as credible force enhancers and form a vital component of force application. Going by the conventional perception and definition of weapon system, a cyber attack on a satellite in a strict sense would be difficult to categorise as an ASAT weapon attack. While this analogy might have been true in the past, cyber attacks and mitigation techniques are being increasingly utilised in all facets of warfare and are now acknowledged as a new dimension in modern warfare. As the modern war-waging equipment relies heavily on information technology for command, control and functionality, cyber warfare now finds itself intricately linked with the operational capabilities of forces fighting in the land, air and sea domains. One may perceive satellites as a complex hardwired system driven by software utilities commanded from the ground to enable precision strikes, improve, and provide for, navigation across the globe; extend communication in otherwise inaccessible terrain; and widen the scope of ISR for successful operations. Like all networked infrastructure on the ground and at sea, satellites in orbits and their controlling ground stations are equally vulnerable and susceptible to cyber attacks. The functionality of all space-based assets or objects transiting through outer space rests to a great extent on onboard embedded software (which is subjected to remote command and control) for provision of services and applications. In view of this, and the future war-waging designs aimed at projection of power towards, and from, outer space, it seems apt to include cyber attacks on space assets as part of the space weaponisation process.

Cyber Warfare and its Link to Space

Prior to establishing the link between cyber warfare and space, it would be prudent to describe what constitutes cyber warfare. Cyber warfare is the unauthorised penetration by, on behalf of, or in support of, a government, into another nation's computers or networks, or any other activity affecting a computer system, in which the purpose is to add, alter, or falsify data, or cause disruption of, or damage to, a computer, or network device, or the objects a computer system controls.[1]

When talking of space-based assets, we can say that space and cyber space are closely interlinked and satellites can be viewed as computers placed in orbit with very long and very vulnerable Wireless Fidelity (Wi-Fi) like data links to the ground stations and users.[2] All satellites are driven by extensive digital controls which are highly vulnerable to interference. The satellite's operation rests on the commands relayed from control stations based on the ground and monitoring the satellite's response. All satellites use Telemetry, Tracking and Command (TT&C) sub-systems to communicate with ground stations. The TT&C is used to monitor the satellite's health, its overall status and exact location in space. It also accepts the required commands for processing of onboard data and manages the application payloads (imaging, communication, navigation, etc) and, in turn, relays the response to the ground. The TT&C relies extensively on the integrated software which, in the modern-day context, can be reconfigured as well as updated remotely from the ground. This reliance on software makes satellites vulnerable to cyber attacks and a number of instances have come to the fore where the satellites' operations have been interfered with. These occurrences or attempted cyber attacks are not restricted to, or against, the military space assets. Satellites, whether military, civil or commercial, irrespective of their ownership, are susceptible targets for state and non-state actors as well as individuals. The attacks may try to elicit effects ranging from temporary irritation to partial or complete breakdown of services. Successful culmination of a cyber attack may involve minimum paraphernalia required in terms of just a computer and an internet connection. The matter gets complicated as cyber attacks are covert and deceptive in nature. Any cyber attack, whether on the ground system or a space asset, would follow similar execution, irrespective of the target, and would be hard to detect. On detection, ascertaining the time of the attack becomes difficult, and attributing the attack to any party is extremely challenging as the attacker, by and large, would have covered his tracks.

While interference with satellites, intentional or unintentional, has been common, there are many instances where hacking of satellites has been reported, with some cases even reporting complete loss of controls. As aptly stated by William J. Lynn III, former US deputy secretary of defence, "The willingness of states to interfere with satellites in orbit has serious implications for our national security. Space systems enable our modern way of war. They allow our war-fighters to strike with precision, to navigate with accuracy, to communicate with certainty, and to see the battlefield with clarity. Without them, many of our most important military advantages evaporate."[3]

Principle Cyber Threats to Satellites

Extensive use of satellites in direct support of operations was witnessed in the Gulf Wars and, since then, there has been an incremental integration of satellite services with the emergence of network-centric warfare amongst the global powers. Moreover, during the Gulf War, instances of blocking satellite services were witnessed and in the aftermath of the war, stray incidences of taking over of complete control by unidentified attackers using cyber means were reported. Cyber attacks are mainly aimed at interfering with and taking over, the controls of a satellite. While military satellites are obvious targets, commercial satellites are also vulnerable during times of conflict. Cyber attacks on satellites and peripheral infrastructure use the techniques of jamming, eavesdropping, hacking and seizing of overall control. The penetration of the cyber and information domain by the hacker community has forced the satellite industry to initiate measures to safeguard satellites and associated sub-systems from cyber threats. While the development of mass-to-target weapons and DEWs continues, new inroads have been made by initiating disruption, degradation or incapacitating a satellite or its services by means of Information Warfare (IW). As new concepts emerge, the development of IW ASAT capabilities now falls in a very different league of a 'silent intrusion system' and due to the capability of IW in degrading, de-orbiting or making a satellite dysfunctional, IW attacks can be categorised in the league parallel to kinetic and directed energy weapons. This categorisation of drawing parallels with kinetic weapons and DEWs can be debated by many, but it must be taken into account that ASAT attacks now ride on the asymmetric applications which no longer demand use of high powered directed energy systems or kinetic kill to impair or damage a satellite. Despite the fact that no satellite has been lost or destroyed by cyber means till date, the occurrence of such an eventuality cannot be ruled out in the future.

Military satellites use hardened protection measures, making it difficult to get them compromised as compared to commercial satellites. Dual use commercial satellites providing support services like communication and reconnaissance are generally devoid of these protection measures as well. As satellites fall under the category of strategic assets, any loss of a satellite or its services is liable to cause economic distress to a nation. Besides this, the possibility of hindering satellite operations as a coercive measure for strong political signalling cannot be ruled out. Cyber attacks on satellites can affect their performance, causing temporary degradation in their services and can extend to cause irreversible, permanent damage. These attacks may be blatant or covert in nature. The attacks may be directed at hampering a particular service, and target satellites irrespective of orbital altitude. While a number of cyber attacks against non-military satellite services have been reported and documented, a majority of instances of cyber attacks or attempts either go unnoticed or even if noticed, are not made public by the satellite operators for fear of losing credibility and standing in the international market. On the military front, such attacks would not be generally publicised as the attacker generally would not be in a position to evaluate the efficacy of his attacks. Only a few cases of cyber attacks and attempts on military satellites have been acknowledged and that too after the required corrective actions to mitigate the threats were put in place.

As will be seen subsequently, a majority of cyber attacks are temporary and reversible in nature. While taking over of complete satellite control is now possible, any destruction of satellites owing to cyber attacks has not been attempted. However, complete takeover of controls may permit the attacker to manoeuvre the satellite and, if need be, the attacker could be in a position to de-orbit the satellite, push it out of orbit into space or manoeuvre it to collide with another space asset.

Satellite Jamming

Satellite jamming is one of the widespread hacking techniques where the attacker deliberately transmits a signal at the same frequency and with higher power so as to interfere with the legitimate signal between the satellite and the user by means of flooding or overpowering of uplink or downlink transmissions. In fact, jamming a satellite would involve subduing of the actual signal in the unwanted noise so that the real signal is no longer legible to the processing circuitry of the receiver system and, thus, cannot reach the user in a comprehensible form. This type of localised jamming would only be of a temporary nature and the jamming effects would be negated in a matter of time with the removal of the jamming signal. All satellites are installed with a number of transponders which amplify the received signal (uplink signal) and then retransmit it towards the Earth at a modified frequency, using frequency converters (downlink signal). A majority of communication satellites are placed in the geosynchronous orbit for continuous coverage and use fixed frequencies for uplink and downlink transmissions. The cyber attack can be directed towards a satellite or can be used to attack the computers and peripheral infrastructure of the ground stations. While modern day military as well as commercial satellites use encoded signals as anti-jamming techniques, a powerful signal at the correct frequency can defeat such protection measures. While many nation-states use dedicated military satellites, the dual use commercial satellites are more vulnerable to jamming attacks and can be exploited in crisis situations. The two types of satellite jamming techniques are orbital jamming and terrestrial jamming.

Orbital Jamming: Here the attacker targets the uplink and overrides the legitimate transmission from the ground terminal to the satellite. Thus, in a real sense, the jamming is directed towards the satellite, preventing the receiver of the satellite from receiving the uplink signal. Further, the efficacy of jamming on a commercial service like communication and television broadcast could be effectively monitored by observing the affected services. This will not be the case in regard to dedicated military satellites as the attacker may not be in a position to process the received signal in the absence of the dedicated configured receiver. As communication and broadcast satellites receive and transmit signals over a wide footprint, it is feasible to carry out cyber attacks on a satellite from any area under its cone of coverage, making it extremely difficult to pinpoint the source of the attack. An attacker jamming the uplink transmission requires that the satellite is visible during the attack. Thus, communication and broadcast satellites would be more vulnerable to such attacks than satellites in LEO. To target satellites in LEO, the cyber attacks additionally would require tracking equipment as the satellites are moving at higher speeds. Further, the attacker will be forced to plan the time of attack over a short duration in a feasible window of opportunity.

Terrestrial Jamming: Similar to the technique used for orbital jamming, terrestrial jamming is aimed to interfere with the downlink signal of a satellite and enables the attacker to inhibit a useful signal reaching the ground station or receivers, affecting a particular service being provided through the satellite. Unlike the jamming of the uplink, the power requirement in this case is much less and, generally, such jammers are positioned in the nearby vicinity of receivers or ground stations. Thus, the source of jamming can be identified and tracked relatively easily. As compared to uplink jammers, downlink jammers are simple and inexpensive. They could be bought off the shelf or built easily by amateurs as well, using instructions available on the internet.

Instances of Satellite Jamming: Satellite jamming has been a common occurrence in the past two decades and has been resorted to by both state and non-state actors, particularly targeting television broadcasts and communication services for censorship purposes. The cases of jamming date back from the time satellites have been used for television and radio broadcast services. In 1995, the Kurdish satellite channel 'Med TV' was jammed by the Turkish authorities claiming that its broadcasts supported terrorism and violence. In the present century, we have had instances of countries like Cuba, Iran, Libya and Ethiopia resorting to jamming satellite communications and television broadcasts originating from Europe and the United States. During the Crimea crisis, Russia reported cyber attacks, originating from western Ukraine, to block TV transmissions. In addition to broadcast transmissions, jamming of GPS signals and satellite telephones has now become a common phenomenon worldwide. For comprehensive occurrences of jamming incidences, one may refer to the list of jamming incidences compiled in the work of Jason Fritz BS; "Satellite Hacking: A Guide for the Perplexed."[4]

The incidences and attempts of jamming instances are not only against commercial and civil satellites, but against military satellites as well. Jamming attacks against satellites providing operational support came to the fore in the Gulf Wars and in the Israel-Lebanon War of 2006. As of today, more sophisticated technologies for jamming satellite signals are readily available and can be procured 'off-the-shelf' from the commercial market. The United States has in its inventory a mobile counter-communications system which may be used to selectively and effectively jam satellite communication during periods of conflicts over a period of interest on a temporary and reversible basis.[5] China also has developed jamming techniques to jam satellite communications.[6]

GPS Jamming: One of the frequently used jamming attacks is against GPS signals which are critical to operations and navigation. GPS signals at published frequencies are transmitted from semi-synchronous orbit (~ 20,000 km) in the power range of 50 watts from a satellite. The power received at the ground equipment is much less and, thus, makes GPS receivers susceptible to jamming. GPS jammers are now widely available and instructions to build a jammer are available on the internet. Thus, a satellite navigation system with investment of billions of dollars can be disrupted with jamming equipment costing a few dollars. Russia markets jamming equipment of the size of a cigarette packet, which, with a power output of one watt, can deny GPS services in a radius of 80 km.[7]

Space-Based Jamming: Space-based jamming would involve the jammer being placed on a satellite in the vicinity of the target satellite. A jammer placed on a satellite would be effective with much smaller power levels as compared to ground-based jammers. However, pointing the jammer power to the satellite antenna and maintaining of the jammer power for prolonged durations is a difficult proposition. Orbiting the jammer in the same orbit is possible but effective jamming power would be lost. Events of space-based jamming have also been reported over contested orbital slots and allocation of frequencies. In 1997, Indonesia used its satellite Palapa B1 to jam the transponder of a communication satellite, APSTAR-1A, leased by the island nation of Tonga from the Hong Kong-based APT Satellite Company over a disputed orbital slot.[8] While many reports termed the incident as intentional jamming, it emerged that the jamming took place due to both satellites being in the near vicinity, owing to disputed orbital slots.[9] Using a satellite platform for jamming equipment does not seem to be a practical proposition as a jamming attack is feasible using ground-based jammers and the attacks planned are bound by the window of opportunity in time and space.

Eavesdropping

Eavesdropping on a satellite would amount to securing unauthorised access to the satellite transmissions without affecting the normal satellite operations, and in a legal sense, would portend stealing of information. This information would be used to decipher the plans of the adversary and could be used effectively to spoof the transmissions for deceiving the enemy. To avoid eavesdropping attacks, hardened encryption algorithms can be used. However, use of complex encryption standards has its own drawbacks in that the cost of operations escalates, and it could result in a drop of overall performance by a margin of 80 percent.[10] Satellite communications without hardened encryption in particular are susceptible to be compromised by off-the-shelf tools and software. One such software called 'SkyGrabber' was sold by a Russian firm, Sky Software, for $26 off the shelf and was used by hackers in Iraq and Afghanistan to capture unencrypted video feeds of the Predator Unmanned Aerial Vehicles (UAVs).[11] While the hackers weren't able to interfere in the operations, they did use the accessed data to pinpoint areas under military surveillance and the pattern followed by the drones for reconnaissance operations for adopting defensive measures.[12] This, in turn, could have helped the insurgents in predicting the position, tracking, locating and destroying the predator drones of the United States during the 2003 invasion of Iraq.[13]

The other type of eavesdropping commonly encountered is the interception of the communications of satellite phones and decrypting the messages using commonly available software on the internet. There are more than 100,000 satellite phone (satphone) subscribers worldwide and these are widely being used in disaster relief and military operations which are sensitive in nature.[14] While satellite phones do use encryption algorithms, these encryption algorithms can be broken easily using software tools readily accessible on the internet.[15]

Hijacking and Spoofing

Hijacking of a satellite involves unauthorised access of a satellite for the purpose of overriding legitimate transmissions with illegitimate ones. The attackers' aim is to make use of the available platform to suit their cause by hijacking a particular service or application. While any permanent damage to the satellite and its sub-systems is ruled out, the attacker overrides or corrupts the legible signal. A successful hijacking involves eavesdropping and spoofing operations. Spoofing can be perceived as an advanced jamming technique where the jamming signal imitates the characteristics of the actual signal and the content of the jamming signal is replaced with a fake signal to deceive the contents. Spoofing, thus, would require additional intelligence on the exact characteristics in terms of frequency of transmission and the power with which the signal is expected at the receiver. Any signals with gross deviations in the received power levels at the receiver are subjected to be filtered out. A hijacking incident would involve replacement of the original content in a televised or radio broadcast. On the military front, such an attack would be aimed to deceive by planting misleading information and feeds. Hijacking incidents of television and radio broadcasts are mainly resorted to as part of psychological warfare and for imposing censorship. For a comprehensive list of occurrences involving hijacking, one may refer to the list in the work of Jason Fritz.[16]

Control

The attacker in these cases penetrates the Tracking, Telemetry and Control (TT&C) using cyber means and modifies the controlling software to manipulate the services, applications and commands to the satellite. Taking over of the functions of the satellite by the attacker would entail gaining complete access to the TT&C link and, thus, confer the attacker with the controls to manoeuvre or destroy the satellite by de-orbiting it out of its slated orbit. The less but still serious type of attack is when the gaining of control is partial, in that the attacker is able to assume unauthorised control on the satellite sub-system. Examples of this type of attack would include taking over the control of the antenna or shifting the orientation of the satellite, making it unusable to the owner. While manipulation of the signal transmission may not necessarily make the satellite defunct, it can render the satellite useless to the rightful owner for prolonged or indefinite periods. One such incident that came into focus was in year 1998 when the high resolution imager of the US-German ROSAT satellite was destroyed owing to exposure to the sun. The investigations by the National Aeronautics and Space Administration (NASA) revealed that the orientation altered as a consequence of the cyber-intrusion at the Goddard Space Flight Centre and the attack allegedly originated from Russia.[17] As of now, while manipulating and controlling of satellite services has been witnessed on numerous occasions, no instance of satellite destruction due to hacking has come to the fore though taking over of the complete controls of a satellite has been reported. In its report to Congress, the US-China economic and security review commission report (USCC 2011) states that "at least two US government satellites have each experienced at least two separate instances of interference apparently consistent with cyber activities against their command and control systems." The report explicitly brought out the following malicious events experienced by the US satellites owing to alleged cyber attacks by Chinese hackers.[18]

- On October 20, 2007, Landsat-7, a US Earth Observation (EO) satellite jointly managed by the NASA and the US Geological

Survey, experienced 12 or more minutes of interference. This interference was only discovered following a similar event in July 2008 (see below).

- On June 20, 2008, the Terra EOS Earth Observation System M–1, a NASA-managed programme for Earth observation, experienced two or more minutes of interference. The responsible party achieved all the steps required to command the satellite but did not issue commands.
- On July 23, 2008, the Landsat-7 experienced 12 or more minutes of interference. The responsible party did not achieve all the steps required to command the satellite.
- On October 22, 2008, the Terra EOS AM–1 experienced nine or more minutes of interference. The responsible party achieved all the steps required to command the satellite but did not issue commands.

While the hackers were able to wrest complete control to command the satellite in the case of the Terra EOS, it is possible that the they were assessing the vulnerability of the satellite control system. The likelihood of these attacks originating from an individual hacker could be ruled out as no motive was established. That leaves the possibility of the attack being attempted at the behest of government sponsored hackers as the attackers incorporated measures to cover up their tracks and keep a window open for further attacks. Issuance of commands to manipulate the satellite in such a scenario tantamounts to an ASAT attack and this has international ramifications. It clearly brings out that unless hardened measures and anti-jamming techniques are adopted, the loss of satellite control could allow the attacker to damage or destroy the satellite by steering it out of the slated orbit. Further, the required anti-jamming measures call for specialised hardware and software encryptions which have to be imbedded into the satellite at the design stage itself. Once the satellite is launched, only limited upgrades in software would be feasible. The hacking of controls would make it possible for the attacker to manipulate the services and the associated network infrastructure. In the evolving network-centric scenario, multiple attacks on a set of satellites could paralyse a nation's network support from space and compromise its operational capability.

Conclusion

The employment of ASAT technology by leveraging cyber attacks will not be limited against military satellites alone; neither will it be restricted for use by the US, USSR and China only. With advent of information systems across the globe, and growing dependence on satellite services in commercial and social structures, a cyber attack can take a toll not only of a nation's economy but also of its will to fight a war. Nation-states not having the requisite technology and wherewithal for launching space assets as well as states without advanced conventional military power, find themselves alienated from the progressive developments taking place in the field of kinetic and directed energy space weapons. The only option to offset conventional and technological disadvantage is to adopt an unconventional and asymmetric approach offered by the covert means of cyber attacks. Occurrences of jamming, hacking and taking over of the controls of a satellite are phenomenal in number and are becoming routine in nature. Many of the cyber attacks on satellites go undetected, and if detected, are not reported. As can be evaluated from the few documented attacks discussed earlier, gaining access to satellite controls would allow an attacker to destroy or damage a satellite, force it to de-orbit, manipulate the transmissions or gain important information on the data collected by the satellite. In the past technology development had not catered for the new kinds of threats, as counter technologies in general never precede new developments. A majority of nations rely heavily on space-based assets and the vulnerability of these assets necessitate protective measures which at times tend to become aggressive so as to deter the adversary. This would hold in conventional conflicts but may not work against non-state actors engaged in asymmetric attacks. A weaker country with the capability of engaging in cyber attacks can exploit the space dependence of its stronger adversary and create chaos without being traced and detected. Asymmetric warfare of this kind is very much prevalent and is now being actively pursued by both state and non-state actors.

Notes

1. Richard Clarke and Robert Knake, *Cyber War* (HarperCollins, 2010), p. 70.
2. Col. M. V. "Coyote" Smith, "Welcome to the Age of Space and Cyber Warfare", presentation at the American Centre for Democracy's symposium on "Energy, Space and Cyber Security-Current and Future Threats," on September 30, 2013, at http://acdemocracy.org/welcome-to-the-age-of-space-and-cyber-warfare/. Accessed on January 13, 2015.
3. William J. Lynn III, "A Military Strategy for the New Space Environment," Centre for Strategic and International Studies, *Washington Quarterly*, 34, no. 3, Summer 2011, pp. 7–16. at csis.org/files/publication/twq11summerlynn.pdf. Accessed on January 21, 2015.
4. Jason Fritz BS, "Satellite Hacking: A Guide for the Perplexed", *Culture Mandala: Bulletin of the Centre for East-West Cultural and Economic Studies*, vol. 10, no. 1, December 2012-May 2013, pp21-50 at www.international-relations.com/CM2012/Satellite-Hacking.pdf. Accessed on January 22, 2015.
5. Jim Wolf, "US Deploys Space Satellite Jamming System", at http://www.rense.com/general59/jam.htm. Accessed on February 5, 2015.
6. Brian Bremner, "As China Stalks Satellites, US and Japan Prepare to Defend Them", at http://www.bloomberg.com/bw/articles/2014-07-17/u-dot-s-dot-japan-prepare-to-defend-satellites-from-chinese-attack. Accessed on February 6, 2015.
7. United States Department of Defence, Rumsfeld Space Commission Report, p. 20, Washington, DC.
8. Fritz BS; n.4.
9. Jeffrey Lewis, "The Role of Non-State Actors in Outer Space Security", Building the Architecture for Sustainable Space Security Conference Report, March 30–31, 2006, United Nations Institute for Disarmament Research, Geneva, Switzerland, p.34.
10. Pierluigi Paganini, "Hacking Satellites… Look up to the Sky", http://resources.infosecinstitute.com/hacking-satellite-look-up-to-the-sky/". Accessed on December 9, 2014.
11. Pierluigi Paganini, "Satellite Infrastructures: Principal Cyber Threats" at http://www.aofs.org/wp-content/uploads/2013/12/131203-Paganini-Satellite-infrastructures-Principal-cyber-threats_Final.pdf. Accessed on December 3, 2014.
12. Paganini, n.10.
13. Chris Cole, "Rise of the Reapers: A Brief History of Drones", October 6, 2014, at http://dronewars.net/2014/10/06/rise-of-the-reapers-a-brief-history-of-drones/#_ednref22. Accessed on January 20, 2015.

14 Benedikt Driessen, Ralf Hund, Carsten Willems, Christof Paar and Thorsten Holz, "Don't Trust Satellite Phones: A Security Analysis of Two Satphone Standards", Horst-Goertz Institute for IT Security, Germany, at http://gmr.crypto.rub.de/paper/paper-1.pdf. Accessed on January 20, 2015.

15. Ibid.

16. Fritz BS, n.4.

17. Keith Epstein and Ben Elgin, "Network Security Breaches Plague NASA", at http://www.bloomberg.com/bw/stories/2008-11-19/network-security-breaches-plague-nasa. Accessed on February 2, 2015.

18. US-China Economic and Security Review Commission Report, Washington, November 9, 2011, pp. 215-217.

6

United States, China and Space Weapons

The eternity of outer space today does not guarantee a safe haven to the space assets as they are progressively utilised in tactical warfare in changing the course of modern-day conflicts and, at the same time, are increasingly vulnerable due to predictability in terms of time and place.

The United States and the erstwhile USSR became embroiled in the pursuit of space technology for military dominance from the time the first satellite was launched. In fact, technology advancements in outer space were mainly driven by the possibility of leveraging space for unleashing of weapons of mass destruction across the globe. The notion of placing weapon platforms in space partly stemmed from the success of the German rocket technology during World War II and prevalent missile-based nuclear arms race after World War II. Both the power centres realised that the one who had the upper hand in controlling space, would control the Earth.[1] As the contest between these superpowers carried on unabated, the idea of using space weapons [conceived in the form of Space-Based Interceptors (SBIs) aimed at intercepting ballistic missiles] started taking shape, and kept gaining momentum, resulting in some credible developments, sporadic evaluations and limited deployments.

The protracted race for deployment of space weapons diminished gradually due to the technological constraints and exorbitant costs involved in launching and maintaining these weapon platforms.

By the late Eighties, almost all major projects designed towards weaponisation of space were shelved or put on hold. However, space-based services and applications saw an exponential growth during the period driven by the strong underpinning provided by the information revolution. As the world tried to assimilate the benefits of seamless connectivity in societal benefits and economic growth, the United States, in the period 1990-91, took the world by surprise and awe with the use of space assets in support of Operation Desert Shield and Operation Desert Storm. While the United States has demonstrated military use of space assets to wage and win a conventional war, the other countries are seeking to emulate and integrate the space support for their conventional forces. The Gulf operations shifted the focus of the military powers to the militarisation of space as use of space applications in support of conventional forces got extensive recognition. The space-based inputs improved the real-time situational awareness and, integrated with ground operations, extended unprecedented benefits in planning terrestrial operations and improving overall force application. The interest in space weapon projects also dwindled to a great extent as they did not provide any distinct advantage over conventional weapon systems. The pursuit for the design and development of space weapons declined further with the break-up of the USSR in the year 1991.

The fall of the USSR saw China's aspirations to assert itself as a growing power in East Asia and its political posturing in this direction saw a reorientation of the geopolitical space and re-emergence of strategic rivalries at the global level. On the one hand, Russia wants to regain its superpower status, while, on other, China, buoyed with its strong economy and growing military, has started visualising itself as the power that can challenge the United States' hegemony in the future. China's belligerent attitude in relation to the Taiwan Strait and its expansionist policy in the South China Sea are assertions of its intent. Realising the importance of space support as one of the pillars that could help it establish its clout in shaping the global affairs, China accelerated its space programme. Though a late entrant in the space race, today, its multifarious space related projects include modern launch systems, space stations, recoverable platforms, space exploration and interplanetary missions. At the same time, it has shown avid interest in military space applications and is reportedly developing wide ranging space weapons, making it a formidable force to reckon with.

The tranquillity prevailing over the issue of use of weapons against space-based assets got a jolt when both China and the United States demonstrated ASAT weaponry in the years 2007 and 2008 respectively. China's intensified efforts in the field of anti-satellite weaponry now challenge the strategic advantage garnered by the United States in the space field. The capability of destroying satellites is not limited to kinetic kill weapons launched from the Earth. As will be brought out subsequently, both these countries have dedicated R & D programmes for development and consolidation of the technology envisaged for a new concept of space-based weapon systems. As one of the advanced space-faring nations, China is at the forefront and continues to work towards building an offensive space capability that will employ space-based and ground-based anti-satellite weapon systems. The primary aim appears to challenge the US' monopolistic space advantages with a vision to balance strategic stability and have its say in the shaping of world affairs.

United States' Space Strategy and Outlook Towards Weaponisation of Space

In the current world order, the United States is the dominant power in the space domain. Its phenomenally successful space ventures have highlighted the fact that states cannot become great powers in the present-day context, unless they demonstrate the ability to control and integrate space-based services in furtherance of national objectives. Over the past two decades, the US has been involved in major conflicts like Operation Desert Storm, Operation Allied Force, Operation Enduring Freedom and Operation Iraqi Freedom. In addition, it has carried out special covert operations on a number of occasions as part of its so-called global war on terror. A close scrutiny and analysis of these conflicts highlights one common thing and that is the superior war-fighting ability that the US forces have accrued from space-based services. The other distinct but more important point is that in these so-called wars (war on terror), the US, as a superior power was pitted against an opponent with inferior weaponry and did not face much resistance due to the opponents' lack of possession of the required capability for retaliation. This one-sided military contest has been a major cause of concern and has infused a sense of insecurity amongst all the nation-states. Today, on the one hand, while the United States relies extensively on the usage of space assets in support of military operations, it is seen as preparing its forces for future combat in, and from, space.

Early Designs for Power Projection from Space

The United States had been interested in power projection from space even before the launch of the first artificial satellite. In the 1950s, both the USA and USSR were embroiled in a race to develop technology to launch objects into space mainly from the perspective of being able to place weapons in space. As the space technology had not evolved, the mere thought process of operating space weapons was enough to create ripples and instil a sense of anxiety and uncertainty in both superpowers. In the latter half of the 1950s, much of the effort was devoted by both superpowers towards the development and demonstration of Intercontinental Ballistic Missiles (ICBMs). The advances in ICBM technology opened up the possibility of delivering firepower across the globe. Further, the ICBM technology on the cards of both the USA and USSR would also permit launching of objects into space—both these powers were now embroiled in a race to demonstrate their preeminence in space technology. As the ICBM technology was still under evaluation, each of these superpowers wanted itself to be in a pioneering position for exploiting the technology. The use of ICBMs also spearheaded apprehensions and speculations about the delivery of nuclear weapons using this platform.

The launch of the Sputnik by the USSR on October 4, 1957, raised speculations and apprehensions within the United States on many counts. The first and foremost was the shocking realisation that it was trailing in technological superiority behind its arch rival, whilst it had always projected itself to be way ahead in R&D in relation to space projects. The successful launch of the Sputnik also substantiated the advances made by the USSR in the field of ICBM technology. This had serious implications for the United States' military as now the USSR could also exploit space-based platforms and ICBM technology for delivery of nuclear weapons. These fears were further exacerbated by the consecutive successful launch of the Sputnik II on November 3, 1957. The United States, in the interim, in order to reclaim the lost ground, had pushed ahead its 'Vanguard project' and announced its launch. The much hyped launch was telecast live, but the Vanguard exploded on the launch pad, denting the image of the US further. It regained some of its lost prestige when it consolidated its presence in space with the successful launch of Explorer-I. Hereafter, both the United States and USSR intensified their efforts in development of space systems and developed better launch capabilities in support of diverse applications, to include manned space flights and reentry modules..

Satellites as Weapon Platforms: Advantage USA or USSR?

As both the USA and USSR succeeded in establishing the presence of their satellites in space, the next step was exploring the possibility of using satellites as weapon delivery platforms. Both superpowers comprehended that placing of weapons in space would bequeath them unparalleled military advantage. The establishing of clout in space was driven by multi-pronged efforts in the development of space weapons. Deployment of weapons in space demanded better launch capabilities and both powers tried to outdo each other by improving the payload capacity. The other area of focus for both powers was establishing a defensive facility against ICBMs and space weapons. A credible defence called for intelligence inputs, observation platforms and detection of launches while catering for tracking capability and developing counter-systems to mitigate imminent threats. Both powers realised that all these capabilities in space were intricately related and any new developments in one field would provide an impetus to the overall developmental programme. Over a short period of time, after some trials, it was realised that the available space technology was still in a primitive stage for positioning and operating weapons in outer space. While launching of space weapons was found to be feasible in spite of technological constraints, the physics of orbital behaviour made it difficult to sustain weapons in space for prolonged periods and restricted their operation in terms of time and place of choice. A credible power projection from space in terms of time and place of choice demanded a constellation of space weapons. Further, such a proposal of deploying a constellation of space weapons was not only marred by issues of reliability and effectiveness but would prove to be exorbitantly costly vis-à-vis the expected yield and effect of conventional weapons.

In spite of the technological impediments, the proclivity to develop space weapons persisted, with both superpowers trying to outwit each other. Any breakthrough in demonstrating or boasting about a concept was enough to keep the other side guessing and on tenterhooks. Consequently, in the USA as well as the USSR, a number of projects were conceived, researched and developed. Edging ahead in this competition, the USSR was successful to an extent in infusing ambiguity amongst the United States' political and military leadership on the nature of space weapons being developed by it. The USSR at this stage had proclaimed the capability of orbiting nuclear weapons, including the hydrogen bomb.

The zeal to develop space-based weapons abated to a great extent in the year 1963. The year witnessed the Partial Test Ban Treaty (PTBT) coming into force which imposed a ban on testing of nuclear weapons in the atmosphere, in outer space and under water. With the treaty coming into force, the focus of both the USA and USSR started shifting towards employing space assets for non-aggressive military applications and bringing about improvements in technology for Intelligence, Reconnaissance and Surveillance (ISR). Use of satellites for ISR missions gained importance as this permitted monitoring of movement of forces and weapon systems in other parts of the globe, allowing preemptive planning and initiating of measures to counter any expected attacks. They also gained further prominence with the then hi-tech applications in support of communication, weather monitoring, navigation and terrain mapping, and the intelligence information streamed in allowed for planning of terrestrial operations.

Primitive Space Weapons and Their Success

Embarking on the perceived role of satellites in the nuclear dissuasion, the United States initiated its anti-satellite programme in 1957 and by 1962, had produced ASAT interceptors employing nuclear warheads on the Nike-Zeus and Thor missile systems.[2] In this period, the US Air Force (USAF) also conceived the Satellite Interceptor (SAINT) programme aimed at inspecting and identifying nuclear weapons in orbit, and if found hostile, their destruction with a 'kinetic kill' capability. The US Navy, in the meantime, worked on another advanced ASAT project in the name of 'Early Spring', employing the concept of a high altitude hovering missile which would launch a payload in the direction of the earmarked satellite and damage it by disintegration of the warhead in the vicinity of the satellite, releasing thousands of metal pellets. The United States, in 1962, also carried out the Starfish Prime nuclear detonation in space which destroyed a number of satellites, created artificial radiation belts and also caused considerable damage to ground infrastructural grids in the resulting Electro-Magnetic Pulse (EMP).

In the 1960s, the USSR unveiled its design of a Fractional Orbit Bombardment System (FOBS) to carry the megaton class of nuclear warheads aboard ICBMs that would achieve Low Earth Orbit (LEO) altitudes and could be brought down on targets around the globe in their reentry phase before the completion of one revolution. A number of test launches demonstrated the efficacy of the launch and de-orbiting manoeuvres, however, over a few years, it was established that the system lacked targeting accuracy. Over a period of time, the advanced Electronic Warfare (EW) system network deployed by the United States to track missile launch signatures eradicated the surprise element of this system and subjugated the decisive advantage of the Soviet ICBMs' unlimited range. This was the also period when, in 1968, the Soviets toyed with the idea of co-orbital ASATs and evaluated the system over a decade and a half, carrying out 20 launches at varying LEO altitudes. The ascendency of the Soviet ASAT systems now posed a major threat to the US as the dependency of satellites for routine functions like ISR, communications and warning had grown considerably. In response to the Soviet advances, the United States, in the 1980s, responded by developing an airborne ASAT. The Air Launched Mini Vehicle (ALMV) made use of the F-15 aircraft to launch a heat seeking Miniature Homing Vehicle (MHV) using a two-stage rocket to destroy the target with a high speed kinetic impact.[3]

Though officially all these ASAT projects were cancelled in due course, stating technological constraints and scarcity of funds, the scrapping of these projects could mainly be attributed to the employment of primitive concepts, with a low rate of success, as well as political compulsions. The other main reason was the PTBT coming into force, resulting in mitigation of the nuclear threat posed by space-based weapons.

Strategic Defence Initiative: A Multi-pronged Approach to Space Weapons

By the late 1980s, the US and USSR were engaged in multi-pronged negotiations on the banning of space weapons. Though both sides engaged in a series of bilateral talks on the issues, each was wary of the possibility of missile attacks with nuclear tipped warheads from the other. In this period of uncertainty and distrust, the projects for development of space weapons slowed down considerably, however, the fear of being attacked by nuclear ICBMs played heavily on the psyche of both sides.

To alleviate the fear from the so-called impending nuclear strikes and to mitigate the threat to the United States, on March 23, 1983, President Ronald Reagan announced the Star Wars programme under the Strategic Defence Initiative (SDI), which once again fuelled the space weapons development programmes. The programme envisaged a new concept in defence strategy involving space and ground-based laser weapons, particle beam weapons and space-to-Earth kinetic attack systems that would be amalgamated to acquire capability to intercept ICBMs in their boost phase. For fruition of the ambitious project, a number of space-based interceptors were conceived, ostensibly christened as 'Rods from Gods' and 'Brilliant Pebbles'.[4] The harnessing of high powered lasers in the ASAT role also gained momentum. The Soviet response to the SDI was a mixed one. In order to tackle the US challenge, on the one hand, the Soviets vowed to refine the existing weapons and missile programmes and, on the other, proposed a ban on space-based weapons. To pressurise the United States to reconsider its approach, the USSR engaged aggressively in negotiations for a space weapon ban and as a step in this direction, declared a unilateral moratorium on ASAT weapon tests.[5]

The much hyped SDI, touted as capable of providing a complete defensive shield over the entire territory of the United States, garnered enormous funding devoted to the research and development of diverse space-based interceptor programmes. However, the US Congress soon realised that the feasibility of such weapon systems would call for a constellation of LEO weapon systems that would be impracticable and expensive. Moreover, even in the case of a successful culmination of the project, the reliability of tackling the missile threats would not be foolproof. Thus, in spite of making a lot of headway in developing the weapon systems, the SDI project was eventually stalled and later called off. In fact, if the projects like Brilliant Pebbles and Rods from Gods had thrived and fructified, they would have imparted more of an offensive capability than a defensive one.

Shifting Focus: Force Projection to Force Enhancement

Both the USSR and USA had contemplated the use of space weapons mainly in a probable nuclear war and devoted much of the work towards use of space weapons in the offensive as well as defensive roles. During this period, space technology had advanced considerably and satellites were incrementally used in support of military operations as information gathering and observation platforms. Besides their military applications, satellites had started to gain prominence in civil and commercial applications, assisting in scientific experiments, weather forecasting, mapping of resources, communication and navigation. This was also the period when development of space weapon projects lost their sheen owing to two main reasons. The first was the reduced possibility of nuclear conflicts owing to various treaties and agreements; and, secondly, it had become more or less evident that space weapons were not practically deployable owing to the existing techno-logistical constraints.

By the beginning of 1990, space science had advanced and proliferated considerably. With more and more nations joining the space club, the near monopolistic hold of the USA and USSR in the space field had started to loosen up. The new and aspiring space-faring nations were eyeing space assets mainly for newfound commercial and civil applications that promised a positive impact on the society and the economy. While the use of satellites for the military services was always coveted by the military powers, the non-military satellite applications became a preferential choice as the same satellites could be used in dual configuration as well.

The last decade of the 20th century was the turning point in transformation of the global outlook on space assets. The United States, in the Persian Gulf War, made extensive use of its satellites in support of terrestrial operations, exploiting the capabilities of communication, reconnaissance, intelligence gathering, information denial, imaging and battle damage assessment. The use of satellites also psyched the global populace, including the political leaders, by bringing in live accounts and imagery of the devastation wreaked by the US forces. The prominent role of space assets in support of land, sea and airborne forces and their dominant role in preventing a military power like Iraq making any headway in controlling operations came to the fore. This war exemplified the use of space support and made it clear to the rest of the world as to how future wars would be fought. The unprecedented success of the Gulf War served as a springboard for steering the space policy from one of force projection to that of force enhancement. This again was aptly visible in Operation Enduring Freedom and Operation Iraqi Freedom.

21st Century: A Renewed Interest in ASAT Technology

Subsequent to the USSR's disintegration on December 26, 1991, the contest for the development of space weapons diminished considerably. The United States, relieved of the competition to develop space weapons, channelled its resources towards integrating satellite services in support of military operations. With this, interest in the development of kinetic kill space weapons saw a decline towards the last decade of the 20th century, and many of the former projects were either shelved or mothballed. However, the United States' concern in respect of the vulnerability of its space assets grew and Congress adopted an aggressive approach in matters related to space security. This was when directed energy technology assumed greater significance and substantial funds were diverted for research and development in the field of high powered microwaves and lasers. The development, testing and evaluation of MIRACL in this direction towards the end of the 20th century succeeded only partially[6] and it was soon realised that the high power laser generation techniques had not matured enough for operational viability.

At the start of the 21st century, Earth-to-space or space-to-Earth weapons were impractical owing to technological constraints, their enormous size, infrastructural requirements and basing complexities, coupled with the high costs. In order to reinvigorate its clout in the space dominion, the United States relied on innovative technologies. With the experience accrued over the past decades, the US not only improved its satellite launch capabilities but also succeeded in orbiting recoverable spacecraft and space planes with experimental payloads.

Destruction of Defunct Satellites

On January 11, 2007, China destroyed its non-functional weather satellite, the Fengyun-1C (FY-1C), using a missile, and demonstrated its advances in ASAT technology. The deliberate destruction of the satellite was attempted after more than two decades by a nation, with the last reported event in the year 1985 when the United States had shot down one of its own satellites using a missile fired from an F-15 aircraft. An aspect that requires attention was the muted response of the US to the experimental evaluations of tests conducted prior to the engagement of the FY-1C and its subdued response to the phenomenal debris created post disintegration. Was it that the US was not confident of the intelligence inputs and had only a hazy picture of the monitored activities? The second important question that arises is, "Was the US able to identify and track the missile launch in real-time?" The answer to both these questions could be contemplated and would bring out the constraints of the Space Surveillance Network (SSN) fielded by the United States. Surveillance and tracking is a complex and costly affair, with vast infrastructural requirements and seamless positioning of sensors in the three-dimensional space. The United States' SSN comprises electro-optical, passive radio frequency and radar sensors. This SSN has inherent limitations as it works on a predictive procedure to keep track of space objects, and it is difficult to track an unannounced activity in space. Thus, even with a precursor of a likely space launch, it is extremely difficult to capture and track a launch event with a limited number of sensors and their geographical distribution,[7] unless information about the exact launch site and timing is available. The other reason why the US may not have reacted to the

Chinese ASAT test, was that it would serve well to project to Congress the requirement for future research, development and testing in relation to space weapons.

The above assertion came true when, following the Chinese ASAT test, the United States once again indulged in destroying its own defunct reconnaissance satellite, the USA-193, at an altitude of 240 km on February 20, 2008, using its Aegis missile defence system aboard a sea-based platform. The United States' ASAT efforts in this period were not limited to kinetic kill capability. In order to gain space supremacy and exhibit its clout to control space so as to emerge as the sole space superpower, it continued investments in new concept laser weapons.

Focus on Laser Technology

The United States, by the end of the 20th century, was well aware of the drawbacks of placing and operating space-based kinetic weapons. With its preeminence in space technology, it was well aware that the one who controls outer space would control the future operations that would provide "freedom of action in space for friendly forces while, when directed, deny it to an adversary, and include the broad aspect of protection of US and US allied space systems, and negation of adversary space systems".[8] Embarking on this premise, it channelised its research in the field of directed energy weapons, with emphasis on laser projects. In the very first decade of the 21st century, it succeeded in fielding a number of high powered solid state laser weapons.

After the successful testing of its Tactical High Energy Laser (THEL) demonstrator from 2000 to 2005, the United States has moved forward and thereafter has introduced low range weapon systems like the Maritime Laser Demonstrator (MLD), Gamma (FIRESTRIKE series of laser), Mobile Active Targeting Resource for Integrated eXperiments (MATRIX), Joint High Power Solid State Laser (JHPSSL), Laser Area Defence System (LADS) and High Energy Liquid Laser Area Defence System (HELLADS).[9] All these weapon systems are based on solid state technology and are in various stages of evaluation. These weapons have been tested in varied configurations aboard sea-based and ground-based platforms and the technology is being upgraded for aircraft operations.

The testing and evaluation of these weapon systems has been incremental in refining the technology to improve the power output with a reduced weapon dimension and weight. One of the evident accomplishments in the laser generation technique has been the use of a modular design where the output from multiple laser sources can now be combined for generation of scalable high power. This concept enables the deliverance of measured scalable power, allowing the feature of controlling lethality. The final aim has been to improve the power gain using a compact apparatus that could well fit into an air-borne platform or spacecraft. Use of laser weapons aboard aircraft or spacecraft would provide an unmatched advantage to the US military and would inherently change the nature of wars to come.

X-37B: Orbital Test Vehicle

The X-37 series of the Orbital Test Vehicle (OTV) was conceived by NASA in the year 1999 and has been developed as a reusable reentry spacecraft. Built as a technology demonstrator, this robotic space plane validates and corroborates the endurance of reusable space vehicle technology. Accorded a classified status by the US Air Force, this mini Space Shuttle-like space plane, characterised by the likes of both an aircraft and a spacecraft, has been designed for a vertical launch using an expendable launch rocket. The X-37B is the modified version in the series of the X-37 spacecraft with the earlier version, the X-37A, being used as an Approach Landing and Test Vehicle (ALTV). Since the year 2010, a total of four X-37B missions has been launched.

Released into LEO, the X-37B can stay in orbits for a prolonged duration spread over months. The third mission was in orbit for a record duration of 656 days and the fourth mission that was launched on May 20, 2015, is expected to last for more than 200 days.[10] This spacecraft derives its auxiliary power from a specially designed solar array and also carries lithium-ion batteries to conserve the propellant fuel.[11] Further, it has been designed for aircraft-like manoeuvrability in space and, thus, would be capable of changing speeds and the altitude or orbit. The spacecraft de-orbits from space under the command from the ground and thereafter autonomously reenters the atmosphere in a glider configuration to land horizontally on a runway. The X-37B programme has intrigued the world from the very beginning on the secretive nature of its mission and profiles. As per the X-37B OTV factsheet displayed on the website of the US Air Force, "The programme is to evaluate and test technology of advance guidance, navigation and control, thermal protection systems, avionics, high temperature structures and seals, conformal reusable insulation and lightweight electromechanical flight systems".[12]

A space plane can be planned for numerous tasks that would include maintenance of space assets, extension of logistic support for improving the life-cycle of satellites and space stations, carrying out ISR missions or acting as a platform for the insertion of satellites. As the mission of the X-37B has been a closely guarded secret, a number of articles and reports have contemplated the use of this spacecraft as a space weapon platform. While it is difficult to judge the exact mission of this space plane, the spacecraft technology would definitely provide an edge to the United States for its future space ventures and open up the possibility for placing weapons in space.

China's Space Strategy and Outlook Towards Space Weaponisation

Towards the end of the 20th century, China was well aware of its potential influence in world affairs as a growing economy. It had already laid out a robust foundation in terms of its manufacturing industries which was driven by earlier investments in mass training and skilling of its manpower. Backed by a strong political will, and timed well to coincide with the break-up of the USSR, the Chinese polity was well aware that it could now assert itself as a regional power and have an influence in shaping world affairs. The economic growth drove its military modernisation and this, in turn, led to its assertive behaviour. With its robust economic outlook, it concentrated on stabilising and sustaining the growth in various fields in spite of the world taking a dim view of its authoritarian policies.

China's Space Ambitions

Following the Sino-Soviet split over deterioration of political and ideological relations in the 1960s, China started to develop a series of indigenous rockets mainly based on the primitive R-series missile procured from the USSR. This led to the development of the Long March launch vehicle family and the first successful satellite launch in 1972.[13] Since then, Long March rockets have been used with reliable consistency. Foraying into the commercial launch market in the year 1990, China successfully launched satellites for varied applications spanning communication, navigation, reconnaissance and meteorology. China has also been successful in launching its Shenzhou series of manned and unmanned spacecraft since November 1999. In 2003, a Long March booster put the first Chinese astronaut into space, thereby making it the third state to launch humans into space.[14] China successfully launched its first mission to the Moon, Chang'e-1, on October 24, 2007, and followed it up with its second Moon mission, Chang'e-2 on October 1, 2010. Presently, its space scientists have planned for an unmanned Mars exploration mission by 2033, and are contemplating the prospects of a manned landing on Mars by the middle of this century.[15] The successful launching of the Tiangong-1 space station on September 29, 2011, followed by a number of rendezvous and dockings of the Shenzhou spacecraft have consolidated China's international standing. On December 14, 2013, China successfully achieved a soft landing on the Moon with its robotic rover 'Yutu', also known as 'Jade Rabbit'. China maintains that its space programme is for peaceful purposes and it is not vying for space dominance. The multi-pronged approach in commercial and exploratory research in space activities is an assertion of China's resolve to achieve the status of a major space power, while reinforcing efforts to bolster its space programme for peaceful purposes.

Foundation Towards Emerging as a Global Space Power

To be recognised as a global power, not only does China want to build up a robust economy, but also seeks to achieve a position whereby it could drive the economies of other nations. To make this feasible, it needs to develop and build a military capability that would be respected globally. The Chinese strategic community rightly understood that development of a competitive space industry and the capability of asserting space dominance were intricately related. Assessing that one of the supporting pillars for acquisition of a global military status rests on a nation's capability to dominate space, it started laying emphasis on its space programmes. In line with this, the Chinese government set up a number of institutions dedicated to space technologies and invested heavily in projects involving satellites, space stations, exploratory research, space weapons and counter-space technologies. In the simplest of terms, China was well aware that its stature as a futuristic global power could be showcased to the world by achieving the status of a futuristic space power. Such a posture also helped it build up its national prestige while covering up its long-term strategic intentions.

The overall space strategy followed by China is two-pronged; one is to explore and exploit space technology for developmental purposes which would provide a boost to the economy, and, the second, to rise as a credible space power. Embarking on this strategy, it would gain on all fronts, in that, the investments made in the research and development of space technologies would complement its civilian, commercial and military programmes, and, in turn, would not only give it a credibility in the exploitation and utilisation of outer space for the economic and societal benefit of mankind but also place it in a position to dictate militarily. While China continues to make strides in its space programme in support of societal and commercial services, it has consistently worked towards integrating, and improvising, space services in the military domain.

Strategy on Weaponisation of Space

China, of late, has been actively pursuing ambitious, incremental and multi-pronged activities related to weaponisation of space, and has made considerable advances in this field. As per China, "The weaponisation of space is an inevitable developmental trend" and the "commanding height" of strategic competition in the 21st century "will not be on Earth, but in space".[16] The recent strides made by China in support of its commercial space ventures coupled, with its bold outlook on military space strategy have raised the concerns of the space-faring nations. China has reportedly also been experimenting with directed energy weapons to attack satellites. PLA writings emphasise the necessity of "destroying, damaging, and interfering with the enemy's reconnaissance ... and communications satellites," suggesting that such systems, as well as navigation and early warning satellites, could be among the targets of attacks designed to "blind and deafen the enemy".[17] The same PLA analysis of the US and coalition military operations also states that "destroying or capturing satellites and other sensors will deprive an opponent of initiative on the battlefield and make it difficult for them to bring their precision guided weapons into full play".[18]

The dichotomous intent of China becomes clear as, on the one hand, it has engaged itself in technology associated with space weapons, while, on the other, it has consistently voiced a strong opinion in support of a weapon free outer space. This is evident from the fact that along with Russia, China has pushed for an international Code of Conduct to prevent weaponisation of space, under the aegis of the UN umbrella. It is also in favour of signing the treaty on Prevention of Arms Race in Outer Space (PAROS). The United States, in spite of having a well-established ballistic missile defence system and possessing technical advantages in potential space weaponry, has consistently refused to negotiate PAROS in the Conference on Disarmament (CD).[19] The failure to ratify this treaty by the US has left little choice for China but to continue research and development in space weapons.

Multi-pronged Approach to Space Weapons

The Gulf War showcased the use of satellites by the United States in support of communication, observation, navigation and dovetailing the information over a network for real-time situational awareness. The striking feature of this campaign for China was the dependency of the United States' military on space assets. An assessment of this dependency pointed out that if China develops a capability to disrupt, deceive, degrade or destroy the satellites or their services, it could significantly counter the asymmetric advantage enjoyed by the US in the space domain. Developing a capability in this direction would also have deterrence value to a limited extent. The Chinese military factored the futuristic importance and the asymmetric advantage that space services would provide in support of military operations and started developing a blueprint for the realisation of the dream of attaining the status of a global power in the years to come.

With this backdrop of expanding its military might, the People's Liberation Army (PLA) revamped its outlook towards new and futuristic weapon technologies and embarked on developments in the fields of lasers, microwaves and cyber warfare. Supported by a number of research institutions, strategic think-tanks and military planners, the Chinese government planned for, and invested heavily in, improvement of existing technologies and encouraged innovative experimentation for future technologies. With a strong base garnered through the indigenised ballistic missile projects, the Chinese amalgamated the technology in the space sector to improve the capabilities of launch vehicles, their payload capacity and the frequency of launch. In doing so, they maintained a fine balance in sharing the space technologies in the scientific, civil and military fields to achieve their goal of emerging as a global space power.

In the aftermath of the 1991 Gulf War, witnessing the space-based capabilities of the United States, the advanced countries all over the world started adopting the concept of 'network-centric warfare' and initiated steps towards improving their space capabilities to support the concept of "informationised" warfare. China, concerned with the increasing US influence in its surrounding region, particularly in the Taiwan Strait, and in the vicinity of the South China Sea became wary of US military might and analysed that it could not match the capability of the US military might in the foreseeable future. The PLA strategists and analysts observed the overt dependence of the United States military on satellite services for C4ISR and the role they played at the strategic, tactical and operational levels of war. One way to counter this was to deny the use of this information to the US forces by denying them access to space-based systems by the use of counter-space technologies. The development of such technology would not only bolster China's deterrent capability against the United States but would also reassert its supremacy as a regional power. These counter-space technologies would involve:

- Weapons directed from Earth-to-space, space-to-Earth and space-to-space.
- Direct ascent kinetic kill systems, directed energy weapons, cyber attacks
- Hard and soft kill capabilities

Adopting a multi-pronged approach, China started building up its ASAT capability to include a mix of weapon platforms using varied technologies aimed at disruption, degradation and destruction of space-based assets. It focussed on the development of kinetic kill vehicles that destroy their targets by ramming them at high speeds, directed energy weapons such as lasers to degrade or disable satellites. In addition, China has pursued development and testing of co-orbital satellites that could be used as weapon platforms and has the capability to interfere with the operation of satellites by cyber means.[20]

Hit-to-Kill ASAT Technologies

The use of kinetic kill vehicles as ASAT weapons was not observed for more than two decades, post the disintegration of the USSR. However, the emerging powers, in the interim, had been contemplating development and testing of ASAT weapons using indigenised launch vehicles. It was on January 11, 2007, that China, using a multi-stage rocket, successfully conducted its first ASAT test, destroying its own inactive polar orbit satellite, the 'FengYun-1C' at an altitude of 865 km. The disintegration of the satellite created one of the largest clouds of space debris, polluting outer space. This space debris is posing a danger to space assets and future space activities. The President Emeritus of the Henry L. Stimson Centre, Michael Krepon, stated that the Chinese ASAT test was predictable and was an indicator to the United States, showcasing its advancement in this field.[21] American intelligence had a precursor of an impending ASAT test as it was already aware of two experimental evaluations conducted on July 7, 2005, and February 6, 2006. These two tests used the solid-fuelled medium-range SC-19 class of missile launched on a mobile launcher, carrying an interceptor designed to crash into the enemy satellites.[22] Though no target was hit, it was not clear if these tests were aimed to destroy any target. However, the experimental evaluations of the SC-19 seem to have contributed to the successful interception of the FY-1C satellite on January 11, 2007. There have been reports suggesting that China may be planning to conduct another ASAT test in Medium Earth Orbit (MEO).[23]

Ballistic Missile Defence System

In January 2010, China conducted another test, this time on ground-based mid-course missile interception technology. With these two tests in 2007 and 2010, it is possible that China has bridged the gap of linking anti-satellite and missile defence systems and made certain headway in "hit-to-kill" technologies.[24] Confirmation that this was indeed another test of the same SC-19 ASAT system comes from a classified US State Department cable that was leaked by Wikileaks in 2011.[25] The technology associated with mid-course BMD technology is strikingly similar to direct ascent kinetic kill ASAT technology and provides an inherent counter-space capability. In January 2013, China publicly reported another "mid-course missile interception test" and, based on similarities of its description by the Chinese media to the 2010 test, one can assume the use of the SC-19 missile series, which is yet to be acknowledged by the US government.[26] It is reiterated that the technologies used for BMD and direct ascent ASAT attacks are complementary to each other, and Chinese research and development in this field has matured significantly.

Sub-Orbital ASAT?

On May 13, 2013, China launched a rocket from the Xichang Satellite Launch Centre in Sichuan province. The rocket reached an altitude of 10,000 km and the ceiling covered was one of the highest sub-orbital launches worldwide since 1976. The rocket apparently did not place any satellites or objects in orbit and as per the Pentagon, this launch could be the first interceptor test aimed at destroying a satellite in higher orbit.[27] While admitting that the launch did take place, China maintains that the rocket carried a science payload to study the Earth's magnetosphere.[28] As per one of the reports, "The system appears to be designed to place a kinetic kill vehicle on a trajectory to deep space that could reach Medium Earth Orbit (MEO), Highly Elliptical Orbit (HEO), and Geostationary Earth Orbit (GEO)".[29]If true, this would represent a significant development in China's ASAT capabilities as no other nation has tested such a system.[30] A detailed analysis of satellite imagery reveals that the research mission was actually the test of a new anti-satellite weapon based on a road-mobile ballistic missile.[31] In this context, one may refer to an exhaustive neutral analysis by Brian Weeden, the technical adviser for the Secure World Foundation, who has scrutinised the event and analysed the technicalities, challenging the feasibility of such a mission.[32] The motive behind the sub-orbital launch is a subject of hypothesis, but China seems to have covered credible ground, reaching new heights in the realm of outer space. The experiment has helped boost the confidence of Chinese space agencies, providing the required thrust for futuristic space missions.

Co-Orbital Technology

China is also reported to have developed parasitic satellites as an additional method to deploy an ASAT weapon.[33] In its annual reports to Congress in 2003 and 2004, the Pentagon asserted that China has "developed and tested an ASAT system described as a parasitic micro-satellite", i.e., a small satellite that attaches itself to a target satellite to disrupt or destroy that satellite on command. Though this report is unconfirmed, the progress made by China in launching a number of recoverable satellites and mastering docking practices do give a strong indication of such a development. In terms of co-orbital ASAT development, China's recent BX-1 microsatellite test, which was carried out as a part of the manned Shenzhou-7 mission, demonstrated technology that can be used as a base for future covert satellite inspection missions, as well as co-orbital ASAT attacks.[34] The BX-1 test could be visualised as a simulated run to test capabilities required for a co-orbital ASAT attack as the satellite passed in close quarters of the International Space Station.[35] The Chinese are also believed to be investing in small (nano) satellites technologies which could be used as space mines.[36]

Robotic Arm in Space

On July 20, 2013, China had launched a set of three satellites called Chuangxin-3 (Innovation-3), Shiyan-7 (Experiment-7), and Shijian-15 (Practice-15).[37] As per available reports, one of the small manoeuvrable satellites was equipped with a robotic arm that was tested to capture another satellite.[38] While reports on the actual mission remain unverified, Pentagon officials believe the small satellite activity is closely associated with China's secret ASAT programme.[39] The report also goes on to state that the robotic arm could have been an experiment to facilitate future maintenance and repair activities in relation to space assets.[40] Experimenting with the robotic arm to physically control space assets or using it for on-station maintenance, points to the advances the Chinese scientific community has made in span of one decade. This technology in future could be sought internationally to manipulate the orbits, improve the longevity of satellites and safeguard satellites from probable collisions with debris. China can also use it as an ASAT system without contravening the legal obligations of placing of weapons in space.

Directed Energy Weapons

China has been pursuing development of DEWs since 1990. Believing firmly that the DEWs and EMP creation by means other than a nuclear blast would be able to change the course of future wars, China has emphasised research and development in the field of ground-based laser systems and radio frequency weapons for degradation of satellites. As per the 1998 Pentagon report to Congress, "China may already possess the capability to damage, under specific conditions, optical sensors on satellites that are very vulnerable to damage by lasers", and that "given China's current interest in laser technology, it is reasonable to assume that Beijing would develop a weapon that could destroy satellites in the future".[41] The assumption gained credibility when, in August and September of 2006, China reportedly used high-powered, ground-based lasers to illuminate US reconnaissance satellites. Reports stated that these were either ASAT tests or relatively "low-power" laser ranging devices intended to precisely determine satellite orbits for ASAT targeting purposes.[42] While China does seek use of laser weapons to disable satellites and is pursuing research in this direction, the generation, handling and focussing of laser beams is a complex affair. Laser weapons capable of attacking a space system will be constrained by the size of the equipment, power feeds, generating a focussed beam of the required intensity, and pointing the beam for the finite time on the target. As per the existing records, the US has reported that its satellites encountered illumination from low powered laser beams. Any experimental laser research directed towards space would result in capturing of this information. Just by citing illumination of satellites, it is not possible to specifically assert that China is in position to generate weapon grade lasers to act against satellites. The United States has been working on weapon grade lasers for more than three decades and has invested considerable resources in various projects, with a modest rate of success. The generation and development of, and targeting with, weapon grade lasers has its own complexities involving power, cooling, equipment size, beam formation and beam pointing. China, being new in this field, would take a few more decades to gain maturity in this technology.

The Chinese mindset of 'inevitability of weaponisation of space' was reinforced in November 2009, when PLA Air Force (PLAAF) Commander Gen Xu Quilang, now the deputy director of the Central Military Commission (CMC), in the course of an interview, stated that space had become a "new commanding height for international strategic competition" and that having control of the air and space "means having control of the ground, oceans, and the electro-magnetic space, which also means having the strategic initiative in one's hands."

Conclusion

In the 21st century, the US is overly dependent on space systems. As its reliance on space assets is high, its vulnerability in space is perceived to be high, and as more and more nations join the space club, this vulnerability is bound to increase. This increased vulnerability of space assets has driven the United States to further its research and development from the combat support role to one of space-based deterrence which inevitably would pave the way to shift its policies towards weaponisation of space. The issue of controlling space was on the cards from the time even before the launch of the world's first satellite. The United States, in the middle of 19th century, was of the firm opinion that power projection from space would help establish overall military superiority, and effective control of space would help garner an unparalleled edge to support combat operations on the ground, at sea and in the air. In view of its concerns on space security, it has adopted a proactive approach in its development of essential infrastructure and components for space weapons.

China is well aware of the ubiquity of the space services used by the United States in varied facets of the societal, commercial and military arenas. China is growing rapidly as a space power and its developmental activities in the space field are advancing at a rapid pace. To circumvent any kind of political, economic or military coercion (in particular from the United States), its focus on exploiting the vulnerability of US space assets is in line with the posturing for minimal deterrence capability. With a robust space programme aimed at the societal and economic well-being of its citizens, China has been a strong supporter of peaceful uses of outer space. China has advocated that outer space should be kept free of weapons and has earnestly made efforts to enforce legal obligations on the international community to prevent weaponisation of space. As the United States has been a stumbling block in the ratification of PAROS, China has been left with no option but to pursue its space advances with an open-ended approach towards space weaponisation. It has exploited and worked on space technologies that would serve to create space weapons at short notice. In this direction, it has demonstrated kinetic kill capability to attack space assets from the ground, and if reports are to be believed, has made considerable progress by experimenting with co-orbital systems capable of maturing as space weapons. China's multi-pronged approach to decimate the adversary's space assets would include incorporating and improvising of directed energy weapons. In the prevailing situation, the proliferation of DEW capabilities by any country would bring in a sense of apprehension amongst the other nations. China has justifiably assessed that until and unless it projects a credible deterrence in some form, it could be subjected to political, economic and military coercion in the future. Thus, in the face of US space assets becoming increasingly indispensable to its grand design, China seeks to build up a minimal deterrence posture focussing on the vulnerability of US space assets.

The technological trends in relation to outer space are fast changing and the ever increasing use of space assets in support of military applications indicates a growing inclination of the space powers for research, development, testing and evaluation of weapons directed from, and towards, space. The eternity of outer space today does not guarantee a safe haven to the space assets as they are progressively utilised in tactical warfare in changing the course of modern-day conflicts and ,at the same time, are increasingly vulnerable due to the predictability in terms of time and place.

Notes

1. S. Rajagopal and Sridhar K. Chari, "Prospects for Stability in a Nuclear Subcontinent", National Institute of Advanced Studies, Bangalore, 2003, p.18
2. Alexei Arbatov and Vladimir Dvorkin, "Outer Space: Weapons, Diplomacy and Security", Carnegie Endowment for International Peace, 2010, Washington DC, p.34
3. Laura Grego, senior scientist, UCS Global Security Programme, " A History of Anti-Satellite Programs", January 2012, at http://www.ucsusa.org/assets/documents/nwgs/a-history-of-ASAT-programs_lo-res.pdf. Accessed on March 7, 2014.
4. Refer to Chapter 4 and 5 for details.
5. Ibid.
6. Refer to Chapter 5.
7. Maj Edward P. Chatters IV, USAF, and Maj Brian J. Crothers, USAF, "Space Surveillance Network", at http://www.au.af.mil/au/awc/space/au-18-2009/au-18_chap19.pdf. Accessed on July 17, 2014.
8. Peter L. Hays, "Current and Future Military Uses of Space", Outer Space and Global Security, UNIDIR, at http://www.unidir.org/files/publications/pdfs/outer-space-and-global-security-307.pdf. Accessed on August 28, 2015.
9. For more details on these projects, one may refer to the chapter on "Directed Energy Weapons", in this book.
10. "Boeing X-37", at https://en.wikipedia.org/wiki/Boeing_X-37. Accessed on October 19, 2015.
11. "X-37B OTV - Spacecraft Information", at http://www.spaceflight101.com/x-37b-otv-spacecraft-information.html. Accessed on August 26, 2014.
12. "X-37B Orbital Test Vehicle", US Air Force, at http://www.af.mil/AboutUs/FactSheets/Display/tabid/224/Article/104539/x-37b-orbital-test-vehicle.aspx. Accessed on August 26, 2014.
13. Prof Keith Hayward, "The Chinese Aerospace Industry — A Background Paper"; Royal Aeronautical Society, at http://aerosociety.com/Assets/Docs/Publications/DiscussionPapers/ChineseAerospaceIndustryDiscussionPaper.pdf. Accessed on January 27, 2014.
14. Ibid.

15. Srinivas Laxman, "China's Space Mission: The Long March to the Moon and Mars", *Asian Scientist*, at http://www.asianscientist.com/features/chinas-space-mission-moon-mars/. Accessed on July 28, 2014.
16. Mary C. FitzGerald, "China's Military Modernization and its Impact on the United States and the Asia-Pacific", March 30, 2007, Statement on "China's Military Strategy for Space" before the U.S.-China Economic and Security Review Commission, at http://origin.www.uscc.gov/sites/default/files/transcripts/3.29-30.07HearingTranscript.pdf. Accessed on January 7, 2014.
17. Office of the Secretary of Defence, "Annual Report to Congress: Military and Security Developments Involving the People's Republic of China 2014," April 24, 2014, at http://www.defense.gov/pubs/2014_DoD_China_Report.pdf. Accessed on July 11, 2014.
18. Ibid.
19. "Proposed Prevention of an Arms Race in Outer Space (PAROS) Treaty", Inventory of International Non-proliferation Organisations and Regimes, Centre for Non-proliferation Studies, at http://cns.miis.edu/inventory/pdfs/paros.pdf. Accessed on March 18, 2014.
20. Kevin Pollpeter et al., "China Dream, Space Dream: China's Progress in Space Technologies and Implications for the United States", a report prepared for the U.S.-China Economic and Security Review Commission at http://origin.www.uscc.gov/sites/default/files/Research/China%20Dream%20Space%20Dream_Report.pdf. Accessed on April 22, 2015.
21. Marc Kaufman and Dafna Linzer, "China Criticized for Anti-Satellite Missile Test", *Washington Post*, January 19, 2007, at http://www.washingtonpost.com/wp-dyn/content/article/2007/01/18/AR2007011801029_2.html. Accessed on August 22, 2014.
22. Michael R. Gordon and David S. Cloud, "US Knew of China's Missile Test, but Kept Silent", April 23, 2007, *The New York Times*, at http://www.nytimes.com/2007/04/23/washington/23satellite.html?pagewanted=print&_r=1&. Accessed on July 9, 2014.
23. Ajey Lele and Gunjan Singh, "China's Space Strategy and Modernisation", *ORF Issue Brief*, February 2013, Observer Research Foundation, New Delhi, at http://www.orfonline.org/wp-content/uploads/2013/02/IssueBrief_49b.pdf. Accessed on November 22, 2013.
24. Rosita Dellios, "China and Outer Space" (2012). *Humanities & Social Sciences Papers*, Paper 571, at http://epublications.bond.edu.au/hss_pubs/571. Accessed on October 29, 2013.
25. Brian Weeden, "Through a Glass Darkly, Chinese, American, and Russian Anti-satellite Testing in Space", March 17, 2014, at http://swfound.org/media/167224/Through_a_Glass_Darkly _March2014.pdf. Accessed on July 9, 2014.
26. Ibid.
27. Andrea Shalal, "U.S. Sees China Launch as Test of Anti-Satellite Muscle: Source", *Reuters*, at http://www.reuters.com/article/2013/05/15/us-china-launch-idUSBRE94E07D20130515. Accessed on July 17, 2014.

28. Ibid.
29. Weeden, n. 25.
30. Ibid.
31. Andrea Shalal, "Analysis Points to China's Work on New Anti-Satellite Weapon", *Reuters*, at http://www.reuters.com/article/2014/03/17/us-china-space-report-idUSBREA2G1Q320140317. Accessed on July 9, 2014.
32. Ibid.
33. M.V. Smith, "Ten Propositions Regarding Space Power", School of Advanced Airpower Studies, Air University, Maxwell Air Force Base, Alabama, June 2001 at http://www.au.af.mil/au/awc/awcgate/saas/smith.pdf. Accessed on August 22, 2014.
34. Ian Easton, "China's Evolving ASAT Weapons Programs and Their Implications for Future U.S. Strategy", Project 2049, Institute, at http://project2049.net/documents/china_asat_weapons_the_great_game_in_space.pdf. Accessed on December 2, 2013.
35. Brian Weeden, "China's BX-1 Microsatellite: a Litmus Test for Space Weaponization," *The Space Review*, October 20, 2008, at http://www.thespacereview.com/article/1235/1. Accessed on March 20, 2014.
36. Ajey Lele and Gunjan Singh, "China's Space Strategy and Modernisation", *ORF Issue Brief*, February 2013, Observer Research Foundation, New Delhi, at http://www.orfonline.org/wp-content/uploads/2013/02/IssueBrief_49b.pdf. Accessed on November 22, 2013.
37. "China Testing New Satellite-Hijacking Space Weapons", October 4, 2013, at http://www.china-defense-mashup.com/china-testing-new-satellite-hijacking-space-weapons.html. Accessed on July 9, 2014.
38. Ibid.
39. Ibid.
40. Ibid.
41. Report to Congress , "Future Military Capabilities and Strategy of the People's Republic of China", (Washington, DC: Department of Defence, November 1998) at http://fas.org/news/china/1998/981100-prc-dod.htm. Accessed on August 22, 2014.
42. Desmond Ball, "Assessing China's ASAT Program", *APSNet Special Reports*, June 14, 2007, at http://nautilus.org/apsnet/assessing-chinas-asat-program/. Accessed on March 20, 2014.

7

Implications of Space Weaponisation and its Global Fallout

The technology invested in ASAT weapons and counter-counter-space capabilities would pave the way for peaceful exploration of space and help mankind reap the benefits in the long run, by exploiting space resources.

From time immemorial, mankind has witnessed conflicts on land and with technological evolution; the *modus operandi* of waging wars has revolved around the ever improvising capability of weapons and delivery platforms. The maritime interests extended the conflict zones into the sea and the evolution of aircraft led to battles being fought from the sky. The evolution of rockets made it possible to launch satellites and this technology, in turn, is being exploited by nation-states to gain control of outer space. The transformation in the war-waging capabilities in the domains of land, sea and air has been bolstered by the acquired war-fighting capability from outer space and grants unparallelled advantage to a nation's firepower. The use of space-based platforms offering real or near real-time inputs not only helps in improving situational awareness and synchronisation of plans but provides opportunities to prepare for future actions for a decisive advantage. In 1958, Senator Lyndon B. Johnson who later assumed the office of the president of the United States, had expressed his view on the importance of space assets in these words, "There is something more important than any ultimate weapon. That is the ultimate position—the position of total control over the Earth that lies somewhere out in space. That is . . . the distant future, though not as distant as we may have thought. Whoever gains that ultimate position, gains control, total control, over the Earth, for the purposes of tyranny or for the service of freedom". Thus, while capability to achieve air superiority is considered as the ultimate expression of military power, the last decade of the 20th century elevated space support as a critical component for force enhancement. As nation-states become more reliant on space systems, the incremental deployment of military satellites and spacecraft is making outer space a contested zone, as it acts as a force multiplier for a military's capabilities.

Space assets or satellites have inherent vulnerabilities stemming from the laws of physics in space. These travel at a known speed, move in well defined fixed orbital slots, and follow a repetitive pattern, making it easy to track and predict their position at any point of time. With the increasing realisation of the potential of space in the boosting of the economy and its military utilisation for the expansion of strategic reach, there is bound to be discord and competing interests, in terms of orbital slots, bandwidth and probable risks of collision resulting from space congestion. It is only a matter of time before future conflicts would involve denial of space services, further exacerbating and escalating the intensity of the conflict for control of outer space. Failure to resolve these contentious issues could flare up into conflicts to a level where targeting of space assets would be considered an option. As has been brought out in the earlier chapters, space weapons are no longer a distant reality, since they provide platforms for the delivery of weapons from and towards space, available with a few selected military powers. Further, with no ratified embargo on the deployment or employment of space weapons, and space assets being intricately linked to economic growth and security, the likely use of these weapons in future conflicts cannot be ruled out.

There is only a handful of countries with credible space programmes. Amongst these, as of now, only the USA, China and Russia have demonstrated the capability of targeting the space assets of an adversary albeit to a limited extent (each country has evaluated and tested weapons against its own space assets at a premeditated place and time of choice). While no recent attempts to place weapons aboard space-based platforms have been reported, the thought of unleashing destructive power from the realm of space has been consistently espoused and attempted since the Cold War period.

As space weapons are being developed, and evolve as a tool of power projection, it would be prudent to examine the impact of these on future warfare strategies, the outer space environment and the consequential impact on society. The aim of this chapter would be to dwell on the global consequences and strategic impacts, resulting from the potential use of these weapons, and figure out if space weapons can help in the rebalancing of global power equations in the face of such an eventuality.

The Initial Steps Towards Space Weaponisation

Space weapons fall into two main categories: one, where the weapon is deployed as an orbital station to target other space assets (including targets transiting through orbital altitudes) or terrestrial targets; and the second, where the weapon is deployed terrestrially (ground-based, sea-based or airborne) in order to target space-based platforms.

In the first category, from available reports and existing literature, we can construe that outer space is free from the deployment of space-based orbital weapons. While this may be true in the present-day context, the accuracy of such a proclamation is debatable, as history does list out instances when space weapons were actually deployed or their launch attempted. A glaring and well documented case in point is of the USSR declaring its co-orbital ASAT capability operational in the year 1973.[1] The other example is the USSR's failed attempt at deploying the 'Polyus-Skif'[2], a laser-equipped ASAT platform in the year 1987, in response to the proposed Strategic Defence Initiative (SDI) of the US. The argument garners further support as one cannot overlook the grand design and efforts by the two superpowers towards deployment and employment of space-based weapons during the Cold War period. As brought out in the preceding chapters, the United States has actively pursued the goal of placing of space-based kinetic interceptors named 'Brilliant Pebbles'[3] and 'Rods from Gods'[4] as part of its SDI. Equally true is the fact that none of these weapon systems was used by the US or USSR against any adversary. These projects were abandoned midway owing to technological shortcomings, practical viability and exorbitant costs. However, the experience gained from testing and evaluating prototype space-based weapons during the Cold War period placed the USA and Russia in pioneering positions for exploiting and advancing innovative concepts. Supporting this view is the ongoing research and development of the project 'Space Based Laser - Integrated Flight Experiment (SBL- IFX)' by the USA as a step towards the much hyped space-based missile defence system.[5] Amongst other emerging global powers, China has shown keen interest in the development of space-based weapons. In fact, all global space powers (with indigenous launch capability) will be in a position to launch and manoeuvre small, micro and nanosatellites to act as parasitic satellites or space mines.[6] In addition, platforms like the space stations, space planes (X-37 series) and space shuttles operated by the USA, Russia or China can be effectively utilised for the deployment of space weapons.

In the second category, wherein the space weapon is deployed terrestrially against space-based or space-transiting targets, a lot of effort has been evident since the launch of the first artificial satellite. Once again, while none of the space assets of a potential adversary has been targeted, the technology for this category of weapon has been tenaciously conceived, evaluated, consolidated and demonstrated on numerous occasions. Through this, space assets can be targeted from ground-based, sea-based or airborne platforms using diverse weapons ranging from kinetic kill technology to making use of directed energy systems. Sub-orbital kinetic kill ASAT capability (land and sea-based) was demonstrated by China (2007) and the USA (2008) when they targeted and destroyed their own defunct satellites. Amongst the air launched kinetic kill ASAT capability, we have witnessed missions like the Air Launch Mini Vehicle (ALMV)[7], pursuance of Micro-Satellite Launch Vehicle (MSLV)[8] project by the USA and the research and development efforts of Russia[9] and China[10] in similar projects. Whereas all nations in possession of a credible satellite launch capability acquire an inherent capability to launch a kinetic kill ASAT weapon, it is the research and development in the field of DEWs which makes it a potential and potent candidate for the destruction of satellites and spacecraft. In the field of DEWs, the USA has carried out testing and evaluation of lasers and high power microwave weapons on a wide variety of platforms[11]. Similarly, Russia has also attempted to exploit an IL-76 aircraft as an airborne platform for laser weapons.

Impact of Technology

The research and development efforts in the varied branches of science perpetuated through the generations of mankind have precipitated some of our greatest technological and social advances. The exploration of a new technology in order to convert novel perceptions into practical applications is a process that propels growth and prosperity. While a new technology can add to our well-being, the same technology could well be laced with a dark lining which can unleash destruction. This is true in the opposite sense as well, as a technology conceived for a destructive mechanism has been used for countless benefits. In fact, the majority of innovations and discoveries have positive as well as negative facets. To name a few, medical, agricultural, nuclear, weapon and internet technologies can be used for general well-being as well as for destructive utilities.

As and when a state-of-the-art space weapon concept develops or comes to the fore, it is considered to be a technological masterpiece (just like the first airplane, the Sputnik, virtual surgeries, etc). Such technology can be used as a stepping stone for the betterment of the national economy and its overall growth. Letting one's imagination run wild, it would not be out of place to state that the fantasised depictions in televised serials (Star Trek) and motion pictures (the likes of Avatar, 2012, Interstellar, Gravity, etc.) could become a reality with technological breakthroughs. Today, as we progress with the newfound concepts of space exploration and space tourism, the future generations may witness beam-based teleportation of objects and even humans. In short, technology by itself is neither good nor bad; it depends on how we reap its benefits. Thus, just like nuclear power, which produced unparalleled devastation in the not so distant past, is now being hailed as a solution to the energy crisis, the development programme of space weapons will provide an impetus towards fulfilment of distant aspirations that have only been dreamed of.

Thus, exploration in scientific research and exploitation of outcomes for the conceptual foundation, and further reaping of the benefits after technology consolidation is a continual and unavoidable process. Just as the weapon engineering process is integral to pioneering technology, similarly, the interest in developing space weapons is no different. The likelihood of a conflict in space can be gauged by the enormous amount of funding dedicated to controversial weapon programmes. The United States' Financial Year (FY) 2016 President's Budget request includes $7.1 billion for the Department of Defence (DoD) Space Investment Programmes and $9.6 billion for missile defence.[12] China, on other hand, spends about $2 billion on its space programme every year.[13] These programmes, additionally seek to exploit new concepts in weapon systems using high energy lasers, high powered microwaves, particle beams and cybernetic attacks against satellites and spacecraft. The inevitable focus on ASAT weapons and counter-counter-space capabilities, while being detrimental in the present context, will pave the way for newer concepts and technologies for peaceful exploration of space and help mankind reap benefits accrued by the exploitation of space resources.

The Inevitability of Space Weaponisation

From these categories of space weapons, it clearly emerges that any statement which directly or implicitly suggests that "outer space is weapons free" is questionable, as the capability to place weapons in space does exist. Even if we go by the premise that there are no weapons in outer space, we are well aware that space basing of weapons is feasible at short notice. From the historical as well as contemporary perspective, the USA, China and Russia are the only three nation-states that have evaluated and demonstrated the technological capabilities of physically destroying space assets. While other states with indigenous satellite launch capability have voiced their interest in space weapons, any serious inclination for, and indulgence in, following it up with concrete steps has been lacking.

Though the number of space-faring nations that can launch weapons into orbit is relatively small, the select major space powers do possess the potential of 'launch on demand'. Thus, while small satellites can be placed into orbit in a matter of a few hours, so can weapons for selective targeting. As there is no embargo on terrestrial deployment of weapon systems, and a majority of states do have the resources to launch ballistic missiles, the possibility of space assets being targeted from terrestrial platforms in future conflicts cannot be overlooked. The progress made in the development of weapons directed towards, and from, space, coupled with the ability of deployment and employment of such weapons is indicative of the fact that space stands more or less weaponised. The R&D in laser techniques, high powered microwave systems, particle beam technology, and use of cyber capabilities has been remarkable and is being perfected for integration on all types of weapon platforms. This coupled with the advances in manoeuvrable and recoverable spacecraft now makes possible the integration of such weapon equipment onto the space-based platforms. With this backdrop, it would not be out of place to mention that space warfare now seems inevitable and is only bound by an event where a space asset is subjected to an attack from an enemy. While weaponisation of space is a potentially contentious subject, in the ensuing deliberations, we assume that space already stands weaponised while respecting the sanctity of the Outer Space Treaty barring use of weapons of mass destruction in space.

Strategic Implications

As space-based services proliferate, the critical dependency on satellite services is witnessing an indomitable growth. In the future, as geopolitical rivalries flare up on issues of economic discrepancies, diminishing natural reserves and expansionist policies of states, the possibility of conflict escalating to the space domain cannot be ruled out. The use of space-based services and applications is directly linked to economic growth, and with a majority of nations making use of these resources in support of military operations, space assets naturally acquire the status of a nation's strategic assets. Being part of a strategic enterprise, these assets have a direct bearing on national security and, thus, need a secure operating environment for freedom of operation.

Now, as the major space-faring nations contest for space supremacy and the emerging space players try to cover the lost ground in the vastness of space, opinions have been voiced on whether future wars could extend to the space domain. As has already been brought out, the capability for the deployment and employment of space weapons already exists. Space-based assets make it possible for a nation to maintain a continuous presence across the globe and help retain situational awareness. The derivation of real-time intelligence makes it possible to dovetail tactics in order to realign the force structures to an advantageous position, and when supported with space weapons, this would reinforce the strategic depth of a nation by realignment to a position of advantage. Space weapons will have an inherent advantage which would provide the states with a capability of force projection without the geographical or physical constraints experienced by the conventional forces.

Role of Orbiting Space Weapons

A weapon in space is more suitable for an offensive role, as space weapons cannot be used to protect satellites.[14] All space weapons in orbit would also be inherently vulnerable as they would be governed by the orbital trajectory as in the case of satellites. We are well aware that placing of any object in an orbit is constrained by its size and payload. While it is possible to launch both Directed Energy Space-Based Weapons (DESBWs) as well as Kinetic Kill Space-Based Weapons (KKSBWs), the possibility of orbiting KKSBWs in space seems more probable till the DESBWs evolve as a credible and cost-effective option. Operation of an independent DESBW sustainable over prolonged periods in orbit is presently constrained by the massive infrastructure required in terms of ancillary systems (power generation, cooling, efficiency, etc.) and, thus, imposes a restriction on the payload that could be carried by the launch vehicle. However, this constraint of payload does not prevent countries like the USA and Russia from operating low powered DEWs aboard a spacecraft or space station as the concept has already been verified using laser weapons on aircraft. These space-based weapons, due to their low yields, would only be suited to target other space assets and are not intended for targets on the ground. As has been brought out in Chapter 4, steering of weapon projectiles from space to Earth[15] would not produce the required bang for the buck as compared to conventional weapons used in terrestrial conflicts.

KKSBWs can be employed effectively in engaging point targets and also as area weapons. However, using KKSBWs as area weapons (to explode in the vicinity of the target) would not only result in fratricide, but would create space debris which would be detrimental for future space endeavours. Thus, using a kinetic kill capability for area targeting would not be practical as the likelihood of taking on multiple targets of choice is slim. Further, as the country originating the attack can be identified and established, the probability of conflict escalation on the ground between the adversaries cannot be ruled out. On the other hand, a DESBW aboard a spacecraft holds the promise of multiple targeting of select assets subject to devising means to aim and fire at targets by manoeuvring the spacecraft's orientation. A DESBW would also come with an inestimable magazine (as it can derive power from an external/independent power source, say, solar energy). As brought out in Chapter 4, such a weapon system would also be silent in nature, in that such a weapon is more likely to aim at the functionality of the target and often not result in disintegration of the target.

In a defensive role, space-based weapons can be used for defence against long range ballistic missiles but this would entail an enormous constellation of weapon platforms which, apart from being prohibitively costly, will also be difficult to maintain and sustain over prolonged periods. Thus, as and when space weapons are exploited, their deployment would be restricted mainly in an offensive role against other space-based assets and not against terrestrial targets.

Role of Terrestrial Space Weapons

Space assets can be targeted using terrestrial-based kinetic weapons as well as DEWs. While kinetic kill weapons have been successfully demonstrated to destroy space assets, the directed energy delivered from a ground or sea-based platform would have to contest the Earth's atmosphere and retain enough beam intensity to cause perceptible damage to the space target. While generation of high powered directed energy would not be constrained by the infrastructural set-up on the ground or on a large ship, use of DEWs aboard an airborne platform would be advantageous even when operated at low power. The advantage of an airborne DEW platform is that the transmitted directed energy beam would be subjected to less atmospheric attenuation; and the platform can be deployed flexibly and employed with prior planning of time and place. Further, the effectiveness of an airborne platform using DEWs has been verified successfully against other airborne targets.

Unlike orbital weapons (which are more suited in an offensive role), the terrestrial weapons to target space assets would be used in both offensive and defensive roles. Owing to the inherent vulnerability of space assets, targeting an earmarked space asset is relatively simpler as compared to manoeuvring a space-based weapon. Further, one of the prominent roles of terrestrial-based space weapons would be to destroy a KKSBW or DESBW suspected to be deployed against one's own space assets. The other more significant defensive role is of Ballistic Missile Defence (BMD) systems to intercept ballistic missiles at sub-orbital trajectories.

Space Weapons, Deterrence and Coercion

Use of space weapons to target an enemy's space assets would help achieve an advantageous position at both strategic and tactical levels where the opponent's space-based asset is being used as a force multiplier. Further, if the adversary is in a position to utilise satellites as force multipliers, it automatically warrants imparting it the status of a space-faring nation. Thus, the attacker targeting an opponent's satellite should be ready for similar consequences, as his own space assets would be equally vulnerable. The capability of launching a space-to-Earth weapon will lend credibility to its deterrent posture and can prevent hostile confrontation between the states. The deterrence value of space weapons against a strong opponent will, by and large, be limited to a defensive posture, in that, both sides would discourage the use of a space weapon for fear of retaliation.

A powerful nation can resort to destroying a weaker opponent's satellite for political signalling and coercing. It is possible that an advanced space power can target a budding opponent's satellite from a punitive perspective. Nonetheless, just the display of a punitive posture can well be used as a tool of coercing the enemy into submission. The obliteration of satellites, besides causing economic distress will have a grave psychological impact on the society. Such an attack could be resorted to against a rogue nation, for example, for supporting and harbouring terrorists. Thus, space weapons can be put to effective use as tools of coercion. The deterrence and coercive value of space weapons will also be much better if matched with the presence of terrestrial forces in the vicinity of the conflict. However, the use of space weapons will incur the wrath of other world powers and, hence, would be avoided, thereby maintaining the status of space as a sanctuary.

The use of space assets as force multipliers in tactical warfare during the course of a conflict has changed the nature of war by making it possible to engage an adversary across the globe. The use of space assets in support of military forces may well obliterate the likelihood of an all-out conventional war. As and when space weapons come to the fore, we will witness a paradigm shift where a nation may impose its resolve on the adversary's political, economic and social fabrics without any face-to-face confrontation.

Can Space Weapons Win Wars?

Before we address the issue of whether space weapons can win wars, we have to realise that space weapons (non-nuclear) can, at the most, be used to destroy other space assets or can neutralise a point target if directed towards Earth. In today's automated and information dominant set-up, any vital service or application is based on a multi-faceted platform. The satellite services and applications run in a layered fashion wherein any disruption of service is taken care of by the built-in redundancies using the services of other satellites or using a fallback infrastructural set-up on the ground. In fact, many services like routine communications use satellite services as a back-up option. A similar analogy applies to military satellites as well. For example, if any satellite goes defunct owing to, say, a technical breakdown, the services could be resumed in a matter of time by the use of other satellites or a fallback application on the ground. Thus, any satellite destroyed in an act of war at the most would be a cause of irritation or have limited economic consequences in a short window of time as fallback options are always factored in. On the military front, satellites are used mainly as force multipliers and not for application of force. Thus, while satellites can provide an advantage to military forces engaged in conflicts for the application of firepower, they cannot be actively used for unleashing destructive force against adversaries. Thus, targeting of adversaries' satellites alone cannot win wars and can only boost the offensive posture of terrestrial forces, putting them in an advantageous position. However, such an attempt may escalate the conflict on the ground and in case the attack involves the satellite of the other space power, the probability of an all out space war would become real. A space war, if fought, will be limited only to the space powers. In the case of conflict between two space powers, even if the attacker attempts and succeeds in the destruction of multiple satellites of its opponent, the targeting of satellites would not result in gaining ground in the conflict zone, rather, it would lead to conflict escalation, with severe ramifications from conventional firepower.

The use of space-to-Earth weapons, on the other hand, is yet to evolve and has not been demonstrated. Even if such weapons come to the fore in the future, they would be exorbitantly costly in comparison to the weapon yield on targets. Further, space-to-Earth weapons cannot match the advantage of conventional weapons launched from terrestrial platforms in terms of either firepower or response time. As has been brought out, a space-based weapon can take on a terrestrial point target across the globe with precision, all by itself, it would not serve as an instrument to win a war in its offensive capacity. Similar to the effect of denial of satellite services to the opponent, taking on the point targets on the Earth from space would confer an advantage to one's own force in a tactical situation. However, use of space-to-Earth weapons alone would not help the friendly forces gain ground.

Thus, it would be apt to infer that any destruction of an opponent's satellite or the use of space-to-Earth weapons on their own would not be decisive in any conflict. As use of space weapons cannot be decisive in a conflict, no sane power would attempt to target satellites during times of conflict as a standalone measure. An attack on satellites could be used as a precursor to break the enemy's will to fight, but this act of commission would rest solely on the overall military might of the opponent on the ground, and could backfire in the face of a strong contender.

Why Crave for Space Weapons?

As brought out, space weapons on their own cannot win wars; neither can they prevent attacks on space assets. Then why is the interest in the development and demonstration of capabilities so pervasive? Development and deployment of space weapons not only exhibits a nation's technological advancement but is also seen as a tool to express space superiority. States are well aware that any technology breakthroughs in the space domain can help garner respect and instil a sense of uncertainty in the eyes of rivals as well as allies. Notwithstanding this sense of pride and prejudice, space weapons do help conjure an image of military might, resulting in instilling a sense of trepidation amongst contenders.

Many analysts may contest that space weapons would neither confer the strategic advantage provided by the conventional weapon systems nor can measure up to the advantage accrued through the militarisation of space. This is because they have been limiting themselves to the measured degree of impact that would be caused by space weapons in the terrestrial protectorate. While space weapons on their own cannot be used to gain ground (this still holds in respect of air power), it must be understood that such weapons would provide for global strategic reach. This extended global reach to deliver munitions makes outer space a strategic military asset. Any instance of the use of such weapons directed to, or from, space would result in a spurt in deployment of these weapons, mainly to exhibit a deterrent posture and declare, "If you can do it, we also can".

The display of might by the possession or demonstration of space weapons is already in progress and helps showcase space superiority. While only a few nations are involved, the competitiveness to spearhead in space weapon technology is amply evident from the efforts and the funding programmes towards launch systems, reentry vehicles and DEWs. As the space weapons programmes are shrouded in a cloud of secrecy, it would not come as a surprise that any demonstration of a new space weapon technology by a nation-state is followed up by a counter-demonstration by its rival faction.

Implications For, and Influence on, Terrestrial Military Forces

The use of space infrastructure in support of military operations permits the armed forces to operate anywhere, irrespective of geographical and physical limits, all across the globe. With the deployment of space and counter-space capabilities, conventional forces will not only receive enhanced inputs for precision targeting but will also be assisted in delivery of precision firepower from the newfound vertical dimension. In addition, they would also be benefitted by the denial of space-based inputs to the adversary, paving the way for freedom of action on enemy territory. Use of ASAT weapons would, thus, improve the protective umbrella for conventional forces and help to dominate over the adversary by ensuring control of information, speed of deployment to garner a superior position and take advantage of precision targeting, whilst denying the same to the enemy.

Space weapons will have a direct bearing on the outcome of future conflicts. As has been brought out earlier, use of space weapons alone cannot win wars. Further, the placing of space weapons and their employment is not feasible in isolation. Placing of weapons in space would call for an infrastructural set-up of an advanced Command, Control, Communication, Computers (C4I) system, a combination of space / ground-based identification and tracking systems, and a system of assessing battle damage. The space ISR capabilities would need to be integrated with existing the Command and Control (C2) network so as to reap the maximum advantage from the new concept weapons using projectiles, lasers, microwaves and soft kill capabilities. Space weapons would, thus, form one of the foci of a space power and contribute to successful operations of ground, maritime and airborne operations. The advent of force projection from, or towards, space-based system will evolve in a manner to minimise the collateral damage with high precision attacks and would have a credible influence on the tactical operations of the army, navy and air force. The hegemonic ambitions of space powers to gain supremacy in space would not only necessitate doctrinal changes resulting in long-term strategic alterations, but would also call for amalgamating the required modifications in the prevalent force structures for maximum efficiency at both tactical and operational levels.

Potential Impact on Global Security and Stability

Militarily, satellites have been used as an instrument in a supportive role for force enhancement and do not have a direct role in force projection. They perform the function of extending communication to the remotest of the areas, intelligence gathering, early warning, navigational services and real-time monitoring of the situation. In short, space assets by themselves are not involved in active conflict and are used only as supportive elements that provide an edge to the war-fighting machinery. The ISR applications provide the requisite intelligence inputs that help in monitoring of, and detecting, ballistic missile launches, to enable a nation to react in a crisis situation and mitigate the impending threat. This, in a way, acts as a deterrence measure and is one of the many factors which help improve global strategic stability.

Weaponisation of space, on the other hand, will have profound implications for global security, with both positive and negative impacts on strategic stability. Introduction of space weapons would create uncertainty and panic due to their potential to subjugate the services of both military and commercial satellites. While on a positive note, possession of space weapons potentially upholds a deterrence capability, the employment of these weapons could also have negative ramifications. Just the fear of the adversary possessing a space weapon would heighten tensions and uncertainty, thereby prompting nations to join the race for acquiring space weapons. Military satellites provide near real-time situational awareness and their obliteration would create a void in the infrastructural set-up used for command and control. Non-availability of satellite services amounts to denial of information superiority at all levels and directly affects the control and coordination of terrestrial forces. The capability of retaliatory strikes would then suffer, as non-availability of intelligence inputs would impinge on the potential of precision targeting.

The launch and placement of weapons in space would lead to global instability as it would pit the world's military powers against one another, and, on the slightest fear or provocation, states might resort to preemptive strikes. As and when a nation's indulgence in development, testing and evaluation of weapons directed to, and from, space translates into deployable weapons, rivalries between power centres will flare up, not only amongst the established space powers but also amongst the other countries that derive space-based services from these nations. In all probability, the coming decade would witness more action in this field with the upsurge of ASAT capability using kinetic kill space weapons and use of directed energy against space assets. Targeting an adversary's satellite systems comes with the promise of blunting the edge of its military might and would have a direct and long drawn impact on its economic growth. Due to the profound impact on national security and stability, nation-states would not only prepare for a first strike capability but would also be compelled to prepare for retaliatory strikes. Paradoxically, all the major and minor space players would be required to adopt counter-measures to safeguard their space assets. As space weapons become part and parcel of a nation's arsenal, they would also be forced to invest in layered fallback infrastructure to cater for uninterrupted services and applications.

Thus, in the case of inevitability of a conflict between two space powers, the nation which strikes the adversary's space assets first would be in an advantageous position. To deny the opponent this advantage, the defender may be forced to use all possible means at its disposal to target the opponent's space assets, thereby, escalating the conflict on the ground. As the attacker would try to avoid such a situation, the likelihood of attacking a space asset would not be attempted in the first place, establishing the deterrence capacity of space weapons. As nations continue to develop and advance the offensive and defensive capabilities of their space weapons, more and more states are likely to join the fray. Though, the initial upsurge in space weapons would result in instability and regional rivalries, the proliferation of ASAT weapons amongst the smaller players would, in the long run, help in rebalancing regional as well as global stability, as the weapons would act as a deterrent for the budding space powers.

Rebalancing of Global Power Equations

The global politics, economics and security in the new world order are driven by the state of the economies, natural reserves, technological advances, military might and the expansionist policy of power centres. The proliferation of space technology will provide a boost to the global economy and its logical extension would force nations worldwide to embrace space capabilities for military operations. The increased dependence on space assets makes them lucrative targets, with potential political, economic and military implications.

While the United States presides as the predominant economic and military power, the global power equation is changing at a fast pace due to the inclination of the international community towards the Asia-Pacific, brought forth mainly because of the rise of China. The United States and China have their vested interests in the Asia-Pacific, with both nations striving hard for maintaining an influential presence in the South China Sea.

China's advances, and demonstrations of its space technology, as well as the increased funding[16] to improve the efficiency and lethality of futuristic space weapons have put forward challenges to the security of space assets of the United States. The development and demonstration of ASAT capability by China not only indicates its rise as a regional space power but has forced the United States to revamp its strategic outlook in the emerging new world order. Thus, developing space and counter-space capabilities would be one of the factors that would impact the balance of future global powers. The introduction of ASAT weapons, on the one hand, would create a hostile and competitive environment by promoting regional rivalries, while, on the other, it would foster new alliances that would seek global partnerships with the established space powers to acquire a protective umbrella for safeguarding own interests in space.

Space Weapons and War on Terror

Historically, at any given time, we find that a number of states had been involved in regional rivalries or embroiled in a state of instability. This trend is visible now, and will continue in the future. The cause of concern in present and future conflict scenarios is the surge in the number of non-state actors that have increasingly resorted to asymmetric warfare, threatening global peace and straining the sanctity of the global social fabric. One of the reasons of this social unrest and proliferation of the number of dissident actors is the cumulative effect of prevailing economic prejudices and unequivocal fractured lines in political systems (resulting from the complexities of diplomatic and cultural differences).

As the affected countries the world over grapple with this phenomenon, the focus is shifting to prevent the scourge of terrorism spreading into the respective territories by targeting their outfits and hubs with the use of standoff weapons that cause minimum or no collateral damage. Tackling the insurgency problem, though difficult, calls for forging of new relationships between countries and building of a universal consensus, irrespective of the prevailing differences and mistrust on other issues.

While use of Unmanned Aerial Vehicles (UAVs) and air attacks with precision strikes would be central to neutralising targets, employment of advanced space weapons in such a situation would facilitate pinpointed attacks, with limited or nil collateral damage. In such a scenario, space weapons can be instrumental in liquidating targets of choice. Though presently, space weapons are cost prohibitive, the advent of space-based directed energy weapons with unlimited magazines would provide for flexible, effective and multi-dimensional capability for selective targeting of earmarked individuals indulging in terrorist activities.

Impact on Outer Space Environment and Fallout

Over the last five decades, from the time humans mastered the technique of placing artificial objects in space, the number of nations that have placed satellites into space for scientific, commercial, societal and military applications has increased manifold. As space technology proliferates, we are witnessing an exponential growth in the number of satellites being launched. Today, we have roughly 22,000 objects larger than a softball orbiting the Earth.[17] Of these artificial satellites, only 5 to 6 percent are in an operational state and the rest can be termed as floating junk in space. The issue becomes complex when we consider the smaller fragments that amount to hundreds of thousands in numbers. This junk in outer space is governed by the laws of physics and the individual elements of this junk move in a fixed orbit, just like satellites. As the inclination of orbits is different, and space objects move at phenomenal speeds of the order of 7.8 km/s in a specific orbital shape, the likelihood of collision between two objects cannot be ruled out. The rising population of fast orbiting small pieces of debris poses a serious challenge to all satellites, spacecraft, space shuttles and, in particular, to the International Space Station (owing to its size), with humans aboard. The likelihood of a collision is more in LEO and decreases with increase in orbital altitudes. While no incident of orbital collision have been reported in GEO, there have been a few instances when LEO satellites have been impacted by stray debris. In fact, three active satellites have been damaged/destroyed since the beginning of the 21st century. Space debris not only threatens all satellites, but any inadvertent collision in outer space leads to the disintegration of satellites in space, resulting in further debris. In February 2009, a defunct Russian satellite collided with an operational Iridium satellite of the United States, resulting in excess of 2,000 fragments larger than 10 cm[18] in size.

One of the major causes of concern is the creation of the debris cloud due to the testing and evaluation of space weapons. The Chinese ASAT test of 2007 created a debris cloud of 3,000 pieces. As and when space weapons are developed, improvised and tested against defunct space assets, the resulting debris would add to the floating junk in space and would be detrimental to future space explorations and projects.

In the event of conflict escalation to outer space, a number of satellites can be expected to be destroyed, leaving a debris field orbiting around the Earth. Thus, space warfare would lead to denial of space usage for all nations in the decades to come. While, reduction of space debris is now gaining prominence amongst the space-faring nations and efforts are underway to adopt mitigation techniques, there is an increasing awareness amongst states to avoid targeting of space assets that would contribute in escalating the debris cloud. While various treaties and codes of conducts come to fore in this respect, the nation-states would continue to exploit newer technologies brought forth by the directed energy and cyber means to target satellites without creating a debris cloud.

Impact of Space Weapons on the Common Man

Use of space weapons against civil and commercial satellites could hamper the day-to-day functioning of not only governments, organisations and military forces but also affect the common man's daily chores by breaking down the communication links and a myriad services. The interruption of communication links would disrupt regular financial transactions, health support systems, personal security systems and routine services like television transmissions, navigation, etc. These services, while not targeting the society directly, may have an indirect consequence, as the society will be bereft of standard services being extended to the common man. However, in today's digitised world and advanced set-up, a nation would always cater for redundancy in terms of fallback options. Many a times, the failure of a satellite would not come to the notice of the common man as the services would be restored in real-time. Thus, isolated attacks on an odd satellite at the most will have a minimal impact on society.

Destruction of military satellites, on the other hand, will have a profound impact on the support services being provided to the terrestrial forces. Any visible destruction, degradation or destruction of these satellites will have psychological connotations on the nation's populace and would raise the level of uncertainty and anxiety.

Employment of space-to-Earth weapons is a distant reality and even if such weapons are deployed and exploited, they would not result in any catastrophic consequences on the ground like conventional weapons. Space-to-Earth weapons would be suitable only against point targets and would not be employed against the masses.

Conclusion

The successful demonstration of kinetic kill space weapons in targeting satellites has fuelled the research towards new concept weapon systems using directed energy technology. While outer space can be construed to be weapons free, countries like the USA, China and Russia possess the capability of targeting space assets, albeit to a limited extent. As weapon technology has been tenaciously conceived, evaluated and demonstrated on numerous occasions, the concept of unleashing destructive power from the realm of space has always been alive amongst the advanced powers. These major space powers have the means and the required infrastructure to place and operate weapons for selective targeting at short notice.

Space weapons would have the same degree of vulnerability as satellites and, with prior intelligence, can become the primary targets in case of conflict escalation to space. Due to the characteristics of space weapons, they are more suited in the offensive role and cannot be used as a viable option for protection of satellites. In the present day context, KKSBWs in space seem more probable till the DESBWs evolve as a credible and cost-effective option. Once the DESBW system evolves, it would be the preferred choice of weapon over kinetic kill systems due to multiple targeting options and avoidance of target disintegration. Terrestrial-based Earth-to-space weapons, on the other hand, can be used in offensive as well as defensive roles against ballistic missiles. Further, space-to-Earth weapons cannot match the advantages of conventional weapons launched from terrestrial platforms either in terms of firepower or response time.

Space weapons would be instrumental in achieving an advantageous position at both strategic and tactical levels. While space weapons by themselves can't win a war, possession of these weapons helps in portraying a deterrence posture. Use of ASAT weapons would improve the protective umbrella for conventional forces and help dominate the adversary by ensuring control of information, speed of deployment at a superior position and allow for precision targeting. The ubiquitous nature of these weapons would also allow them to be used as a tool for coercing the adversary and for punitive means. As and when space weapons come to the fore, we will witness a paradigm shift wherein nation-states may impose their will on the adversary's political, economic and social fabric without a face-to-face confrontation.

Space war, if fought, will be limited only to the space powers. Even in the case of a conflict between two space powers, if the attacker attempts and succeeds in the destruction of multiple satellites of the adversary, targeting of satellites would not result in gaining of ground in a conflict zone, rather, it would lead to conflict escalation. Attacks on satellites could be used as a precursor to break the enemy's will to fight war, but this act of commission would rest solely on the overall military might of the opponent on the ground and could backfire in the face of a strong contender. Introduction of space weapons would create uncertainty and panic with their potential to subjugate the services of both military and commercial satellites. While on a positive note, the possession of space weapons potentially upholds a deterrence capability, the employment of these weapons could result in negative ramifications such as the testing and evaluation of space weapons, creating space debris. Furthermore, a conflict in outer space would leave a debris field orbiting around the Earth and would be detrimental for future space explorations and projects.

As rival countries compete for space weapons, it is more of the contest for technology demonstration and possession of unique capability which would propel them into a position of advantage. Though the initial upsurge in space weapons would result in instability and regional rivalry, the proliferation of ASAT weapons amongst the smaller players would help in the long run, in rebalancing regional as well as global stability as the weapons would act as a deterrent measure amongst the budding space powers. We can only hope that the technology invested in ASAT weapons and counter-counter space capabilities would pave the way for peaceful exploration of space and help mankind reap the benefits in the long run, by exploiting space resources. Thus, space weapons would definitely come to the fore as the stepping stone for exploratory research in the field of space exploration and help reap the benefits of technology (for example, the possibility of extra-terrestrial settlements).

Development of space weapons is a process emanating from the evolution of technology which cannot be curbed owing to the inquisitive nature of humans and the stiff competition between states. In this context, it is safe to infer that technological realisation of space weapons would dictate the process of space weaponisation.

Notes

1. Laura Grego,"A History of Anti-Satellite Programs", Union of Concerned Scientist, January 2012, at http://www.ucsusa.org/nuclear_weapons_and_global_security/solutions/space-weapons/a-history-of-anti-satellite.html. Accessed on August 13, 2014.

2. Amy Teitel, "The Laser-Toting Soviet Satellite that Almost Sparked a Space Arms Race", at http://www.wired.co.uk/news/archive/2013-05/16/soviet-laser-satellite. Accessed on February 19, 2015.
3. Donald R. Baucom, "The Rise and Fall of Brilliant Pebbles", *The Journal of Social, Political and Economic Studies* (Washington DC), vol. 29, no. 2, Summer 2004, p. 145 at, http://highfrontier.org/oldarchive/Archive/hf/The%20Rise%20and%20Fall%20of%20Brilliant%20Pebbles%20-Baucom.pdf. Accessed on August 9, 2014.
4. Yevgeny Miasnikov, "Precision-Guided Conventional Weapons", in Alexei Arbatov and Vladimir Dvorkin, eds., *Nuclear Reset: Arms Reduction and Nonproliferation*, (Moscow: Carnegie Endowment for International Peace, 2012) at http://carnegieendowment.org/files/nuclear_reset_Book2012_web.pdf. Accessed on August 9, 2014.
5. "Megawatt Laser Test Brings Space-Based Lasers One Step Closer", Accessed at http://www.spacedaily.com/news/laser-00e.html on November 10, 2014.
6. David Wright, Laura Grego, and Lisbeth Gronlund, "The Physics of Space Security", in a reference manual, *American Academy of Arts and Sciences* (Cambridge MA, 2005), at http://www.ucsusa.org/sites/default/files/legacy/assets/documents/nwgs/physics-space-security.pdf. Accessed on March 6, 2014.
7. Steven M. Kosiak, "Arming the Heavens: A Preliminary Assessment of the Potential Cost and Cost-Effectiveness of Space-Based Weapons", Centre for Strategic and Budgetary Assessment, Washington DC, 2007, at http://csbaonline.org/publications/2007/10/arming-the-heavens-a-preliminary-assessment-of-the-potential-cost-and-cost-effectiveness-of-space-based-weapons/. Accessed on July 11, 2014.
8. Wright, et. al., n. 6, p. 83.
9. *IHS Jane's Weapons: Strategic 2013-2014*, p. 319.
10. "Shenlong Space Plane Advances China's Military Space Potential", at http://www.strategycenter.net/research/pubid.174/pub_detail.asp. Accessed on August 7, 2014.
11. Refer to Chapter 4 for a brief description of projects like Zenith Star, MIRACL, Airborne Laser (ABL), Tactical High Energy Laser, Advanced Tactical Laser (ATL), CHAMP, etc.
12 "United States Department of Defense Fiscal Year 2016 Budget Request: Overview", Office of the Under Secretary of Defense, at http://comptroller.defense.gov/Portals/45/Documents/defbudget/fy2016/FY2016_Budget_Request_Overview_Book.pdf. Accessed on May 9, 2016.
13. Kelly Dickerson, "China's Space Program Could Completely Crush its Competition", at http://www.businessinsider.in/Chinas-space-program-could-completely-crush-its-competition/articleshow/47697593.cms. Accessed on May 9, 2016.
14. "An Introduction to Space Weapons", *Ensuring Space Security*, a project of the Union of Concerned Scientists, Fact Sheet No.1, at http://www.ucsusa.org/sites/default/files/legacy/assets/documents/nwgs/intro-to-space-weapons.pdf. Accessed on March 20, 2015.

15. The projects conceived for weapons under the Strategic Defence Initiative i.e. Rods from Gods and Brilliant Pebbles were shelved as they were cost exorbitant, were difficult to sustain, and did not provide for any distinct advantage over conventional weapon systems.
16. Dickerson, n. 13.
17. Steven A. Hildreth and Allison Arnold, "Threats to U.S. National Security Interests in Space: Orbital Debris Mitigation and Removal", CRS Report to Congress, January 8, 2014, at https://www.fas.org/sgp/crs/natsec/R43353.pdf. Accessed on November 10, 2014.
18. Ibid.

8

Space Weaponisation and the Legal Framework

Enactment of a law on the use of a new technology weapon system can, by and large, never precede the event itself.

The positioning of a satellite in outer space allows for its use for extending numerous types of interoperable services and enhances the nation's global footprint. In the last six decades, the world has become increasingly dependent on space technology for a multitude of civilian and military applications. As satellites play the role of a key enabler in economic growth and security, outer space support is increasingly becoming instrumental for states to safeguard and enhance their security needs. The access to, and maintaining presence in, space, whether on one's own, or through the help of others, is increasingly assuming a crucial role in ongoing scientific research, commercial well-being, and in accruing societal benefits ranging from the global to the individual level. For the military, outer space support is now central to all operations and directly impacts the planning and execution of activities in the land, maritime and air domains. The post Gulf War conflicts and operations executed in support of the global war on terror have established the fact that nations (or conglomerations of) capable of exploiting space services in furtherance of their national (and international) objectives, tend to have a remarkable edge over rival opponents in a competitive environment. In parallel, there are also states that are working towards denial of space-based services to their adversaries by devising ways and means to counter space-based assets and their applications. This concept of assimilating counter-space capabilities involves use of deceptive, disruptive, destructive and damaging techniques to degrade/harm space-based assets or services and, thus, adds a vulnerability dimension to the issue of space security. The first and foremost requirement of space security is a set of rules and regulations governing the activities—both permitted and prohibited—in outer space. Space law, thus, can be described as the body of law governing space-related activities and defines the legal responsibilities of states vis-à-vis their conduct in outer space.

With the increasing number of nations adopting space services, space resources like communication bandwidth and orbital slots are increasingly becoming scarce and contested resources. This, along with two events of profound significance of the early 1990s, has had a profound impact on the world space order. The first event was the spectacular and effective demonstration of space power by the United States in the Gulf War. This war showcased how space assets could be effectively employed as force multipliers to win a conventional war. The second event was the restructuring of the world space order, post break-up of the erstwhile Soviet Union and, consequently, the United States assuming a de-facto position as the dominant space power.

Since a majority of satellites are dual use ones, security and safety of satellites and associated infrastructure is not limited to their role as military assets, but also adds to the vulnerabilities of civil and commercial space ventures. The aim of this chapter would be to examine the laws and regulations relevant to space security, with emphasis on space weaponisation; it would also dwell on the multilateral processes and institutions under which space security issues are being discussed.

Space Law

Principally, space law comes within the larger gamut of international law. As outer space is a global commons and there are no demarcated boundaries in space, no individual nation can assert its jurisdiction on any area or portion thereof. Thus, any law in relation to space will be governed by consensually accepted international arrangements. Space law would, thus, encompass a set of international rules that are enforced by a body of law governing activities in outer space. The domain of international space law encompasses a wide range of issues of international concern that help regulate the global commons of outer space; this includes issues such as the space environment, launching and sustaining objects in space, research and development activities, management of space-based services and applications, space-related military activities and security of space assets.[1] While states would own, and be responsible for, their own space assets and their functionality, the governing international law would ensure that there is no clash of interest with other parties or states.

On the domestic front, nations can carve out their own space laws that would principally govern domestic space policies flowing out of the ambit of international space law. These will constitute a set of domestic rules for regulating the national space policy on the use of space resources. The never seen before advances in commercial space technology and the ever increasing exploitation of outer space resources is now occurring at a much more rapid pace than current international space legislation can account for.[2]

Further, as brought out in the preceding chapters, select nations continue to explore means and methods towards weaponisation of space. The realisation of space weapons will have a lasting impact on international relations and future space activities. Citing research and development in space technologies and issues relating to space security, these nations have so far been successful in creating stumbling roadblocks in reaching an international consensus towards realisation of binding agreements and treaties. Further, there have been eclectic disagreements and resistance in the acceptance of a framework on an international code of conduct for outer space activities. Thus, there is an urgent need to invigorate and elaborate the debate on the existing set of space agreements and treaties to reach consensually agreed and globally accepted binding actions. This would pave the way for institutionalising a law that would establish a binding obligation on nations to adhere to these and be accountable for their outer space activities.

Concerns of Weapons in Outer Space

The debate on the issue of force projection using weapons in, and from, space-based platforms was at its peak during the period of the Cold War when both the US and erstwhile USSR were embroiled in pursuit of ASAT weapons for eliciting an explicit advantage, militarily as well as psychologically. Both these superpowers invested heavily in the design and development of space weapons and carried out continuous evaluation and testing till the dissolution of the USSR. The space weapon projects involved pursuance of Anti-Ballistic Missile (ABM) programmes, kinetic kill capabilities as well as use of directed energy weapons, including use of the nuclear arsenal in space. Both the USA and USSR believed that deploying a space weapon before the opponent would come with huge benefits and would deter the adversary in deployment and employment of space weapons.

The Cold War period was marred by mistrust, uncertainty and discontentment. The possibility of an apocalyptic event paved the way for discussions on a series of arms control measures to help de-escalate tensions. As apprehensions of the potential use of space weapons increased and created alarm amongst nations the world over, the issue of banning the positioning of weapons in space gained prominence and called for debates, negotiations and treaties concerning disarmament measures through legal instruments, institutional mechanisms and political channels.

Space Law and the United Nations Office for Outer Space Affairs

The term "space law" is most often associated with the rules, principles and standards of international law appearing in the five international treaties and five sets of principles governing outer space which have been developed under the auspices of the United Nations (UN).[3] In addition to these international instruments, many states have national legislations governing space-related activities. The general laws governing activities in space are formed to address a variety of matters, such as the preservation of the space and Earth environment, liability for damage caused by space objects, the settlement of disputes, the rescue of astronauts, the sharing of information about potential danger in outer space, the use of space-related technologies, and international cooperation.[4] A number of fundamental principles guide the conduct of space activities, including the notion of space as the province of all humankind, the freedom of exploration and use of outer space by all states without discrimination, and the principle of non-appropriation of outer space.[5]

At the end of World War II, which left an enormous trail of destruction and devastation, the United Nations Organisation was formed for maintenance of international peace and security. Its work is guided by the principles contained in its founding charter, which, in its preamble, had set an objective: "To establish conditions under which justice and respect for the obligations arising from treaties and other sources of international law can be maintained".[6] The UN Security Council (UNSC) has the primary responsibility for international peace and security wherein it works to prevent conflicts; helps to achieve peaceful solutions between conflicting states; operates and controls peacekeeping operations; and creates the conditions to allow peace to hold and flourish.[7] As part of its charter, efforts in the United Nations to maintain outer space for peaceful purposes began in 1957, months prior to the launch of the first artificial satellite into the Earth's orbit.[8]

The requirement of rules and regulations in regards to outer space started taking shape after the launch of the Sputnik in the year 1957. In relation to dealing with issues in maintaining peace and tranquillity in outer space, a small division by the name of the United Nations Office for Outer Space Affairs (UNOOSA) was established by the United Nations General Assembly (UNGA) via its resolution 1348 (XIII) of December 13, 1958.[9]

UNCOPOUS and Space Law

The General Assembly, in 1959, set up a permanent body reaffirming the mandate under Resolution 1472 (XIV), consisting of 24 members and established the United Nations Committee on the Peaceful Uses of Outer Space (UNCOPUOS). This body was instituted to govern the exploration and use of space for the benefit of all humanity, for peace, security and development.[10] It laid the foundation of space-related activities that could be undertaken by the United Nations, encouraging space research programmes, and studying legal problems arising from the exploration of outer space.[11] The committee[12], under Resolution 1962 (XVIII),[13] declared the legal principles governing the activities of states in the exploration and use of outer space. The text of this resolution is the mother document, providing the basic guidelines for instituting the framework for various laws, treaties and codes of conduct in relation to space; the resolution is summarised below.

- The use of outer space is free for exploration and use by all states for the benefit, and in the interests, of all mankind. In doing so, it is not subject to national appropriation by any means and would be carried out in accordance with international law, without jeopardising international peace and security.
- The responsibility for national activities in outer space would be that of the state, whether carried on by governmental agencies or by non-governmental entities.
- States shall conduct all their activities in outer space with due regard for the corresponding interests of other states and avoid harmful contamination of space and celestial bodies. When such activity is likely to have any detrimental effect on other state(s), it shall inform, share and take the consensus of the affected party (parties) before proceeding with any such activity or experiment.
- The state shall retain jurisdiction and control over an object launched by it and shall be liable for any damage caused anywhere by its space objects.
- States shall regard astronauts as envoys of mankind in outer space.

The adoption of this crucial resolution laid down the foundation for the creation of the five UN treaties and agreements on space law. As this book is focussed on the topic of space weapons, and space law in itself is a vast subject, the emphasis in the remainder of the chapter will be accorded to the Articles of law related to space weapons and their deployment.

Outer Space Treaty of 1967

Titled the "Treaty on Principles Governing the Activities of States in the Exploration and Use of Outer Space, including the Moon and Other Celestial Bodies", the treaty has been framed under UN Resolution 2222 (XXI). In 2015, a total of 103 nations ratified the treaty, and thus, are officially bound to comply with its provisions. In addition to these 103 nations, 25 nations are signatories to this treaty and ratification from these signatories is awaited.[14] The signatory states are those that have expressed the intention to comply with the treaty (but are not bound by it).

The Outer Space Treaty (OST) is mainly derived from UN Resolution 1962 (XVIII), while adding a few new provisions. In relation to placing and using weapons in space, the relevant clauses,[15] with analyses, are presented below:

Article II

- *"Outer space, including the Moon and other celestial bodies, is not subject to national appropriation by claim of sovereignty, by means of use or occupation, or by any other means."*

  Analysis: Occupation or subjugation of outer space territory (including any celestial body, planet and the planets natural satellite(s)) by virtue of infrastructural or human presence, using any means, is prohibited.

Article IV

- *"States parties to the Treaty undertake not to place in orbit around the Earth any objects carrying nuclear weapons or any other kinds of weapons of mass destruction, install such weapons on celestial bodies, or station such weapons in outer space in any other manner."*

Analysis: The treaty has clearly spelt out that the member states will not place Weapons of Mass Destruction (WMD) on any satellite (which will generally follow a fixed orbit), spacecraft (like a space plane with manoeuvrable capability that allows it to change its orbit a number of times), any celestial body or sustainable weapon platform in space.

- Thus, the treaty prohibits any use of Chemical, Biological, Radiological, Nuclear (CBRN) weapons in outer space that can destroy a sizeable community of humans or cause catastrophic damage to man-made infrastructure, natural resources and the biosphere, including on the Earth.
- The concept of WMD in a strict sense revolves around the catastrophic damage to humans and their life supporting nature. The clause of Article IV of this treaty, thus, forbids use of WMDs in relation to 'space-to-Earth weapons'.
- Further, as WMDs cannot be orbited in space, targeting any space-based asset or other celestial body with such a weapon system (space-to-space weapon) is prohibited.
- The Article does not prohibit launch of WMDs using ballistic missiles that traverse through outer space in part of their trajectory (Earth-to-Earth weapons transiting through space).
- The treaty does not have provisions on the prohibition of the use of conventional weapons (weapons not categorised as WMDs) towards and from space.

- *"The Moon and other celestial bodies shall be used by all States Parties to the Treaty exclusively for peaceful purposes. The establishment of military bases, installations and fortifications, the testing of any type of weapons and the conduct of military manoeuvres on celestial bodies shall be forbidden. The use of military personnel for scientific research or for any other peaceful purposes shall not be prohibited. The use of any equipment or facility necessary for peaceful exploration of the Moon and other celestial bodies shall also not be prohibited."*

Analysis:

- This clause clearly states that the military forces of nation-states cannot establish themselves on any celestial body. The nations also cannot have any infrastructure set-up and claim jurisdiction on any territory or part thereof (read in conjunction with Article II) on any celestial body.
- All kinds of military exercises and military manoeuvres on celestial bodies are prohibited. Also, the clause prohibits testing of any kind of weapon system and, thus, forbids placing of weapons and thereby, use of such weapons on any celestial body.
- The clause above explicitly permits military personnel on celestial bodies to carry out scientific research for peaceful purposes. Now, the immediate response would be as to why 'military personnel' have been specified, in particular. As the earlier part of this clause deals with military forces and puts a restraint on military activities, the latter part clarifies that military personnel are free to take part in scientific research and experiments conducted towards peaceful uses of space. Had this not been clarified in these words, the use of military personnel in any mission could have been objectionable.
- If we consider both the clauses of Article IV concurrently, the OST does not allow any kind of weapon system on a celestial body. However, placing and use of conventional weapons (other than WMDs) on satellites or as independent weapon platforms in space is not prohibited.
- The term 'Moon', while itself being a celestial body, figures not only in this clause but throughout the text of the OST. This is because most of the space missions planned during this time and the discussions on the treaty involved the perception of the Moon's exploration and aimed for the landing of humans on the Moon.

Thus, even after the treaty came into force, the Cold War period witnessed the race for development of conventional space weapons. As no major international law bans the testing and evaluation of conventional weapons in space, the progress of weaponising continues even in the 21st century. A case in point is that of the demonstration of the ASAT weapons by China in 2007 and the USA in 2008. Further, while these instances of evaluation are few in number, the matter that is of greater concern is the unabated positioning and orbiting of spacecraft that could serve as future space weapon platforms. This, in conjunction with the progressive development of new concept weapon systems (read DEWs) makes conflicts in outer space inevitable and that too without violating the provisions of the Outer Space Treaty.

Follow-up on Outer Space Treaty

After the Outer Space Treaty came into force, it acted as a guiding factor for four additional treaties that reiterate and strengthen the legal principles governing the activities of states in the exploration and use of outer space, brought forth by Resolution 1962 (XVIII).

- Agreement on the Rescue of Astronauts, the Return of Astronauts and Return of Objects Launched into Outer Space (1968). This agreement expands the role of state parties on the duties and responsibilities in dealing with astronauts in distress and expands on the provisions of Article V[16] of the OST.
- Convention on International Liability for Damage Caused by Space Objects (1972). This treaty expands the liability clauses laid out in Article VII[17] of the OST. In this, it elaborates the liability on state parties in case any damage is caused by an outer space object to the Earth, aircraft, any other object in outer space or on a celestial body.
- Convention on Registration of Objects Launched into Outer Space (1975). This expands the principle of registration and makes compulsory the disclosure on the nature of space objects when demanded and, thus, expands on the provisions of Article VIII[18] of the OST.

- Agreement Governing the Activities of States on the Moon and Other Celestial Bodies (1979). The Moon Agreement complements the OST and expands on its provisions to ensure that the Moon and other celestial bodies are exclusively used for peaceful purposes; it prohibits any military presence or operations on its surface.

Other Outer Space Related Treaties of the United Nations

After the Outer Space Treaty came into force, no further international rules and regulations have come forth to address specific issues and those concerning possible use of weapons in outer space. As has been brought out earlier, the OST is also limited, in that, it only imposes a ban on placing and using of weapons of mass destruction in space, leaving open the window for the use of deployment and employment of other conventional weapon systems that do not qualify as WMDs. Thus, the treaties introduced till this time do not prevent any nation attacking satellites from the Earth, aircraft or from another space asset, and in the process, the very essence of the OST in maintaining and using outer space for peaceful purposes is not fulfilled in entirety.

It is not that efforts have not been made for the implementation of comprehensive mechanisms that could address the shortcomings of the OST in relation to placing and preventing placing of weapons in space. The United Nations has been active in proposing disarmament measures and has supported the efforts by member states to prevent an arms race in outer space. Since the early 1980s, the UNGA has been conducting a Conference on Disarmament (CD) to consider proposals under the agenda item "Prevention of an Arms Race in Outer Space (PAROS)", including draft treaties aimed at preventing the placement of weapons in outer space and prohibiting the use of anti-satellite weapons.[19]

Prevention of Arms Race in Outer Space (PAROS)

The Cold War period saw rapid advances in space sciences and technology. While satellites provided an unprecedented reach and inputs that would serve the peaceful use of space for mankind, the placing of weapons in space was also looked upon as a lucrative option. Both the United States and the USSR were involved in different space weapons projects and had a firm belief that space-based weapons would place them in an advantageous position. Over a period of time, both these superpowers realised that the proposals to place weapons in space was not only a complex affair but was challenging in terms of positioning and sustaining a large number of weapon platforms due to the exorbitant costs. In spite of ensuing failures and not achieving the desired results commensurate with the efforts and money spent on space weapon projects, both parties, while being wary of each other, continued investing and evaluating the space weapon systems particularly those with potential to neutralise the nuclear threats posed by ICBMs. Concurrent to these developments, both powers were also contemplating the formulation of regulatory mechanisms to avoid any arms race in space.

In August 1981, the Soviet Union, in the UN General Assembly, placed a proposal to prohibit the placement of weapons in outer space.[20] The UNGA recognised the possibility of an arms race in outer space and in the process, vide its resolution A/RES/36/97 dated December 9, 1981, directed the committee on disarmament to consider negotiating an effective and verifiable agreement on PAROS and therein reach a consensus on prohibition of anti-satellite systems.[21] PAROS was aimed at preventing any military confrontation in outer space. Subsequently, in 1985, the Conference on Disarmament (CD) established an ad hoc committee to begin talks on the PAROS Treaty.[22] The committee was convened each year from 1985 to 1994 and worked towards identifying and examining issues relating to development, testing and deployment of weapons in space, legal protection of space assets, orbital debris, etc. and proposed various Confidence-Building Measures (CBMs). However, the United States and Israel were not enthusiastic and supportive of the PAROS initiative and the treaty could not be negotiated. The United States opined that the issue of an arms race in space was inconsequential, supporting its argument by stating that neither has any country placed any weapon in outer space, nor there has been any indication of a significant ongoing development by any state with respect to placing arms in space. Thus, it was against accepting any legally binding instrument or a review of existing agreements in this respect. The United States was the only country to vote against the resolution, while Israel abstained.[23] In the wake of this stand, the treaty negotiations faced a roadblock and the committee has yet to reconvene, despite an annual, near-unanimous vote by the UNGA and CD approving the PAROS Resolution.[24]

However, the members of the Group of 21[25] and China continued their efforts to bring in a legal instrument that would help avoid future weaponisation of space. The committee followed up the agenda of PAROS and continued to meet in the subsequent years. The main highlights of the sessions and reports are summarised below:

- In 1994, the delegations of Russia and Group of 21 maintained that the provisions of the OST were far from preventing an arms race in outer space, in that, the legal instruments do not prevent the "launching into space and testing in space of conventional weapons as well as weapons based on new physical principles, such as lasers, very high frequency weapons, particle beam weapons and others" and that the "unrestrained development of ballistic missile defences could lead to the development of ASAT weapons".[26] Some delegations opined that Article IV of the OST should be amended to include a prohibition on all kinds of weapons in space, and referred to the testing, development and deployment of ASAT weapons.[27]
- China, in 1999, put up an agenda point for the reestablishment of an ad-hoc committee on PAROS, and, in 2000, submitted a working paper and put forward tentative ideas on new international legal instruments. The working paper reiterated,

With the accelerated development of outer space weapons, anti-ballistic missiles and other weapon systems, individual countries have stepped up efforts to secure military superiority in outer space and have mapped out, and are pursuing, plans to secure military superiority on the ground from space. In these circumstances, preventing outer space from becoming a new venue for an arms race without prejudice to its peaceful uses has obviously become the most important and pressing task of the Conference.[28]

In 2001, China also submitted a working paper titled "Possible Elements of the Future International Legal Instrument on the Prevention of the Weaponisation of Outer Space". Under the instrument titled "Treaty on Prevention of Weaponisation of Outer Space", the basic obligations proposed were: not to test, deploy or use in outer space any weapons, weapon systems or their components; not to test, deploy or use on land, in the sea or atmosphere any weapons, weapon systems or their components that can be used for war-fighting in outer space; and not to use any objects launched into orbit to directly participate in combatant activities.[29] Taking the cue from this paper, the delegations of China and the Russian Federation, along with Vietnam, Indonesia, Belarus, Zimbabwe and Syrian Arab Republic submitted for circulation another working paper titled "Possible Elements for a Future International Legal Agreement on the Prevention of the Deployment of Weapons in Outer Space, the Threat or Use of Force against Outer Space Objects". The basic obligations proposed were revised as under (CD/1679)[30]:

- Not to place in orbit around the Earth any objects carrying any kinds of weapons.
- Not to install such weapons on celestial bodies, or not to station such weapons in outer space in any other manner.
- Not to resort to the threat or use of force against outer space objects.
- Not to assist or encourage other states, groups of states, international organisations to participate in activities prohibited by this treaty.

- The United States in the same year, in a letter dated July 10, 2002, (circulated under CD/1680) stated that it respects and abides by the OST of 1967, however, "The peaceful exploration and use of space does not rule out activities in pursuit of national security goals". Citing Article 51 of the UN Charter on the right of individual and collective self-defence, and the new threats faced in today's world (read Russian and Chinese space projects), the United States submitted that it "requires the right to be exercised both on the Earth and above it", and "this right depends on its ability to operate in space".[31] Reiterating its stand, the United States opined that in the OST of 1967 there already exists an extensive and comprehensive system for limiting the uses of outer space to those that are peaceful and providing a framework for the legitimate military uses of outer space and, thus, there is no need for additional outer space treaties.[32]

- In June 2003, Russia, in an initiative to promote openness and in a bid to build confidence in the domain of outer space activities, proposed its willingness to provide advance notification of forthcoming spacecraft launches and their purpose and main parameters. The Russian Federation also called on the other space players with indigenous launching facilities to join this initiative.[33]

Thus, from the conference proceedings, it is quite evident that the Russian Federation and China have shown keen interest in legitimising the ban on the deployment and employment of any type and kind of weapons in space and in this endeavour, they have been wholeheartedly supported by the majority of member nation-states. It was only due to fierce opposition from the Western members (read the United States and Israel) that a committee on PAROS could not be established. However, efforts for a legal regime on the outer space weaponisation issue never died down. In the ensuing years, PAROS was redrafted and proposed as a draft treaty newly christened as Prevention of the Placement of Weapons in Outer Space.

Prevention of the Placement of Weapons in Outer Space and Threat of Use of Force Against Outer Space Objects

On February 29, 2008, the Russian Federation and the People's Republic of China put up a draft proposal on the "Treaty on Prevention of the Placement of Weapons in Outer Space[34] and of the Threat or Use of Force against Outer Space Objects[35] (PPWT)".[36]

The draft treaty states, "The States Parties undertake not to place in orbit around the Earth any objects carrying any kinds of weapons, not to install such weapons on celestial bodies and not to *place*[37] such *weapons in outer space*[38] in any other manner; not to resort to the *threat or use of force against outer space objects*[39]; and not to assist or induce other States, groups of States or international organizations to participate in activities prohibited by this Treaty."

The United States, unsurprisingly, opposed the provisions proposed in the treaty and went on to raise a number of contentious issues on its text. This was followed by outright rejection of the proposal, stating that it was fundamentally flawed[40]. The United States also made it clear that its space policy opposes any arms control concepts, proposals, and legal regimes that seek prohibitions on military or intelligence uses of space; or fail to preserve the rights of the United States to conduct research, development, testing, and operations in space for military, intelligence, civil, or commercial purposes.[41] Further, it went to the extent of declaring that the proposals laid out in this proposed treaty were even more unacceptable than the draft agreement outlined in the Chinese-Russian working paper of 2002 (CD/1679).[42]

Limitations of Draft PPWT

The draft PPWT was once again updated in June 2014 with almost similar provisions as in the first draft of February 2008; however, this treaty, as can be seen from the following deliberations, still left a window open for future weaponisation of space. The basic concerns in respect of the PPWT are:

- If a nation wants to raise an objection against a satellite of another nation or wants to project a threat to its own outer space object from any other country's space object, how would it prove that such a threat does exist? Further, the likelihood of verification of such a threat by a third party becomes difficult.
- An attack on the space asset of the aggrieved state party may involve (a) a soft kill function, say, interference, temporary malfunction, induced changes in orbital parameters or functional damage; (b) a hard kill function, say, partial or complete physical damage, obstruction or force change of orbital parameters. In the eventuality of a soft kill attack, the verification of such an attack itself would be challenging, and if verified, the attribution of such an attack to any particular state would be extremely difficult. Further, in the case of a hard kill, while the possibility of identifying the hostile source exists, there exists no provision in the treaty that bans ASAT attacks carried out from the terrestrial realms.
- State parties can take advantage of Article V[43] of the treaty and in this garb, can indulge in an attack on a space asset, citing the right of self-defence.
- The draft PPWT is silent on any attack that could be directed towards space assets from weapon systems on the Earth and also any weapon like missiles launched from one point of the Earth to another point and transiting through outer space.
- The proposed treaty has no provisions to curb research, development and evaluation of space technology that could be integrated on weapon platforms. Further, the deployment of a weapon system within terrestrial limits makes possible the use of ASAT weaponry without any legal constraints. Thus, the treaty leaves enough space for any party to evaluate its ASAT weapon launched from the limits of the Earth and its surroundings to destroy its own space asset, thereby arming the state with a proven ASAT technology.
- The issue of polluting outer space with debris as the fallout of use of space weapon needs to be incorporated.

Thus, the draft PPWT in many ways does not restrain the use of ASAT weapons and only prohibits placing, orbiting and testing of space-based weapon platforms. Further, the provision to inspect any suspected space-based platform is also not present in the treaty.

International Code of Conduct in Space

The European Union has proposed an International Code of Conduct (ICoC) for Outer Space Activities, a voluntary international instrument aimed to enhance the safety, security and sustainability of activities in outer space.[44] This non-legally binding revised draft (3rd of the series) released on September 16, 2013, lays down the broad "Transparency and Confidence-Building Measures (TCBMs) in Outer Space Activities" in pursuance of UNGA Resolution 61/75 and provides guidelines for the establishment and implementation of policies and procedures to minimise the risk of accidents in space, collisions between space objects, or any form of harmful interference with another state's peaceful exploration, and use, of outer space.[45] The ICoC does not address the issue on restrictions of use of space weapons or call for imposing a ban on space weapons. The proposed code neither extrapolates nor interpolates the existing provisions in the United Nations Charter and in the OST.

Future Prospects on International Law Against Space Weapons

The process of establishing regulatory international space laws or to conclude a treaty would flow from the broader perspective of general laws that have been accepted and enacted under the provisions of the UN Charter. In the context of international relations, space laws and treaties will have to deal with two categories of space objects. The first category is celestial bodies and the second type comprises man-made objects (artificial satellites and spacecraft). Thus, any law in respect of celestial bodies will be for their exploration, and for the conservation of the universal commons of outer space. In relation to space, the most important largely acknowledged resolution is that outer space and the natural components within it are global resources and no state can assert any right on these (corroborated in the OST). While an agreement on the prohibition of use of any weapon on or against celestial bodies does exist, a broad consensus on laws governing artificial satellites and spacecraft is yet to be evolved.

The international consensus on the establishment of the space law on the use of satellites, spacecraft, space weapons and weapon platforms is marred by the fact that space is now increasingly getting congested and contested. As states compete for exploitation and utilisation of space resources, the outer space environment and sustainability of space activities is under immense pressure as far as the safety and security of space-based assets is concerned.

Generally, it has been experienced that enactment of a law on use of a new technology weapon system can never precede the event itself. Any law generally will be enacted to prevent the occurrence of an untoward accident/incident, and in the case of an untoward event that is not governed within the existing provisions, that it is not repeated. For institutionalising a law on space weapons, or for that matter any weapon, the establishment of various international treaties and laws generally comes to the fore only after the weapon has been put to use. History is replete with examples where the laws on the use of nuclear, biological and chemical weapons were enacted only after these weapons were put to use. It was only after experiencing the devastating effects of these weapons that the process of enactment of laws banning such weapons was initiated. In short, any law will be formed only post demonstration of capability, and one cannot lay down a law on something that does not exist. As of now, we are yet to witness use of space weapons in a direct conflict role. Thus, we can comprehend to a certain extent that no comprehensive international law on 'space weapons and their use' will be formed until and unless the weapon technology is exploited.

One of the major impediments in the establishment of a comprehensive law for space weapons is that such a law would directly or indirectly curtail research and development in space technology. This is more so in the case of space weapon development as the associated technology (and in that, the use of directed energy weapons) is still in the nascent stage. It is also a well-established fact that any technology, particularly in the development of weapon systems and their platforms may come with unprecedented benefits for humanity. Just like the technology associated with rockets (as a weapon system) was later used to launch satellites, and atomic weapons paved the way for harnessing of nuclear energy to meet electricity requirements, the technology of space weapons and delivery mechanisms could open up the possibility of exploring the unknown and unfamiliar protectorate of the universe. Thus, until we reach the pinnacle in space weapon technology, the issue of curbing the innovative process by prohibitive laws will be met with resistance.

Any international law or treaty can be instituted only after it is accepted and ratified by a specified minimum number of nations (and be binding on them only). In the case of the United Nations Security Council, a treaty can come into force only if a specified minimum number of nations endorse it and the proposal is not vetoed by any of the permanent members. Armed with the veto power, the five permanent members of the council can quash any non-procedural matter, including the formation of international rules and regulations, irrespective of overwhelming international support. Thus, the draft treaties on PAROS and PPWT are yet to be negotiated as the United States is opposed to them.

Conclusion

Reliance on space-based services and applications is crucial for a nation's progress. The development in the technology in relation to outer space comes with widespread benefits that not only assist in bringing the world community together but also help in bridging the societal and economic gaps between nations. The access to, and maintaining a presence in, space, plays a crucial role for scientific research, commercial well-being and societal benefits. However, dual use of this technology for military applications is undermining the security of space assets. The issue of space security assumes a new dimension as we are in a transition, to graduate from militarisation to weaponisation of space. A lot of technological progress for the development of new concept weapons has been made and this is being further refined to include high powered lasers and high powered microwave weapon systems. With the introduction of reentry manoeuvrable spacecraft which can stay in orbit for prolonged periods, these could be used as platforms to orbit these weapon systems. Though these weapon systems are still in the evaluation and testing phase, the United States has already inducted such weapon systems in the inventory of its terrestrial forces and, as brought out in the preceding chapters, is improvising them for use on space platforms.

While there are laws and treaties relating to outer space, they are grossly inadequate. The reasons for the inadequacy of the space laws can be attributed to not keeping pace with the advances in space technology, the innovations in weapon technologies and the inexorable reach of mankind in the outer space domain. This, in turn, has acted as a catalyst in escalating commercial aspirations and space security related issues. The concern about space weapons becomes more prominent as an international consensus on legal instruments to regulate activities in space is hampered by the political and expansionist ambitions of some nations.

As space weapon technology is still evolving and new concept non-lethal weapons are being evaluated and tested, any law prohibiting technology innovation will be met with resistance. Till such time that the technology is exploited to its full potential (matching of theoretical hypothesis with practical implementation), invigoration of the law against space weapons will face insurmountable challenges.

Notes

1. "International Law", Global Issues, United Nations, at http://www.un.org/en/globalissues/internationallaw/. Accessed on September 1, 2015.
2. Michael Beaver, "Current Space Law Limitations and Its Implications on Outer Space Conflicts", *E-International Students*, June 16, 2015, at http://www.e-ir.info/2015/06/16/current-space-law-limitations-and-its-implications-on-outer-space-conflicts/. Accessed on September 29, 2015.

3. "Space Law", United Nations, Office for Outer Space Affairs, available at http://www.unoosa.org/oosa/en/ourwork/spacelaw/index.html. Accessed on September 1, 2015.
4. Ibid.
5. Ibid.
6. Ibid.
7. Ibid.
8. "Outer Space", United Nations Committee on Disarmament, at http://www.un.org/disarmament/topics/outerspace/. Accessed on September 1, 2015.
9. "History", United Nations, Office for Outer Space Affairs, available at http://www.unoosa.org/oosa/en/aboutus/history/index.html. Accessed on September 1, 2015.
10. "Committee on the Peaceful Uses of Outer Space", United Nations, Office for Outer Space Affairs, available at http://www.unoosa.org/oosa/en/ourwork/copuos/index.html. Accessed on September 1, 2015.
11. Ibid.
12. "Resolutions Adopted on Reports of First Committee", United Nations, General assembly, available at http://www.unoosa.org/pdf/gares/ARES_14_1472E.pdf. Accessed on September 2, 2015.
13. "Declaration of Legal Principles Governing the Activities of States in the Exploration and Use of Outer Space", Resolution adopted by the General Assembly,1962 (XVIII), available at http://www.un-documents.net/a18r1962.htm. Accessed on September 1, 2015.
14. "Status of International Agreements relating to Activities in Outer Space", at http://www.unoosa.org/pdf/limited/c2/AC105_C2_2015_CRP08E.pdf. Accessed on September 2, 2015.
15. "Treaty on Principles Governing the Activities of States in the Exploration and Use of Outer Space, including the Moon and Other Celestial Bodies", Resolution adopted by the General Assembly, available at http://www.unoosa.org/pdf/publications/ST_SPACE_061Rev01E.pdf. Accessed on September 1, 2015.
16. Article V of the OST deals with provisions in relation to all possible assistance to astronauts in the event of an accident, distress, or emergency landing on the territory of another state party or on the high seas.
17. Article VII of the OST states "Each State Party to the Treaty that launches or procures the launching of an object into outer space, including the Moon and other celestial bodies, and each State Party from whose territory or facility an object is launched, is internationally liable for damage to another State Party to the Treaty or to its natural or juridical persons by such object or its component parts on the Earth, in air space or in outer space, including the Moon and other celestial bodies".
18. Article VIII of the OST deals with the registry of an object launched into outer and lays out the rules on jurisdiction and control over such object.
19. n. 8.
20. Ambassador (Retd.) Paul Meyer," The Conference on Disarmament and the Prevention of an Arms Race in Outer Space", *UNIDIR* Resources, at http://www.

unidir.org/files/publications/pdfs/the-conference-on-disarmament-and-the-prevention-of-an-arms-race-in-outer-space-370.pdf. Accessed on September 3, 2015.

21. "Prevention of an Arms Race in Outer Space", UNGA Resolution A/RES/36/97 at http://www.un.org/documents/ga/res/36/a36r097.htm. Accessed on September 30, 2015.
22. "Prevention of an Arms Race in Outer Space", at http://fas.org/programs/ssp/nukes/ArmsControl_NEW/nonproliferation/NFZ/NP-NFZ-PAROS.html. Accessed on February 22, 2015.
23. "Report of the Conference on Disarmament to the General Assembly of the United Nations", CD/1281, September 13, 1994, at http://daccess-dds-ny.un.org/doc/UNDOC/GEN/G94/643/22/PDF/G9464322.pdf?OpenElement. Accessed on September 4, 2015.
24. Meyer, n. 20.
25. Non-Aligned Nations in the Conference on Disarmament.
26. Conference on Disarmament, Report of the Ad Hoc Committee on Prevention of an Arms Race in Outer Space, document CD/1271, 24 August 1994 at http://daccess-dds-ny.un.org/doc/UNDOC/GEN/G94/639/71/IMG/G9463971.pdf?OpenElement. Accessed on September 24, 2015.
27 Ibid.
28. Conference on Disarmament, letter from the permanent representative of China transmitting a working paper entitled "China's Position on and Suggestions for Ways to Address the Issue of Prevention of an Arms Race in Outer Space at the Conference on Disarmament", document CD/1606, February 9, 2000, at http://daccess-dds-ny.un.org/doc/UNDOC/GEN/G00/604/81/PDF/G0060481.pdf?OpenElement. Accessed on September 24, 2015.
29. Conference on Disarmament, letter from the permanent representative of China transmitting a working paper entitled "Possible Elements of the Future International Legal Instrument on the Prevention of the Weaponization of Outer Space", document CD/1645, dated June 6, 2001, at http://daccess-dds-ny.un.org/doc/UNDOC/GEN/G01/622/44/PDF/G0162244.pdf?OpenElement. Accessed on September 24, 2015.
30. Conference on Disarmament, letter from the permanent representatives of China, the Russian Federation, Vietnam, Indonesia, Belarus, Zimbabwe and Syrian Arab Republic submitted for circulation titled "Possible Elements for a Future International Legal Agreement on the Prevention of the Deployment of Weapons in Outer Space, The Threat or Use of Force Against Outer Space Objects", document CD/1679, dated June 28, 2002, at http://daccess-dds-ny.un.org/doc/UNDOC/GEN/G02/624/84/PDF/G0262484.pdf?OpenElement. Accessed on September 24, 2015.
31. Conference on Disarmament, letter dated July 10, 2002, from the permanent representative of the United States circulated under CD/1680, at http://daccess-dds-ny.un.org/doc/UNDOC/GEN/G02/628/69/IMG/G0262869.pdf?OpenElement. Accessed on September 24, 2015.
32. Ibid.

33. Conference on Disarmament, CD/1710, June 26, 2003, at http://daccess-dds-ny.un.org/doc/UNDOC/GEN/G03/624/63/PDF/G0362463.pdf?OpenElement. Accessed on September 24, 2015.
34. The term "outer space" means the space above the Earth in excess of 100 km above sea level.
35. The term "outer space object" means any device designed to function in outer space which is launched into an orbit around any celestial body, or located in orbit around any celestial body, or on any celestial body, except the Earth, or leaving orbit around any celestial body towards this celestial body, or moving from any celestial body towards another celestial body, or placed in outer space by any other means
36. Conference on Disarmament, CD/1839, dated February 29, 2008, Draft "Treaty on Prevention of the Placement of Weapons in Outer Space and of the Threat or Use of Force against Outer Space Objects (PPWT)", at http://daccess-dds-ny.un.org/doc/UNDOC/GEN/G08/604/02/PDF/G0860402.pdf?OpenElement. Accessed on September 24, 2015.
37. A weapon shall be considered to have been "placed" in outer space if it orbits the Earth at least once, or follows a section of such an orbit before leaving this orbit, or is permanently located somewhere in outer space.
38. The term "weapon in outer space" means any device placed in outer space, based on any physical principle, which has been specially produced or converted to destroy, damage or disrupt the normal functioning of objects in outer space, on the Earth or in the Earth's atmosphere, or to eliminate a population or components of the biosphere which are important to human existence or inflict damage on them
39. The "use of force" or the "threat of force" mean any hostile actions against outer space objects, including, *inter alia,* actions aimed at destroying them, damaging them, temporarily or permanently disrupting their normal functioning or deliberately changing their orbit parameters, or the threat of such actions.
40. Conference on Disarmament, CD/1847, August 26, 2008, at http://daccess-dds-ny.un.org/doc/UNDOC/GEN/G08/628/51/PDF/G0862851.pdf?OpenElement. Accessed on September 24, 2015.
41. Ibid.
42. Ibid.
43. Article V of proposed PPWT states, "Nothing in this Treaty may be interpreted as impeding the exercise by the States Parties of their right of self-defence in accordance with Article 51 of the Charter of the United Nations".
44. "Code of Conduct for Outer Space Activities", European Union External Action service, at http://eeas.europa.eu/non-proliferation-and-disarmament/outer-space-activities/index_en.htm. Accessed on October 8, 2015.
45. Ibid.

9

Space Weapons: Indian Context and Futuristic Roadmap

While a nation's economic growth and security complement each other, so does weapon technology and the technology used in the service of mankind.

India, with its economic resurgence, is aiming to push beyond its traditional sphere of interest focussed on regional dominance and is perceived to be emerging as a future global power. Successive elected governments have aptly assessed and recognised that a prominent position in the global world order calls for a robust economy, intricately and inseparably intertwined with a befitting political expression and military strength. Much of military strength is derived from the assimilation and incorporation of advances made in science and technology. More often than not, indigenous and innovative efforts in the development of weapon systems provide capabilities unique in nature and character for the conduct of warfare across the broad spectrum of challenges. Fully aware of the fact that the outcome of future conflicts will be driven by technology and technological superiority, India is now increasingly focussing on bridging the capability gaps to optimally structure, equip and orient its armed forces for the desired combat effectiveness across the entire spectrum of conflict.

India's armed forces are the third largest in the world and much of its military strength in the future will depend on how it is poised to harness the technology potential for enhancement of its war-waging capabilities in the decades to come. The military-technological differential will be one of the key factors for competitive advantage against an adversary, and superior military technology will help dominate the opponent during times of both peace and war.[1] As the Indian government is making all efforts to modernise, and provide a cutting edge to, its land, maritime and air forces, the time is now ripe to focus on integrating space-based support to harness its military might. Knowing well that space support would play a decisive role in future conflicts, it is imperative for India to institutionalise a broad framework for fast tracking and consolidating efforts that will help it in employing space-based platforms for force enhancement and, if need be, exercising the option for power projection from space.

Asia and Outer Space

The space domain, earlier dominated by the US and USSR (Russia), now involves more than 50 national space agencies. The advances in space research and technology demonstrated by these two countries in the 20th century prompted the Asian nations to initiate and accelerate their space programmes in the 21st century. The last two decades have witnessed an increased number of nation-states, particularly from the Asian subcontinent, embracing the space services for the following reasons:

- Lowering of the technological and economic barriers for entry into the space arena.
- Proliferation of satellite technology.
- Increasing trend of outsourcing of launch capabilities.
- Leasing of onboard satellite resources.

The harnessing of advanced space technology and capability that is derived from an ever-escalating horde of space-based assets is one of the reasons that seems to be creating a divide in the economic, political and security state of affairs between space-faring and space-aspiring nations. This, in turn, has bolstered the efforts for emerging Asian space players like China, India and Japan to progressively enhance their own space capabilities. Apart from these, Iran, Israel and North Korea also have independent satellite launch capability. Space-based services now play an indispensable role in providing benefits to the civil populace, national economy and national security. The importance of gaining credibility in the space sector is closely associated with the stronger economic growth rates, coupled with political aspirations and societal benefits. This can be gauged from the efforts invested by the new emerging economies like China and India in a multitude of space projects and experimental endeavours.

Indian Space Programme

The Indian space odyssey began with the setting up of the Indian National Committee for Space Research (INCOSPAR) in 1962. After the first rocket for scientific studies was launched from Thumba on November 21, 1963, a number of sounding rockets were launched at regular intervals. The Indian space programme has by far been driven by the use of space technology for socio-economic development and has centred on the notion of peaceful use of outer space in the service of mankind. The vision of Dr. Vikram A. Sarabhai, the founding father of the space programme in India, has been the guiding force for the Indian space programme and reaffirmed the Indian government's conviction about the potential of space technology and its applications as an effective instrument for national development. The launch of the first indigenous rocket, the RH-75, in 1967, was followed by bolder steps. In 1969, the Indian Space Research Organisation (ISRO) was formed, superseding the erstwhile INCOSPAR. Since the time of its foundation, ISRO has been guided by the vision of Dr. Sarabhai, articulated in 1968:

> There are some who question the relevance of space activities in a developing nation. To us, there is no ambiguity of purpose. We do not have the fantasy of competing with the economically advanced nations.......But we are convinced that if we are to play a meaningful role nationally, and in the community of nations, we must be second

to none in the application of advanced technologies to the real problems of man and society.[2]

The above quote by Dr. Sarabhai clearly and succinctly summed up the prevailing economic condition and the newfound interest in space science at that time. This quote, which was at the home page of the ISRO website till year 2014, has now been removed. The quote, "*We do not have the fantasy of competing with the economically advanced nations*" is no longer relevant. Bolstered by strong economic growth and unremitting efforts in realisation of its aspiration of becoming a future global power, India now competes in the league of the developed nations. Further, the Indian government has realised that in spite of its being a staunch supporter of peaceful uses of outer space, space enabled information has become increasingly integral to the war-fighting capability of its armed forces.

Indian Space Research Organisation

Dr. Vikram Sarabhai, having identified the role and importance of space technology in a nation's development, provided ISRO the necessary direction to function as an actor in, and agent of, development. ISRO then embarked on its mission to introduce space-based services and to develop the technologies to achieve the same independently. Aryabhatta, the first Indian-made satellite, with scientific payloads, was launched in 1975, using a Soviet launch vehicle. This was followed by the launch of the Bhaskara series of satellites with onboard cameras.

India's entry into the space club was marked on July 18, 1980, when it successfully demonstrated the launch of its first launch vehicle, the SLV-3, that carried a 40 kg class satellite, the Rohini (RS-1), into a 400 km orbit above the Earth.[3] With this launch, India joined the exclusive space club of the USA, Soviet Union, Europe, Japan and China that had capability of launching satellites. The successive efforts of ISRO thereafter have not only been laudable but have established it as an organisation that stays at the cutting edge of technology. With the launch of successful space missions and more than 70 satellites, ISRO has cut a niche for itself among the space-faring nations.

The two main satellite systems—Indian National Satellite (INSAT) system and Indian Remote Sensing (IRS) satellite—have received world acclamation. The INSAT series of satellites placed in geostationary orbits is one of the largest domestic communication satellite constellations in the Asia-Pacific region used for communication, television broadcasting and meteorological applications.[4] The IRS series of satellites is the largest civilian remote sensing satellite constellation in the world, providing imageries for varied applications covering agriculture, water resources, urban development, mineral prospecting, environment, forestry, drought and flood forecasting, ocean resources and disaster management.[5]

ISRO has two satellite launch vehicles: the Polar Satellite Launch Vehicle (PSLV) and Geosynchronous Satellite Launch Vehicle (GSLV). The PSLV is meant for launching Earth Observation (EO) satellites into Sun Synchronous Orbit (SSO) and small satellites into Low Earth Orbit (LEO), whereas, the GSLV is used for launching telecommunications satellites into a 36,000 km Geostationary Earth Orbit (GEO).

Research and development in space projects by ISRO now includes lunar and interplanetary missions that encourage and promote science education, apart from providing valuable data to the world community for scientific enrichment. On October 22, 2008, ISRO launched the Chandrayaan-1, its first mission to the Moon in a lunar orbit at a height of 100 km for chemical, mineralogical and photo-geologic mapping of the Moon. The Chandrayaan-1 mission has gained considerable international standing by discovering evidence of water on the Moon. Thereafter, ISRO achieved a new milestone when its first interplanetary space flight carrying the spacecraft christened 'Mangalayaan' (Mars Orbiter Mission) succeeded in its very first attempt, creating history on September 24, 2014.[6] With this, India became the first Asian country to insert a satellite in the Martian orbit; that too, in the very first attempt. ISRO became the fourth space agency in the world after NASA, the Russian Federal Space Agency and European Space Agency to accomplish a Mars mission. The project, completed at a meagre spending of Rs. 450 crore[7], is the cheapest interplanetary mission in the world at almost one-tenth of the cost of similar missions undertaken by other countries.

The success of the Chandrayaan and Mars Orbiter Mission (MOM) helped ISRO in accomplishing the objective of maturing the required designs of satellites and launch systems. From these missions, ISRO gained substantial experience in the fields of propulsion and power systems, automation, robotics and sensors for its future space assignments. These missions have helped it to establish the tradeoffs between existing and newer technologies like cryogenic fluid management, solar power, nuclear propulsion, nuclear power, communication systems and spacecraft autonomy.[8] In addition to the research and development that went into these projects, ISRO has benefitted immensely in the fields of planning, management and operations from the scientific, commercial and military perspectives.[9]

India's Outlook Towards Space Security in the 20th Century

India has always considered space technology as an important element for scientific, economic and societal growth and this is aptly encapsulated in ISRO's vision statement of "harnessing space technology for national development, while pursuing space science research and planetary exploration".[10] ISRO, under the aegis of the Government of India, has been strictly abiding by this vision statement and has been a strong supporter of "peaceful uses of outer space". Even during the Cold War period, when the USA and USSR were embroiled in a space race for the development of ASAT weapons, India had conveyed its dissent on the proposals framed under the Strategic Defence Initiative (SDI) and similar space weapons projects. The Indian concerns were voiced during the United Nations 38th session, when Prime Minister Indira Gandhi, on September 28, 1983, said,

"The crisis which confronts our civilisation today is unprecedented in history.... We appeal to the great powers to give up mistrust, engage in sincere, forward looking negotiations in a spirit of shared good faith to reach agreement on various disarmament measures..." while further conveying India's dissent on the issue of using outer space for future wars.[11] Levelling criticism on the developments in ASAT technology, India called for negotiations for negating the possibility of an arms race in outer space, while, on the other hand, it did not voice its aversion to the use of satellites as platforms for surveillance, communication, and other functions in secondary support of the military.[12]

Further, India has always supported global cooperation in space developmental activities to favour all nations. The chairman, ISRO, in his statement to the United Nations conference on the exploration and peaceful uses of outer space at Vienna, in 1999, had stated, "The widespread development of peaceful uses of outer space by all countries will be possible only with unhindered access to technology and knowledge on a global basis. Global cooperation in this regard should be further strengthened to remove impediments to the access of technology, equipment, materials and knowledge for use in peaceful and developmental activities."[13]

Space Security: Concerns for India in the 21st Century

While India's space activities have been primarily focussed on promoting all round development of the nation, this outlook gradually started to change, partly due to the alteration of the security scenario in the Asia-Pacific region. After witnessing the use of space assets by the United States post 1990 in support of military operations, the realisation of the use of space applications in future wars started dawning on India. In 1999, the Indian government initiated its own Ballistic Missile Defence (BMD) system to tackle the growing threats from China and Pakistan. Further, it also started initiating steps to improve its capability to use space assets in support of military operations.

In India's immediate neighbourhood, China continued to stride ahead in its space advances in support of societal and commercial services, while consistently working towards integrating, and improvising on, space services in the military domain. Since the beginning of the 21st century, China has demonstrated rapid expansion in its space capabilities that may not only prompt an Asian space race but also have a long-term impact on the global space environment.[14] China's multi-pronged approach in commercial and exploratory research in space activities reinforces its outlook towards the use of space programmes for peaceful purposes, but its space ambitions seem to be highly nationalistic. However, if we scrutinise its space programme from close quarters, it is evident that the technological advances accrued from its space exploration programmes and peaceful projects are actively integrated into the military design.

The inexorable rise of China in the last decade succeeded in creating turbulence in the existing global power equations and one of the visible assertions has been its expansionist space policies, including an ambitious space weapon programme. China's indulgence in developing and acquiring technology for space weapons has raised serious concerns amongst other space-faring nations on the security of their space assets. In the last decade, the demonstration of anti-satellite capability by China forced India to reconsider its stand on outer space in support of military applications.[15] India's space security concerns are mainly in relation to China's pursuit of the following space and counter-space capabilities.

- **Space-Based ISR Capabilities:** Since 2009, China has launched more than 70 satellites[16] to include Electro-Optical (EO) satellites for digital imagery in the visual and near infrared spectrum; synthetic aperture radar satellites for night time and all weather imagery; and Electronic Intelligence (ELINT) satellites for acquiring electronic signatures.[17] The interest in developing a space-based ELINT and SIGINT (Signal Intelligence) sensor network would have implications for the air defence networks, ballistic missile defence systems, communication security, and counter-space operations in the Asia-Pacific region.[18] The intelligence inputs will help it deny and disrupt the terrestrial as well as the satellite services of adversaries in future conflicts.

- **Kinetic Kill ASAT Weaponry:** China has demonstrated its capability to destroy satellites in LEO[19], has improvised its missile defence system technologies[20] and has also conducted experiments that could help it in destroying satellites in higher orbits[21]. Besides this, China is reportedly pursuing development of parasitic satellites, co-orbital ASATs, and robotic arms in space.[22] It could also be developing nanosatellites to be used as space mines.[23]
- **Directed Energy Weapons:** China has been devoting significant resources to directed energy weapon systems, particularly ground-based lasers, and has purportedly used them to target US reconnaissance satellites.[24]
- **Cyber Attack Capability:** China is said to be pursuing formation of cyber warfare units to hack into space control systems for effects ranging from temporary irritation to partial or complete breakdown of satellite services.[25]

China's strides in counter-space activities have already impacted the global space environment to a great extent, bringing about far-reaching economic, political and social repercussions. The demonstration of ASAT capability and evaluating technologies used for space weapons has not only raised concerns amongst the global space powers but has also prompted its neighbouring countries like Japan to revise the policy on the use of space for "peaceful purposes" to "extending of space activity for national security". Another case in point is the apprehension of the United States on the vulnerability of its space assets and subsequent follow-up in terms of strategic recalibration and speeding up the development of new concept weapon systems.[26]

The Shifting Dynamics of Space Security

The advances in ASAT technologies by China, in particular the 2007 ASAT test, escalated the uncertainty in the Indian mindset and rekindled its view on following its acclaimed motto of "peaceful use of outer space". While there was no reaction by the government immediately after the test, India, at the United Nations General Assembly, on October 25, 2007, was discreet in voicing its opinion without direct reference to China. Dr. Rameshwar Oraon, a member of the Indian delegation, while reasserting India's commitment on "peaceful uses of outer space" conveyed that peaceful uses of outer space could be undermined by deployment of weapons in outer space and there was a need to initiate steps to avoid its weaponisation through multilateral engagement.[27]

While the Chinese test was seen largely as a manifestation of its geopolitical ambition to challenge the American hegemony in space, it was enough to perturb the Indian Ministry of Defence and officials of the armed forces. The disquiet amongst the Indian military brass was visible as opinions were expressed on future space security and, challenges faced for protection of space assets. The then Army Chief, Gen Deepak Kapoor, voiced his concerns in no uncertain terms, "China's space programme is expanding at an exponentially rapid pace in both offensive and defensive content", adding that space was increasingly becoming the "ultimate military high ground" to dominate in the wars of the future.[28] As per Dr K. Kasturirangan, former chairman of ISRO, "China's military capabilities in space, as demonstrated in 2007, by destroying a satellite, was a cause for worry for India",[29] and "India cannot be immune to the rapidly changing international security environment, the emergence of a new space order, the threat to its national security from the nuclear and missile capabilities in its neighbourhood, and the vulnerabilities of its space assets. Space security becomes important in the context of not only the Indian civilian programme but also in the context of its national security."[30]

Thus, while India has a well developed indigenous space programme to meet its socio-economic needs, of late it has started voicing concerns on the vulnerability of its space assets. These concerns, in turn, are persuading it to consider measures that would ensure the security of its space assets. However, it is yet to formulate its vision on the protection of its space assets.

Rhetoric of Space Weapons Development

The Indian polity is well aware that its space assets could be subjugated in the future and, thus, it needs to develop a minimal deterrent capability to secure them. This calls for building up indigenous counter-space capabilities which may or may not incorporate the capability of power projection from space.

On the sidelines of the 97th Indian Science Congress in the year 2010, the Defence Research and Development Organisation's (DRDO's) Director General V K Saraswat, who also happened to be the scientific adviser to the defence minister, told reporters, "India is putting together building blocks of technology that could be used to neutralise enemy satellites".[31] He also stated that "the scientists were planning to build the weapon which would have the capacity to hit and destroy satellites in low earth orbit and polar orbit" and that, "We are working to ensure space security and protect our satellites. At the same time, we are also working on how to deny the enemy access to its space assets".[32] He further elaborated, "Basically, these are deterrence technologies and quite certainly many of these technologies will not be used. I hope they are not used".[33] The other highlight of the conference was that though India had only a civilian space programme, the inherent dual use nature of satellite technology could be adapted for military purposes as well.[34]

If one carries out an analysis of these statements, it clearly emerges that India is keen to pursue asymmetric capabilities that would ensure protection to its space assets. India has learned from the various conflicts that to sustain peace, one must be able to defend peace, and this capability would come by developing modern warfare capabilities that would constrict the required space needed by the adversary for manoeuvre and feel the pressure.[35] In this regard, it was rightly quoted by James Mc Donnell "The creative conquest of space will serve as a wonderful substitute for war."[36]

Why India Should not be Averse to ASAT Technology

The United States, in addition to being a pioneer in evaluation and testing of ASAT weapons in the 20th century, is well ahead of other nations in space technology. Its progress in the space weapon technology was unchallenged post Cold War period. While it had always been inclined to evaluate new concept weapons (read DEWs) and had continued research and development in this field, its shaky rationale and wavering motivation prevented it from investing heavily in new concept weapons. With its 2007 ASAT test, China broke the monopoly of the United States. The United States, at this point in time, while being still way ahead of China in ASAT technology, lost no opportunity in allaying fears about the danger to its space assets and, in the bargain, revived a few of the earlier ASAT projects. The renewed interest in ASAT systems was not limited to resumption of projects but paved the way to bolstering the design and development of new concept weapon systems that could possibly be integrated into space platforms from a futuristic perspective. When the United States, tagged as a world military power with an unparalleled global reach, takes cognisance of Chinese ASAT technology and reacts by furthering its military prowess, why shouldn't India—now vying to be a global and regional power—build up on capabilities that would help it secure a prominent place in the new world order?

As has been brought out earlier, India at this juncture has been exhibiting a mixed response as far as acquisition of ASAT capabilities is concerned. Even in the face of the prevailing uncertainty, it is not lost upon the government that until and unless it projects itself as a credible military power, with competitive capabilities in space, its economy and security may be at risk. The emergence of China as a global power has notable consequences for India. While both countries have exercised caution in dealing with contentious issues, they lack a substantive rapport in their bilateral relationship (like the prevailing border and trade disputes). Further, the uncertainty and trust deficit between these two has been apparent as India has been wary of China's support to Pakistan, and China has voiced concerns on India's interest in the disputed South China Sea. In the eventuality of deterioration of bilateral relations with China, the possibility of China using its ASAT weaponry to cripple the command and control system of the Indian armed forces and subjugate its ability to respond effectively in the course of a conflict cannot be ruled out.

However, while India does possess the capability to design and develop basic space weapons, it is still entangled in the uncertainty of venturing into ASAT developments. This uncertainty is not unfounded as development of space weapons could invite international ramifications that would have a cascading effect on the country's economic growth, without substantial gains. Thus, while India mulls over this ambiguity on whether it should initiate steps to develop space weapons, it cannot afford to neglect China's advances towards weaponising space and allow the asymmetry to widen to an extent that it loses out even in projecting a minimal deterrent capability. Thus, the Indian government needs to consider and build up a robust counter-space capability to project a minimal deterrence posture. As China apparently leads India in a wide range of space projects and launch vehicle configurations, and has been evaluating an extensive range of counter-space capabilities, it is imperative for India to match these capacities at least qualitatively, if not quantitatively.

Space Weapons Enabled: To Be or Not to Be?

The question of whether or not India should develop space weapons is a contentious one and is debatable on many counts. As has been brought out in the earlier chapters, firstly, though space weapons have been tested and evaluated by select nations, outer space is still free of weapons. Secondly, development of space weapons is a complex affair and is an exorbitantly costly proposal. Thirdly, the majority of space weapon projects by the USA and erstwhile USSR resulted in failure and were shelved after preliminary assessments. Fourthly, physical destruction of space assets using kinetic means will pollute the space environment with debris and there is increased consensus at the international level on banning the use of such weapons. Further, creation of space debris would be detrimental to future space endeavours, whether own or those of others. Fifthly, the use of new age weapon systems (DEWs) is yet to mature and the technology for the same is yet to fully evolve. Lastly, but most importantly, use of space weapons alone cannot win wars.

On an optimistic note, India's indulgence in development of space weapons will boost its technological prowess and this technological superiority will help India not only to deter its adversaries but also to gain experience that will help in future development of new age weapon systems for its conventional forces. The research and development would provide the nation with critical technologies that would prove to be the game changer in establishing India as a global power.

As military support from space assets is an accepted global norm, it is essential that we enhance the military use of space. As technological superiority will be a decisive factor in determining the outcome of future conflicts, much of the intelligence gathering for military operations and successful culmination of plans will depend on space-based assets. Space-related military potential will empower the country for a well-coordinated and synchronised tactical capability, communication, resource management, enhanced ISR and network-centric capabilities. Technological innovations spurred by employment of high power lasers, high powered microwaves and charged particle beams will also contribute to new age weapon systems for use by the terrestrial forces. Space weapon projects will open the avenues for the development of unmanned aerial platforms and spacecraft that would augment the nation's military potential, and the technology will simultaneously boost the commercial airline industry and avionics segment.

While the Indian leadership may decide against weaponisation of space in view of its outlook on 'peaceful uses of outer space', it is high time to understand that the design and development of

ASATs, spacecraft and new concept weapons are not to be treated in isolation as instruments of war-mongering. The derivatives of the investment in development of space weapon systems and platforms will be far too many. The technology of space weapons will help not only in exploitation of space for military gains but also to gain access to the vast protectorate of the universe in the service of mankind. These services may include extraterrestrial settlements, harvesting of resources from outer space and channelling of energy from the Sun/stars[37] for improvement of living conditions on the Earth. Further, the innovation and subsequent modernisation would boost our national confidence and open up new avenues for overall economic growth.

Ballistic Missile Defence Projects

India, as a first step in the development of its space weapon programme, will have to invigorate its multi-layered ballistic missile project to strengthen its strategic agility and operational flexibility. The ballistic missile technology, while providing for a global strike capability, will also enhance the technology used in space launch vehicles.

The DRDO initiated development of its own Ballistic Missile Defence (BMD) system in 1999. India's BMD is a two-layered system supposed to tackle incoming missiles with exo-atmospheric interception using the Prithvi Air Defence (PAD) system (range of 80-120 km) and endo-atmospheric interception using the Aakash missiles for the Advanced Air Defence (AAD) system (range of 15-30 km). The PAD system is devised for mid-course interception of the attacking missile in its cruise phase and the AAD is a terminal phase interception system which is designed to counter incoming missiles after their entry into the atmosphere.[38] PAD and AAD were successfully tested in November 2006 and December 2007 respectively and with this, India became the fourth country possessing the capability of developing an anti-ballistic missile system after the United States, Russia and Israel[39].

India is also seeking the help of Israel to jointly develop an Integrated Anti-Missile System (IAMS) to be deployed against nuclear and conventional missiles. As per reports, the proposed system will integrate India's long-range Prithvi air defence missile system with a mobile radar system [being developed by Bharat Electronics Limited (BEL) in partnership with Israel Aircraft Industries (IAI)].[40] Collaboration for IAMS will definitely propel the ongoing BMD project.

The advances in a full-fledged BMD project over the next few decades would help establish a multi-layered missile defence system and space-based sensor systems that would serve as components for a futuristic Indian space weaponisation programme.

Kinetic Kill Space Weapon

India has already established itself as one of the select nations to possess indigenous satellite launch vehicle capability. Thus, with an intrinsic ballistic missile knowledge base and maintaining a strong footing in launching of space assets, India can keep open the option of exercising the use of kinetic kill capability to destroy a satellite. The technology to target a satellite using a ballistic missile is much simpler when compared to positioning a payload in precise orbit. If India decides on demonstration of such a capability in line with the ASAT activities of the USA and China, all it has to do is to launch a rocket equipped with onboard detection, ranging and tracking systems for a physical kill or use a proximity fuse to trigger the explosive warhead in the vicinity of the target satellite. Such a demonstration would, however, go against India's stand of peaceful uses of outer space. Further, India would like to project itself as a responsible player in the space field and it would take all possible steps to avoid such an exhibition that would further pollute space with debris.

On the other hand, a better option for India would be to build up expertise in the field of air launched kinetic kill projectiles to target satellites. While such a capability may not be demonstrated against space-based assets, the evaluation and testing of the projectile on a virtual earmarked trajectory in the shadow of a space experiment can always be attempted. This way, we could gain confidence in possessing the capability of second strike against an adversary's space assets, and bolster space deterrence. Further, technology of air launched projectiles will help strengthen the conventional strike capability.

Co-orbital Weapon Technology

India's indigenous satellite launch capability also allows for deploying co-orbital ASAT weapons, parasitic satellites and space mines. Modern technology permits better sensor systems for homing and tracking for selective targeting of space assets. In addition, with the advent of ASATs, the concept of 'watchdog satellites' to guard other satellites could also be explored.[41] However, launch of co-orbital satellites is not an attractive concept as the satellites will have to shadow the target satellites for an indefinite period and the co-orbital asset is subject to detection from the launch phase itself. Thus, a stronger placed adversary can destroy a co-orbital satellite in a preemptive strike that could well result in an outer space conflict.

A better opportunity would lie in possessing 'launch on demand' capability for launching smaller satellites and space mines as per the need of the hour. Such a facility would also enable replacement of dysfunctional satellites at short notice. This would also help boost the overall commercial satellite industry as the overseas demands of launching satellites at short notice could be met.

Directed Energy Weapons

The use of directed energy weapons is fast emerging as an operational reality as they confer distinct advantages over conventional weapon systems. While DEW technology is still undergoing evolution, it does offer promising options as a war-waging instrument that would involve technologies incorporating high energy lasers, high power microwaves and electromagnetic pulse systems.

As DEW systems would provide capabilities that would provide an unparalleled impetus to tactical as well as strategic options, it will be crucial for India to invest and flourish in this field. It is widely debated that the 'blast and fragmentation' weapons cannot progress much technologically and future military strength will lie with the nation-states that succeed in development of DEW systems.[42] Such systems will possess the capability to completely and irrevocably neutralise, incapacitate and help isolate a stronger adversary without any collateral or biological damage to human beings.[43]

From India's perspective, the technological superiority of DEWs over KEWs can give the capability to cope with threats in the emerging geostrategic arena and this would need timely investments and focus on building directed energy weapon capability.[44]

The Way Forward

The scientific innovations and discoveries, even if exploited in support of weapon systems, have proved that such technology has more often than not been used to transform human life for a better existence. The technological breakthroughs and realisation of new age weapon systems, gradually, with the passage of time, start assuming a secondary role. The primary role would be in the areas wherein indigenous development of spacecraft and advances of laser technology, microwaves and charged particle beams are pursued for the benefit of mankind, while simultaneously opening up newer opportunities in the field of space exploration, medical applications, mapping and garnering of extraterrestrial resources. Thus, the forward path in national interest can be summed up as "while a nation's economic growth and security complement each other, so does weapon technology and the technology used in the service of mankind".

For pursuing and achieving technological superiority, it is imperative for India to continue research and development in space projects that will result in improving the existing launch vehicle platforms and space-based infrastructure. Therefore, the investments in the design and manufacture of new generation spacecraft and manoeuvrable space planes capable of serving the dual purpose of civilian and military applications will be prudent.

As there are ample indications that future military conflicts may involve power projection from space, the Indian government should seriously consider the advanced space projects and space ventures, for fulfilling commercial aspirations in the international space market as well as work diligently in amalgamating the technology with military objectives. Thus, while not seeking to evaluate and demonstrate space weapons, it would suffice that India validates the technology required for space weapons.

The validation of technology for space weapons would involve multifarious requirements that could be planned out over the duration of the next five decades. While the main aim is to be dovetailed towards exploitation of space for emerging as a global player, the component of evaluating, demonstrating and, if need be, of utilising space weapons should automatically be imbibed in the grand design. Thus, the Indian government should enhance the existing space-based capabilities while expanding its space infrastructure by investing in projects involving anti-ballistic missile systems, space-based and near space surveillance systems, augmenting of satellite launch facilities, advanced launch vehicles, global satellite constellations and deployment of spacecraft and space stations. In parallel, it should pursue innovative efforts to achieve technological breakthroughs in the field of directed energy and new concept weapons using particle beams.

- The augmentation of satellite launch platforms and improvement in the payload capacity of our launch vehicles would help capture a sizeable market share in the competitive international satellite launch market. At the same time, it would improve the turnaround times for satellite launches and provide a 'launch on demand' capability.
- With multiple satellite launch capability using a single launch vehicle, India is already in a position to launch micro, mini and parasitic satellites.
- The refinement in the kinetic kill capability using ballistic missile technology is feasible by the conduct of scientific experiments at varied orbital altitudes.

- The technology for the design and development of recoverable spacecraft and space planes is already under evaluation and should be followed up with a concrete plan, with specified timelines. Efforts to improve the payload capacity of these space vehicles would be a continual process.
- The scientific community should initiate methods by which India leads in the commercial sector for removal of space debris. One could consider development of a manoeuvrable spacecraft with a robotic arm that would help de-orbit objects from space or develop other innovative concepts that could help in reduction of space debris. Not only will such a proposal earn global revenue but the technology will help militarily in adopting an attacking as well as defensive posture in space.
- Research and development in directed energy and particle beam weapon systems should be given high priority. The testing and evaluation of such systems on the ground is not prohibited and on successful testing, the endeavour should be to integrate these weapons on an airborne platform. Demonstration of laser and high powered microwave weapons from an airborne platform would itself have a deterrent effect against future space adversaries.
- Efforts in the reduction of the size of these new concept weapon platforms, without compromising on power and propulsion, would enable positioning such weapons on space-based platforms.

Challenges and Complexities

- **Political Will:** The Indian polity generally adopts a non-aligned posture by avoiding a tenacious position that could lead to controversies on the international front. However, it needs to be understood that space related weapons are yet to evolve technically and the steps initiated by select nations are for exploiting the scientific potential that would help them acquire unique capabilities in support of national security as well as for societal benefits. While India may not engage in active evaluation and testing of space weapons, any breakthrough in space science and new concept weapon technology could result in leapfrogging success to help bridge the asymmetrical gap or even gain a decisive advantage over the advanced space-faring nations.

- **National Space Policy:** India does not have a consolidated national space policy. The Indian leadership should take on the responsibility of floating a national common space vision to derive a policy on all space related activities that would help it deter, warn and provide the capability to secure the national space assets. The nation is in need of a comprehensive space doctrine that would help expand the exploratory research and space application missions to ensure space security in the years ahead. While supporting the development of space-based weapon systems, it should lay down the broad framework on the course of action to be followed by the earmarked agencies.
- **Long-Term Perspective Planning:** The progress in the space domain will be one of the central precursors for India's emergence as a global power. It is, thus, essential that the Indian government lays out a Long-Term Perspective Plan (LTPP) for the futuristic space activities to bolster space technology and innovations in space sciences. Design and development of satellites, improvement in launch configurations, augmentation of launch facilities and manufacture of new generation spacecraft not only require a considerable lead time but also involve huge investments in research as well as infrastructural development. Thus, the government needs to invest in a manner whereby we transform the advances in dual use space technology into affordable and critical military capability. The formulation of the LTPP should identify critical technologies for indigenous development and, simultaneously, lay out a broad framework for the development of new concept weapon systems.
- **Revitalising the Indian Defence Industry:** While the Indian government has established wide ranging production

facilities with the help of Defence Public Sector Undertakings (DPSUs) and the Ordnance Factories (OFs), the indigenisation, development and the production in defence sector has been far from satisfactory. The government, and in that the Ministry of Defence (MoD), should initiate steps to foster the required confidence in the Indian PSUs in the development of the latest space and weapon technologies. One of the drawbacks in the majority of the defence related projects has been the deficit in accountability. The sense of accountability can be bolstered by ensuring effective interaction with, and, the participation of, the PSUs, MoD and armed forces which would rest on mutual trust and cooperation in achieving the desired degree of self-reliance and timely completion of space related projects.

- **Public-Private Partnership***:* Over a period of time, the country has realised that until and unless it opens up the defence industry to the private sector, the national endeavour of achieving self-reliance in defence production would be extremely difficult. Successive governments have made significant progress in formulating policy reforms in this direction, and the role of the private sector is now progressively shifting from that of being a supplier of raw material and small components to one of partnership in the manufacture of advanced weaponry and systems. The rise of India as a global power will be shaped by technological advances, thereby promoting self-reliance in its manufacturing sector. One of the recent steps to bolster self-reliance is the initiative of the 'Make in India Programme (MIIP)', that promotes investment opportunities, fosters innovations, protects intellectual property rights and encourages all round development. In addition to the MIIP, the government has further increased the Foreign Direct Investment (FDI) limit in defence, with 49 per cent now permitted under the automatic route, 75 per cent where technology transfer is involved, and up to 100 per cent in cases involving significant new technology.[45]

- **Technological Superiority:** Future conflicts would largely be shaped by innovative technology, and the nation-states which display technological superiority, will have a crucial edge over their adversary. Development of cutting edge technology, particularly in the field of space sciences, entails considerable investment in terms of time, money and human resource. This will also contribute to India's emerging status as an economic powerhouse. The development of space technology to meet the requirements of space security calls for broad-based defence related research and development programmes. The strategy on defence technology should be aimed to achieve a technological breakthrough before other nations to maintain the much needed crucial edge at all times. This is visible in the challenge that was thrown at the DPSUs by Prime Minister Modi, who said, "If the world is coming up with some products in 2020, can we come in the field prepared with products in 2018?"[46]

The importance of indigenisation and thereby attaining self-reliance in defence manufacturing and production is not only of critical strategic and national importance but also an essential component of national power.[47] It should be clearly understood at this juncture that no nation will share critical technologies, particularly those related to a space weapon programme, and their platforms (spacecraft). It is for this reason that it becomes imperative to invest in, and concentrate on, research and development in technologies related to new concept weapons like DEWs and charged particle beams. The R&D in this field should be accorded due emphasis at all levels. New age weapon systems can thereafter be integrated on varied platforms, including the space assets.

Conclusion

The Indian government has been aware that its national security has a profound impact on economic development, which, in turn, is also dependent to a certain extent on the security of space assets.

The outcome of future conflicts would be driven by the development of new concept weapon systems which would provide unique capabilities in the conduct of warfare. As space support would play a decisive role in future conflicts, the innovation and advancement of technology from the perspective of power projection from, and towards, space-based platforms is gaining momentum. Under the garb of the growing trend of weaponisation of space, it is now the right time for India to reexamine its long-drawn-out vision of peaceful uses of outer space. Opening up to the idea of using space support in military operations, India needs to understand that weaponisation of space has now become an inevitable reality and there is a need to develop a minimal deterrent capability to secure its space assets. Just like air dominance was accorded high priority in the 20th century, space dominance will be vital for conflicts in the 21st century.

India's development of space weapons will not only deter its adversaries but also help develop new age weapon systems for its conventional forces. The research and development would give the nation crucial technologies that would help India gain a prominent position on the global platform. Advances in space weapon projects will help it develop unmanned aerial platforms and spacecraft that would augment the nation's military potential. The investments in technology would also help it gain access to the unexplored protectorate of the universe and open up new avenues that may ameliorate the global standards of living.

While India's space security outlook is gradually changing and it has voiced concerns over the events that would lead ultimately to weaponisation of space, it is still embroiled in an uncertainty on venturing into this domain. While India basks in this ambiguity on whether it should initiate steps to develop space weapons, it cannot afford to neglect China's advances towards weaponising space and allow the asymmetry to widen. As China apparently leads India in a wide range of space projects, it is imperative for India to match these capacities at least qualitatively, if not quantitatively.

India needs to strengthen its BMD capability and progress work in the direction to establish a multi-layered missile defence system, space-based sensor systems and airborne interceptor missiles. While its indigenous space programme may permit launch of missiles (rocket) for physical destruction of space assets, building up on the capability of air launched kinetic kill vehicles on the lines of the ALMVs will bolster space deterrence and help strengthen the conventional strike capability. Another area of interest that would boost the commercial space sector while augmenting space security would be to establish a launch on demand capability.

The most important area for India is the research and development in DEW systems that would set it apart from, and help bridge any asymmetrical capability gaps with, the strongest adversary. India should look towards to development of a credible weapon system with the desired lethality over a specific range using directed energy (high powered lasers and microwaves) that is mountable on a conducive and flexible platform. This will not only provide a cutting edge in controlling the course of future warfare, but would help India to achieve surmountable gains over future adversaries. Use of the DEW technology would open up new concepts in space weapons and provide for counter-space capability.

At this point in time, as well as in the future, it is to be clearly understood that it is only the breakthroughs in science (emphasis on space science) and new concept weapons technology that have the potential to tilt the course of future wars, irrespective of the military might of a nation. Unless India sheds its inhibition on weaponisation of space, it may not be in a position to leverage its resources in becoming a military space power. This calls for institutionalising a broad framework and a long-term perspective plan, conceptualising space policies, creating organisational structures and investing in R&D activities related to civil, commercial and military exploitation of space.

Notes

1. Col SC Narang (Retd.), *New Defence Policy of India: A Perspective* (Delhi: Prashant Publication House, 2010), p.164.
2. Dr. Vikram Ambalal Sarabhai, at http://www.isro.gov.in/hi/node/417. Accessed on January 11, 2016.
3. "SLV", at http://www.isro.gov.in/launchers/slv. Accessed on January 6, 2014.
4. "ISRO", http://www.isro.org/satellites/geostationary.aspx. Accessed on January 6, 2014.
5. "ISRO", http://www.isro.org/satellites/earthobservationsatellites.aspx. Accessed on January 6, 2016.
6. "Mars Orbiter Mission", at http://www.isro.org/mars/updates.aspx. Accessed on September 24, 2014
7. Ibid.
8. P A Patil, "India's Maiden Mars Mission Puts ISRO on a New High", *In Focus*, Centre for Air Power Studies, September 24, 2014.
9. Ibid.
10. ISRO: Vision and Mission Statement, available at http://www.isro.org/about-isro/vision-and-mission-statements. Accessed on August 25, 2015.
11. Speech by Mrs Indira Gandhi, September 28, 1983, at the 38th session of the United Nations General Assembly, at https://www.pminewyork.org/adminpart/uploadpdf/73201lms32.pdf. Accessed on August 25, 2015.
12. Rajeswari Pillai Rajagopalan and Arvind K. John, "A New Frontier: Boosting India's Military Presence in Outer Space", Observer Research Foundation, New Delhi, occassional paper#50, January 2014.
13. Statement of Dr. K. Kasturirangan, chairman, Indian Space Research Organisation, Head of Indian Delegation to UNISPACE III, July 19-30, 1999, at http://www.un.org/events/unispace3/speeches/19ind.htm. Accessed on August 25, 2015.
14. James Clay Moltz, "It's On: Asia's New Space Race", at http://www.thedailybeast.com/articles/2015/01/17/why-china-will-win-the-next-space-race.html. Accessed on January 19, 2015.
15. "Technology Perspective and Capability Roadmap (TPCR)", April 2013, Headquarters Integrated Defence Staff, Ministry of Defence, Government of India, at http://mod.gov.in/writereaddata/TPCR13.pdf. Accessed on October 29, 2013 .
16. UCS satellite database 2015, at http://www.ucsusa.org/nuclear-weapons/space-weapons/satellite-database.html, Accessed on October 28, 2015.
17. Ian Easton, "China's Evolving Reconnaissance-Strike Capabilities: Implications for the U.S.-Japan Alliance", Project 2049, Institute and Japan Institute of International Affairs, February 2014, at http://www.project2049.net/documents/Chinas_Evolving_Reconnaissance_Strike_Capabilities_Easton.pdf. Accessed on accessed on August 26, 2015.
18. Ian Easton and Mark A Stokes, "China's Electronic Intelligence Satellite Developments: Implications for U.S. Air and Naval Operations", Project 2049 Institute, at http://

project2049.net/documents/china_electronic_intelligence_elint_satellite_developments_easton_stokes.pdf. Accessed on December 2, 2013.

19. On January 11, 2007, China successfully conducted its first ASAT test destroying its own inactive polar orbit satellite, the 'FengYun-1C', and creating one of the largest clouds of debris, posing danger to global space assets and future space activities.
20. Rosita Dellios, "China and Outer Space", *Humanities & Social Sciences Papers*, Paper 571, at http://epublications.bond.edu.au/hss_pubs/571. Accessed on October 29, 2013.
21. Andrea Shalal, "US Sees China Launch as Test of Anti-Satellite Muscle: Source", Reuters, at http://www.reuters.com/article/2013/05/15/us-china-launch-idUSBRE94E07D20130515. Accessed on July 17, 2014.
22. PA Patil, "China's Burgeoning Anti-Satellite Activities", *Defence and Diplomacy*, Journal of the Centre for Air Power Studies, New Delhi, vol.3 no.4, July-September 2014.
23. Ibid.
24. Ian Easton, "The Great Game in Space: China's Evolving ASAT Weapons Programs and their Implications for Future U.S. Strategy", *Project 2049 Institute*, at https://project2049.net/documents/china_asat_weapons_the_great_game_in_space.pdf. Accessed on December 2, 2013.
25. Ibid.
26. Ibid. Also refer to Chapter VI on development of new concept weapon systems.
27. Statement by Dr. Rameshwar Oraon, member of Parliament and member of the Indian delegation, on agenda item 31: international cooperation in the peaceful uses of outer space in the general debate of the special political and decolonisation committee [fourth committee] of the 62nd session of the United Nations General Assembly, on October 25, 2007, available at https://www.pminewyork.org/adminpart/uploadpdf/94822ind1364.pdf. Accessed on August 25, 2015.
28. "Space Command Must to Check China", at http://timesofindia.indiatimes.com/india/Space-command-must-to-check-China/articleshow/3135817.cms. Accessed on August 26, 2015.
29. "Ex- ISRO Chief Calls China's ASAT a Cause for Worry", September 14, 2009, at http://www.outlookindia.com/news/article/exisro-chief-calls-chinas-asat-a-cause-for-worry/666156. Accessed on August 26, 2015.
30. Arvind Gupta, Amitav Malik and Ajay Lele, eds., *Space Security: Need for Global Convergence*, Pentagon Security International (New Delhi, 2012), p. 12.
31. "India Readying Weapon to Destroy Enemy Satellites: Saraswat", at http://archive.indianexpress.com/news/india-readying-weapon-to-destroy-enemy-satellites-saraswat/562776/. Accessed on August 26, 2015.
32. Ibid.
33. Ibid.
34. Graham Gibbs, "An Analysis of the Space Policies of the Major Space-Faring Nations and Selected Emerging Space-Faring Nations", at http://www.spacepolicyonline.com/pages/images/stories/Graham%20Gibbs%20Analysis%20of%20National%20Space%20Policies.pdf. Accessed on March 13, 2014.

35. Brahma Chellaney, "China's Antisatellite Weapon Test: Implications for India", *Stagecraft and Statecraft*, February 9, 2007, *Japan Times*, at http://chellaney.net/2007/02/27/chinas-anti-satellite-weapon-test-implications-for-india/. Accessed on March 9, 2015.
36. James Smith "Mac" McDonnell (April 9, 1899 – August 22, 1980) was an American aviator, engineer, and businessman. He was an aviation pioneer and founder of McDonnell Aircraft Corporation, later McDonnell Douglas, and the James S. McDonnell Foundation.
37. PA Patil, "Wireless Power Transmission from Space", *In Focus*, Centre for Air Power Studies, New Delhi, April 30, 2015, at http://www.capsindia.org
38. Frank O' Donnell and Yogesh Joshi, "India's Missile Defense: Is the Game Worth the Candle?" August 2, 2013, at http://thediplomat.com/2013/08/indias-missile-defense-is-the-game-worth-the-candle/? Accessed on February 13, 2014.
39. "A Look at the Indian Ballistic Missile Defence Programme", at http://www.indiatvnews.com/news/india/a-look-at-the-indian-ballistic-missile-defence-programme accessed on February 13, 2014. Also refer "Indian Ballistic Missile Defence Programme", at https://en.wikipedia.org/wiki/Indian_Ballistic_Missile_Defence_Programme. Accessed on February 13, 2014..
40 "India, Israel to Build Anti-Missile System", at http://www.defensenews.com/article/20140206/DEFREG03/302060025/India-Israel-Build-Anti-Missile-System. Accessed on February 13, 2014.
41. "Technology Perspective and Capability Roadmap (TPCR)", April 2013, Headquarters Integrated Defence Staff, Ministry of Defence, Government of India at http://mod.gov.in/writereaddata/TPCR13.pdf. Accessed on October 29, 2013.
42. Air Cmde Jasjit Singh (Retd.) "Threats, Challenges and Capabilities-2050" (New Delhi: Centre for Air Power Studies), pp. 120-121.
43. Ibid.
44. Ibid., pp. 180-181.
45. "The Key is Technology, not Money", at http://www.thehindu.com/opinion/op-ed/fdi-in-defence/article7102328.ece. Accessed on September 2, 2015.
46. Ibid.
47. n. 41.

Index

9789381904886 • Rs 995

9789380502076 • Rs 680

9789380502281 • Rs 750

8187966475 • Rs 620